BEYOND THE LAND

T0281797

Praise for *Beyond the Land*

"Using the bold category of 'Diaspora Israeli Culture,' Weininger's timely and thought-provoking book guides us through contemporary Jewish literature and art in Israel, America, and Europe. Moving deftly between speculative fiction and multimedia projects, Hebrew in the Midwest and New York and poetic haflas in Berlin, the book illuminates current globalized, translingual, transnational Jewish cultures."

—Shachar Pinkser, professor of Middle East studies
and Judaic studies, University of Michigan

"In this rich, compelling, and timely study of the productive entanglement of diaspora and exile in Israeli culture, Melissa Weininger brilliantly maps the new cultural horizons that contemporary Israeli art imagines, and even activates, beyond its national borders."

—Adriana X. Jacobs, associate professor of modern
Hebrew literature, University of Oxford

"Weininger's book challenges the standard construction of home(land), diaspora, and the relationship between the two. Combining attention to detail, insightful reading, and lucid prose, it rewrites the Israeli literary landscape, bringing coherence to an unruly bookshelf of contemporary must-read novels."

—Nancy E. Berg, professor of Hebrew and comparative
literature, Washington University in St. Louis

BEYOND THE LAND

Diaspora Israeli Culture in the Twenty-First Century

MELISSA WEININGER

Wayne State University Press
Detroit

ISBN 9780814350591 (paperback)
ISBN 9780814350607 (hardcover)
ISBN 9780814350614 (e-book)

Library of Congress Control Number: 2022947186

On cover: Detail from *Die ganze Welt in einem Kleberblat* (The Entire World in a Cloverleaf) by Heinrich Buenting, 1581. Cover design by Will Brown.

Wayne State University Press rests on Waawiyaataanong, also referred to as Detroit, the ancestral and contemporary homeland of the Three Fires Confederacy. These sovereign lands were granted by the Ojibwe, Odawa, Potawatomi, and Wyandot Nations, in 1807, through the Treaty of Detroit. Wayne State University Press affirms Indigenous sovereignty and honors all tribes with a connection to Detroit. With our Native neighbors, the press works to advance educational equity and promote a better future for the earth and all people.

Wayne State University Press
Leonard N. Simons Building
4809 Woodward Avenue
Detroit, Michigan 48201-1309

Visit us online at wsupress.wayne.edu.

For my parents,
Michael and Susan Weininger

Contents

Acknowledgments

This book has been many years in the making, through a number of personal, professional, and global upheavals and transitions, and like all projects of this nature, it would not have been possible without the help and support of many colleagues, friends, and family. First among these are the many scholars who have read parts of this manuscript and offered their thoughtful and nuanced critiques or with whom I have had crucial conversations about the material that enhanced or changed my thinking, including Yael Almog, Nancy Berg, Dean Franco, Olga Gershenson, Denise Grollmus, Karen Grumberg, Rachel Harris, Adriana Jacobs, Steven Kellman, Allen Matusow, Tahneer Oksman, Ranen Omer-Sherman, Shachar Pinsker, Adam Rovner, Allison Schachter, and Shayna Weiss, as well as the anonymous peer reviewers of the manuscript. Liora Halperin helped me come up with the title. I also am deeply grateful for my contact with many of the subjects of this volume, writers and artists and activists whose work I deeply admire and who have been very generous with me, including Yoav Avni, Shani Boianjiu, Hanno Hauenstein, Tal Hever-Chybowski, Ruby Namdar, Mati Shemoelof, and Ayelet Tsabari.

While working on this book, I have been surrounded by wonderful colleagues at two different institutions. I am grateful to Susan Lurie and Helena Michie of Rice University's Center for the Study of Women, Gender, and Sexuality for making a comfortable space for me there and to my colleague Josh Furman in Rice's Program in Jewish Studies for being my closest colleague and staunchest supporter. Much of this manuscript was written while sharing an office with the best program administrator and private investigator anyone has ever been blessed to work with, Starr Dickerson. Since arriving at California State University, Northridge, my colleague Jennifer Thompson has proven to be the ideal mentor, ushering me through the disorienting process of learning the ropes at a new institution and making me feel appreciated and welcomed.

Portions of some of the chapters have appeared in print in various places over the last few years, and I am grateful to those publications and the editors I worked with for helping to refine my ideas. Some portions of chapter 1 and chapter 2 appeared in "Translingual at Home and Abroad: Israeli Literature Unbound," in *Since 1948: Israeli Literature in the Making*, ed. Nancy Berg and Naomi Sokoloff (SUNY Press, October 2020). Elements of chapter 3 have appeared in "Hebrew in English: The New Transnational Hebrew Literature," *Shofar: An Interdisciplinary Journal of Jewish Studies* 33, no. 4 (2015): 15–35, and "Language Politics: The Boundaries of Homeland in Translingual Israeli Literature," *Studies in the Novel* 48, no. 4 (2016): 477–93. And parts of chapter 5 were published in "Haunted Dreams: The Legacy of the Holocaust in *And Europe Will Be Stunned*," in *The Palgrave Handbook of Holocaust Literature and Culture*, ed. Victoria Aaron and Phyllis Lassner (Palgrave Macmillan, February 2020).

Finally, on a more personal note, much of this book would literally not have been written without my valued writing partner, Sara Ronis. Our regular Zoom writing sessions sustained me through the isolating years of the pandemic and inspired me to dedicate myself to my work even on days when I didn't want to. I have also been lucky in life to have many groups of friends, mostly women, from high school, college, graduate school, and beyond, who form a kind of cushion that has caught me at my worst moments and insulated me from their worst effects, and their influence and support is the background to everything I do. The list is too long to include everyone here, but special thank-yous go to Amy, Amanda, Emily, Katie, Alex, Becca, Maia, Jen, Sharon, and Kelsey. I am also indebted to the many childcare workers and babysitters who cared for my children over the years, as well as the wonderful women who have cleaned my home—their own labor freed me to do mine.

My final thanks are reserved for family, who are the center of my support network and my home no matter where I am: my brother Noah and sister-in-law Rebecca; my partner Mike; my children, Noam and Shayna; and my parents, Michael and Susan, without whom none of this would have been possible.

Introduction

A Home Away from Home

The Problem of Diaspora

> The solidarity within a dispersed people can be material, as we have
> seen, or it can be symbolic and affective: "Jerusalem" can be invoked
> in a purely spiritual sense. The reference to a place of origin is on the
> order of the imaginary, but people live also in and by the imaginary.
>
> —Dominique Schnapper and Denise L. Davis[1]

Flute music plays as leafy reeds wave in the wind against a blue sky. A
voiceover solemnly intones the opening lines of Psalm 137 in Hebrew,
"By Babylon's streams, / there we sat, oh we wept, / when we recalled
Zion," while the date—538 BCE—appears in the upper right-hand cor-
ner of the screen.[2] The camera fades in to a scene of a small group of
people dressed in long tunics and turbans sitting on the banks of a body
of water and chatting in modern Israeli Hebrew. Thus opens a skit on
the popular Israeli sketch comedy show *Hayehudim Baim* (The Jews Are
Coming), a program known for skewering biblical, Jewish, and Israeli
history.[3]

   As the camera focuses on a group of three exiles sitting on the
banks of a river, they one by one lament their fate, each professing their
desire to return to their beloved Jerusalem, discussing places and people they know.[4] One claims, "There is nothing I wouldn't do to return

[to Jerusalem]." Suddenly, someone runs up and breathlessly informs them that the Persian king has issued an edict allowing all the Jews to return: The exile has ended. Are they coming? One by one, each of the three reiterate their desire to go back coupled with an excuse as to why they can't: "My children are in the middle of school. . . . We can't take them out right now"; "I'm dying to come, dying, but right now we're building a second story above the pool"; "I just signed up at a gym" (figs. 1 and 2). Eventually, the messenger is persuaded to sit down with them and decides not to return to Jerusalem either. It seems life isn't so bad in Babylon.

Exile has been, since the destruction of the First Temple in Jerusalem in 586 BCE, a central fact of Jewish existence.[5] Its centrality to Jewish self-conception is evident in the way that the longing for return is enshrined in the texts, liturgy, and practice of Judaism. The longing for return to Zion is reiterated by religious Jews three times daily, as part of the *Shemoneh Esreh* (also called the *Amidah*), and embodied in the stance of the prayer, which is meant to be said while facing Jerusalem. Each year, the holiday of Tisha b'Av (the ninth day of the Hebrew month of Av) commemorates the destruction of the Temple as well as the inception of the Babylonian Exile that accompanied it. And that exile is represented in the text of Psalm 137, the text that is the starting point for *Hayehudim Baim*'s humorous mocking of the Jewish longing for Jerusalem, represented as a rote and superficial component of Jewish culture that takes second place to everyday life in the diaspora.

The concept of exile is not just internally definitive of Jewish identity and culture. The very idea of national or ethnic dispersion has come to be at least partially synonymous with the historical Jewish condition of exile. The first definition of "diaspora" in the *Oxford English Dictionary* refers specifically to the exilic condition of the Jewish people: "The body of Jews living outside the land of Israel; the countries and places inhabited by these, regarded collectively; the dispersion of the Jewish people beyond the land of Israel."[6] Only the second definition points to the "extended use" of this term as a general designation for dispersed peoples. Exile and its accompanying dispersion, or diaspora, have been

FIGURES 1 AND 2. Scenes from *Hayehudim Baim* (The Jews Are Coming), in which exiled Babylonian Jews make excuses not to return to the land of Israel.

deeply, perhaps inextricably, linked to Jewish history and both self-conceptions and external perceptions of the Jewish people.

The persistence of this linkage is at least partly attributable to the continuity of Jewish diaspora: already more than twenty-five hundred years after the Babylonian Exile, communities of Jews still live as Jews around the world. As the historian Shimon Dubnov observed, "The nature of Jewish emigration and wanderings is not peculiar in itself. It is the persistence of the Jewish people as a recognizable group through centuries of such wanderings in countries where they constituted a compact minority, which never enjoyed the powerful and dependable protection or support either of a homeland or of any foreign ally, that makes the Jewish Diaspora a rare and significant phenomenon."[7] This persistence of the Jewish people in dispersion points to one of the paradoxes of Jewish life, one made explicit by the comedy sketch: that for all the expressed longing for Zion, from the biblical period on, Jews have always made their homes elsewhere. Often, they have chosen diaspora, even when other options were available. As *Hayehudim Baim* reminds us, even after Cyrus the Great issued an edict allowing for the return of the exiled Israelites from Babylon, most of them remained in diaspora, which had become, despite any longing for Zion, a new home.

Indeed, in the ancient world, diaspora was not uniformly lamented and homeland was not necessarily privileged over the diasporic home.[8] Rather, the elevation of homeland—Zion, Jerusalem, the land of Israel—over diaspora is a modern phenomenon, largely driven by the rise of Zionism in the late nineteenth century. As Sidra DeKoven Ezrahi observes, "In the modern Jewish experience, 'home' has been overdetermined by the ideology and enactment of a collective repatriation in Israel while at the very same time, for Jews of European extraction, at least, even an imagined return to native grounds has been preempted by devastation."[9] This reterritorialization of a people long defined by a transnational, diasporic existence changed the historical valence of homeland and diaspora in Jewish culture, causing a shift in Jewish self-conception that continues to preoccupy contemporary thinkers, artists, and writers.

DIASPORA AND POSTCOLONIALITY

The post-Enlightenment—both the European Enlightenment and the Jewish *haskalah* that followed—understanding of Jewish diaspora, coupled with postmodernity, has led to a broadening of the meaning and application of the notion of "diaspora." Beginning in the 1990s with scholars like Stuart Hall and James Clifford, diaspora began to gain currency within the growing field of postcolonial studies and was defined more broadly, as well as used metaphorically or symbolically to refer to a condition rather than a specific community or group. Diaspora, and its implication of marginality or exclusion from hegemonic power structures, became a useful symbol for postcolonialism's challenge to nationalism and the nation-state. Explaining the value of diaspora to contemporary thought, Stéphane Dufoix notes that "postmodern thought gives pride of place to paradoxical identity, the noncenter, and hybridity"—all features of diaspora and diaspora communities.[10] In the first issue of the journal *Diaspora*, whose existence itself is a sign of the increasing power of the term within certain scholarly circles, Khachig Tölölyan noted in his introductory article that "diasporas are emblems of transnationalism because they embody the question of borders, which is at the heart of any adequate definition of the Others of the nation-state," and that these Others challenge the vision of a homogeneous nation underlying hegemonic national narratives.[11]

Thus diaspora has become a powerful tool in both the social sciences and the humanities for understanding the circulation and migration of populations in a globalized world. Diaspora can help to explain political, social, and cultural currents against the old national models, which do not adequately account for subjugated, silenced, or marginal populations. And in doing so, diaspora offers a challenge to nationalist modes of thinking about language, borders, and homelands. Primarily, the hybrid and migratory nature of diasporas—their movement across established boundaries—blurs or breaks down the binary categories entrenched by nation-states both physically—in the form of national borders—and metaphorically—in considering what is allowed inside or relegated to the outside of those borders.

Borders, as Daniel Boyarin has noted, are places where identities are performed and contested and also, in reality, are "places where people are strip-searched, detained, imprisoned, and sometimes shot. Borders themselves are not given but constructed by power to mask hybridity, to occlude and disown it."[12] Thus the function of reclaiming and performing the kind of hybridity that is a feature of transnational diasporas is also to expose the fallacy of the natural border, calling into question national claims to authenticity. As James Clifford notes, "It is now widely understood that the old localizing strategies—by bounded *community*, by organic *culture*, by *region*, by *center* and *periphery*—may obscure as much as they reveal."[13] In this understanding, diaspora becomes a way of pulling back the curtain on hegemonic assumptions about community and identity. But the adoption of diaspora as a tool for critique of sovereignty also risks reifying a conception of "diaspora" that itself reveals the limits of this critique. This study seeks to complicate both the critiques of sovereignty offered by a conceptual diaspora as well as the idea of diaspora itself as a place, or an idea, separate from and always in opposition to homeland.

HYBRIDITY AND DIASPORA

The hybridity of diaspora existence offers a challenge to this binarization in its implicit challenge to traditional dichotomies, particularly those of center and periphery, homeland and exile, by its very transnationality. According to Clifford, despite any national aspirations on the part of diaspora cultures, "diasporic cultural forms can never, in practice, be exclusively nationalist. They are deployed in transnational networks built from multiple attachments, and they encode practices of accommodation with, as well as resistance to, host countries and their norms."[14] The fluctuation of diaspora communities, their displacement and migration, both exposes and resists the reification of culture, nation, and identity. In cultural terms, diasporic practices foster what has been called an "imaginary of exile" to construct and maintain a given diaspora community.[15] Often, although this imaginary relies on an attachment to homeland and the idea of return, diasporic representations "tend to defer that fantasy in favor of a practice of 'dwelling (differently)' in a global network of interchange and circulation."[16] In other words, cultural expressions of diaspora metaphorize national longing while at the same time challenging national norms and the idea of the nation-state itself.

Nonetheless, a valorization of diaspora runs the risk of entrenching new dichotomies and reinforcing its own boundaries. Nico Israel notes that writers of diaspora still tend to adhere in some way to a system of binaries—insider/outsider, center/periphery, national/trans- or extra-national—even if they adopt the marginal terms in those dichotomies.[17] This points to one danger of the adoption of diaspora as a symbolic antidote to the nation-state, its power, and its problems. Rather, as Dominique Schnapper and Denise L. Davis warn, "The 'scholarly' concept of diaspora would have to eliminate at once both the suspicion prevalent during the era of the nation-state's triumph and the current lyricism of partisans of particularity."[18] Marianne Hirsch and Nancy K. Miller argue that the "post-millennial moment" demands "mutual imbrication rather than clear opposition between a desire for roots and an embrace of diasporic existence."[19] These scholars point to the dangers of valorizing the diaspora at the expense of preserving our understanding of diaspora not as a static concept, reified by its elevation to metaphor, but rather as fluid, shifting, and contingent.

DIASPORA AND JEWISH STUDIES

The danger of valorizing diaspora is particularly evident in the foundational Jewish studies scholarship that began the project to recuperate the idea of diaspora within Jewish thought and culture. This recuperation of diaspora arose as a scholarly response to a political problem: the increasing influence of Zionism and Israel on Jewish life and culture, even in the diaspora, and a decreasing tolerance for critique of either. The turn to diaspora, then, can be seen as a desire to redefine Jewish identity, and Jewish studies, away from Zionism. In 1993, Daniel Boyarin and Jonathan Boyarin published their influential article, "Diaspora: Generation and the Ground of Jewish Identity," in the journal *Critical Inquiry*, marking the beginning of a long-term project to reevaluate the significance of diaspora to Jewish history and identity. This article was a crucial intervention in certain universalizing discourses of Jewish identity then current in European thought, exposing the problems with constructing the Jew as a trope of difference without allowing for the preservation or activation of actual difference.[20] However, at the same time, their theory of diaspora entrenches an opposition between the poles of Israel and diaspora, or homeland and exile, that also tends to exclude marginal identities. Because the Boyarins' theory of diaspora in many ways underlies contemporary scholarly approaches to diaspora within Jewish studies, a close examination of both its value and its pitfalls is necessary to fully understand the non-binarist approach to diaspora established in my own analysis.

In place of a homogenized Jewish identity that has come to be conflated with state power in Zionist ideology, the Boyarins proposed a critical construction of cultural identity in general and Jewish identity in particular, one that "would simultaneously respect the irreducibility and the positive value of cultural differences, address the harmfulness, not of abolishing frontiers but of dissolution of uniqueness, and encourage the mutual fructification of different life-styles and traditions."[21] This critical construction of Jewish identity is based in a model of diasporic existence, one that recalls what they document as a long Jewish tradition of privileging diaspora, in certain biblical and prophetic texts as well as rabbinic discourse, as well as recasting the "dangers" of diaspora, generally perceived to be assimilation and cultural dilution, as strengths, reminding us that Jewish culture has continued to exist and thrive as a result of a cultural hybridity that is particularly diasporic. Their contentions constitute an important critical intervention into a discourse increasingly dominated by Zionist definitions of Jewish identity that reproduce the homogenizing constructions subject to critique here.

The Boyarins developed their critique of Jewish power and the reproduction of its discourses in Jewish studies and contemporary Jewish life in their book, *Powers of Diaspora*. And despite the important work their theory of diaspora has done to recuperate elided discourses and histories, the formulation of diaspora offered by the Boyarins, as well as the valorization of diaspora as a model for resistance to state power and the preservation of a particular conception of "Jewishness," has troubling aspects. First, this theory of diaspora appears to imagine a seemingly monolithic Jewishness, one that enshrines a particular ethics that tends to appropriate the spaces of heterogeneity that it theoretically celebrates. That is, this diasporic Jewish identity depends upon the appropriation or erasure of certain internally marginal identities—especially women and non-European Jews—and this appropriation has real implications for those disempowered elements within the diaspora culture. Second, the definition of Jewishness as diasporic over and against a Zionist Jewish identity that is defined by sovereign power preserves and strengthens an Israel/diaspora binary that closes off other interpretive possibilities for Jewish identity, which may include certain expressions of nationalism, political Zionism, or Israeliness, including those under consideration in this book. Third, their model does not consider other possible modes of resistance to state power, even those that come from within the sites and institutions of that power.

One of the marginal groups sidelined or excluded in the Boyarins' conception of diaspora as a valorized space for resistance to Zionist hegemony is women. The understanding of Jewishness presented in this account of diaspora is defined by powerlessness, and that powerlessness is characterized as feminine. What the Boyarins, in particular, fail to engage with (although they raise the critique) are the implications for women and gender of their definition of a diasporic Jewish identity as contiguous with a disempowered femininity. In an argument begun in his book *Unheroic Conduct*, Daniel Boyarin employs gender as a mode of understanding and reclaiming a diasporic Jewish identity in an age of Jewish sovereignty. But, as even Boyarin admits, this appropriation of "the feminine" as a universalized description for the very condition of diaspora has problematic consequences. In *Unheroic Conduct*, Boyarin notes parenthetically (and the parentheses are important in marking this observation as an aside, as set off from the central part of his argument) that we must be "ever mindful, at the same time, of the absolute necessity of an equally trenchant critique of that culture for its own systems of oppression of women."[22] To the extent that he is able, within the context of a project that is centered on masculinity and male subjectivity, Boyarin does point out the ways in which even a culture that valued a certain kind of what he calls "femminization" in men enforced the subjugation of women.

But this footnote to his project does not account for the problem of understanding Jewish identity writ large as a diaspora identity predicated on this appropriation of femininity (as construed in its particular historical and cultural contexts). Tania Modleski has written of this process of appropriation generally, "We need to consider the extent to which male power is actually consolidated through cycles of crisis and resolution, whereby men ultimately deal with the threat of female power by incorporating it."[23] In *Powers of Diaspora*, Daniel Boyarin notes Modleski's critique but dismisses it, suggesting that the oppression (or, I would argue, erasure) of women does not "exhaust the meaning" of submission or powerlessness as a cultural value.[24] This may be true, but if the valorization of diaspora is here posited as a foundational element of a monolithic Jewishness, and that valorization is based on the appropriation of the feminine and the erasure of women, this effectively enshrines the erasure of women in the meaning of "being Jewish."

Part of this definitional elision of women rests on a confusion between the subjugation of women and their erasure from the discourse of diaspora through appropriation. While Daniel Boyarin credits that diasporic Jewish culture did enforce the subjugation of women (without offering a solution to the adoption of that culture as a model without the attendant subjugation) he at the same time argues, "In a cultural system within which there are only two genders, the only way to symbolize 'refusing to be a man' may be an assertion that one is, in some sense, a woman."[25] But if traditional Jewish men, in refusing the gender-normative dictates of the dominant Christian European culture, are perceived as women, then what happens to actual women? If Jewish men are symbolically coded as women, how can one be a Jewish woman? Do Jewish women, materially or representationally, exist within this conception of diaspora?

Likewise, this diasporic model elides consideration of other forms, locations, and cultures of "Jewishness." In the Boyarins' formulation, Jewishness is a strangely monolithic concept, one located primarily in a history of European Jewish diaspora and centered on masculinity. Their argument is rooted in cultural conceptions of a diaspora Jewishness specific to Europe and the Jewish encounter with a dominant Christianity. For example, they write of diasporic Jewish culture as a form of resistance:

> In resisting through becoming "Muscle Jews," it could be argued, the early Zionists were simply assimilating and capitulating to general European values (since "Muscular Christianity" was a dominant movement of that time as well), while through maintaining themselves as weak and passive, the Torah Jews of Eastern Europe were engaged in a more successful act of cultural resistance to the hegemony of Christian culture.[26]

But what about those Jewish communities not located in Europe or those who had no need to resist a muscular Christianity because they were surrounded instead by a dominant culture that was Muslim? Are these diasporas irrelevant? Do they not contribute to the monolithic category of "Jewishness" as defined here? If not, diasporic Jewishness is also predicated on an erasure of the non-European Jew. Just as this argument about diaspora is concerned with the historical and cultural contingency of gender only insofar as it is related to men, it is concerned with the contingency of Jewish identity and practice only insofar as it is related to Europe.

These elisions have the potential to obscure crucial voices within the field of Jewish studies and to render invisible the role of marginal identities within our construction of "Jewishness." Who is included in this definition, and who is excluded? In *Powers of Diaspora*, Daniel Boyarin privileges a rabbinic model of Jewishness that eschews certain types of power, primarily state power. This notion is encapsulated in an epigraph from the Babylonian Talmud, "Be obscure and live!" (Sanhedrin 14a). In the book, this epigraph is offered without a specific citation, which, once the whole passage in which it appears is taken into account, seems to be a deliberate obfuscation that proves the point: that the uncritical valorization of diaspora reproduces some of the very homogenizing discourses it was intended to work against. The entire passage reads:

רבי זירא הוה מיטמר למיסמכיה דאמר רבי אלעזר לעולם הוי קבל
וקיים כיון דשמעה להא דא"ר אלעזר אין אדם עולה לגדולה אלא א"כ
מוחלין לו על כל עונותיו אמצי ליה אנפשיה

> The Gemara relates: Rabbi Zeira would habitually hide himself so that they would not ordain him. He did this due to the fact that Rabbi Elazar said: Always be obscure and remain alive, meaning the more humble and unknown you make yourself, the longer you will live. When he heard that which Rabbi Elazar also said: A person does not rise to greatness unless all his sins are forgiven, *he understood that there are also benefits to greatness*, and he presented himself to the Nasi in order that he would ordain him.[27]

Like so much of rabbinic tradition, this tale relates a lesson about power that contains its contradiction: Rabbi Elazar cautions that one must be wary of power and yet admits that there are also benefits to it.

But the Boyarins choose to cite only the first part of the story, eliminating its nuance and its lesson: that power is sometimes necessary and one should not shy away from it completely. The chapter in which this epigraph appears is devoted to exposing the way that the rabbis opposed Roman power through obscurity and deception, essentially tricking the authorities in many instances in ways that allowed them to remain alive in order to study the Torah, in this case the "cultural power" that is being preserved in the face of an oppositional "state power." But what this celebration of tricksters does not account for are the ways that obscurity may have different implications for those who are marginal even within a marginal community. Obscurity often means voicelessness, and trickery is often valued in leaders but denigrated in outsiders. And it is those outsiders for whom the second half of the lesson of Rabbi Elazar is essential.

One instance of this double standard can be found in the Boyarins' own example of a story involving Rabbi Eliezer, on trial for sectarianism, offering outward acquiescence to the Roman regime while at the same time resisting that regime through a complicated double entendre that undermines the meaning of his consent.[28] This celebration of Eliezer's tricky deception ignores the fact that for many, especially women, outward consent to domination often cannot function as a variety of resistance but rather has much more serious consequences. This is evident even in several of the rabbinic stories used as support, in which deceptive practices for women often end in forced prostitution and rape. Indeed, in recounting a rabbinic story in which Rabbi Hanina is punished partly by the banishment of his daughter to a brothel, the Boyarins metaphorize her forced prostitution to conclude, "The approved practice of the Jews is gendered feminine, while the behavior of the Roman is gendered masculine."[29] Although they again mention in passing the victim blaming this story engages in, the focus, for purposes of theorizing and valorizing diaspora, is on the men in power and specifically the male gaze. Here, the lives of actual women and the violence committed against them become a useful metaphor in a theoretical stance against state power. This valorization of powerlessness clearly has different, and dire, consequences for women, non-European Jews, and non-white Jews, and to celebrate this powerlessness is to ignore the dangers of obscurity.

DIASPORA IN THE AGE OF SOVEREIGNTY

Is it possible to retain the value of diaspora as a critical term, to recuperate the heterogeneous and multivalent understanding of Jewish identity and culture that diaspora indicates, *without* valorizing an image of powerlessness that may endanger or erase the marginalized as its central feature? In this book I propose considering a group of works of contemporary Israeli literature and art, created in and about the diaspora, as an intervention into the discourse of the valorization of diaspora and an expansion of understandings of diaspora both within Jewish studies and in postcolonial theory. This artistic work also intervenes in broader public political and sociocultural conversations and debates about the relationship of diaspora Jewry to Israel and the Israeli state relationship to diaspora Jews.

The importance of literature to these broader political, social, and theoretical debates, particularly in the case of Israeli literature, has been charted by Omri Asscher, in his study of translational and critical practices between Israeli and American literature from the 1940s through the 1980s. While Asscher considers the two literatures as distinct and oppositional, even characterizing them as "competing Jewish ident[ities] across the ocean," his conclusion nonetheless points to the kind of enmeshment between Israel and diaspora I argue for here.[30] Asscher concludes, "The seemingly dichotomous existence of two separate Jewish cultures, in Israel and America, was in fact merely a point of departure, a premise to understand how each intellectual discourse was not only permeable to but also intermingled with and dependent on the other Jewish culture."[31] The literature considered here, which centers this permeability in its content, language, and location, offers a contemporary perspective on the complex relationships, in many different directions, between Israel and the Jewish diaspora.

As Gil Hochberg has written of using literary works to draw conclusions about issues that have been largely discussed as political or social problems, literature can offer new insights into such conversations because "it not only *reflects* historical and sociopolitical realities but further *competes* with them, introducing alternative actualities, which might find expression only at the level of cultural imagination, but which, as such, are nevertheless part of our times."[32] The art and literature considered in this book represent one possibility for constructing a more nuanced conception of Jewish identity and the relationship to both state power and the idea of homeland that underlies the impulse to sovereignty. This conception of Jewish identity resists homogenizing Zionist discourses and embraces the excluded and marginal but at the same time understands Rabbi Elazar's dictum that there are benefits to power and works in the interstices of that paradox.

Rather than privileging a European, male, rabbinic conception of diaspora, reinscribing the very boundaries that diaspora itself repudiates, this work takes an expansive view of diasporic cultures and identities, complicating the discourse of privilege around diaspora. Many of the works discussed here are created by women and center characters who have previously been marginal: women, Mizrahim, members of the LGBTQ community, noncitizens, refugees, and others. They also focus on places and spaces rendered within Zionist discourse as at best peripheral and at worst detrimental to Jewish life, from Europe to New York to discarded or forgotten alternative homelands. The inclusion of these elided identities and spaces has the effect of challenging the very binary terms that are often reified by both postcolonial thought and Jewish recuperations of diaspora: center and periphery, hegemonic and marginal. Rather than simply replacing one term with the other, the introduction of multivalent and coexistent constructions of community and home suggests that these binaries are not sufficient to contain the possibilities offered by diaspora, breaking them down from the inside.

These works deconstruct not only binary oppositions around the idea of diaspora but sometimes even the terms of the binary themselves. For example, the category of literature and art under consideration in this book is most simply described as "diaspora Israeli culture." In the binarist approach, this phrase is self-contradictory: "diaspora" and "Israel" are two mutually exclusive terms, bounded by geography and, in the case of Israel, borders. But the imbrication of these terms necessarily calls into question the possibility of a definition in which one does not exclude the other. As we will see, "diaspora Israeli culture" brings Israel into diaspora and diaspora into Israel or perhaps simply exposes the way that each of these places and concepts always already contains the other. There is no "pure" Jewish diaspora, no place entirely separate from Israel. Likewise, Zionism, despite its best attempts to construct an autochthonous, authentic Israeli culture, cannot erase the foundational traces of diaspora on which it was built and continues to exist. Thus the very term "diaspora Israeli culture," as uncomfortable as it might seem, suggests the very kind of intersectional and critical approach embedded in the work itself.

The abrasion created by the phrase "diaspora Israeli culture" also points to its slipperiness or to its pointed imprecision. What is diaspora Israeli culture? Is it literature and art created by Israelis in the diaspora? Is it composed in Hebrew or in other languages? Is it work about the diaspora created in Israel? It is all of these things: an exploration of place, exile, home, language, nation, and nationalism undertaken by Israeli writers and artists living in both Israel and the diaspora, in Hebrew and diasporic vernaculars, about both diaspora life and Israel. This slippage mirrors the inherently migratory nature of diaspora, its ability to violate boundaries, to expose the limits of categorization and definition. In his work on S. Yizhar, Shaul Setter has proposed a new way of reading "Israeli literature"—and here the quotation marks are deliberate, indicative that the mode of reading calls into question the category itself, much as the work in this volume does—in which seemingly stable categories of nation, sovereignty, and collectivity, for example, are destabilized and in which there is no representative Israeli voice or audience.[33]

This slippage across definitional boundaries allows for the production of a more contingent accounting of Jewish identity and history than that of the dominant theoretical models of Jewish diaspora. As noted above, those models have largely emerged in opposition to Zionism and the state of Israel and have thus cast Zionism and Israel as monolithic entities. This is, in part, because as an aspect of its nation-building enterprise, Zionism constructed a homogenous, synthetic Jewish-Israeli national identity. As Oz Almog puts it, "The Zionist national religion, like other traditional religions, sought to create cultural as well as ideological homogeneity. (The transition from the multitude of Diaspora cultures to a uniform Israeli culture is also evident in the phrase 'the ingathering of the exiles,' which became a common idiom during the mass immigration.)"[34] This homogenous Israeli identity was founded "on the triad of settlement, communality, and soldiering," which were represented as the primary values of the New Jew.[35]

These values, and the unification of Israeliness around a homogenous image of newness, were formulated specifically in rejection of the diaspora. Amnon Raz-Krakotzkin has extensively explored the meaning and function of exile in Israeli consciousness and historiography. He notes that the "negation of exile," the common phrase for Zionist disparagement and rejection of Jewish diaspora cultures, is "a central axis of an all-embracing viewpoint that defines the self-consciousness of the Jews of Israel."[36] Like other theorists who have embraced diaspora as a mode of critique of Zionism and Israel, Raz-Krakotzkin recognizes the critical power of exile as a subaltern position, one that can offer a challenge to the dominant majority. However, he also emphasizes that this critical stance is not just a condition of powerlessness but also a position with regard to the existing order. Rather than claiming the powerlessness of exile as a virtue, Raz-Krakotzkin suggests an embrace of exile as a mode of understanding the suppressed elements of the Jewish past that might reflect on the Israeli present and offer "possibilities of a new consciousness," one that acknowledges multiple narratives of Jewish and Israeli history and identity.[37]

Raz-Krakotzkin's work is part of a body of critical scholarship largely originating from within Israel, developed beginning in the 1980s, that is characterized as "post-Zionism." Post-Zionist critiques sought to open Israeli discourse, to create a more democratic cultural space, by emphasizing diverse voices and perspectives that had been subsumed under the hegemonic Zionist narrative of Jewish-Israeli identity and culture. Laurence Silberstein's 2008 book, *Postzionism: A Reader*, which collected material from historians, philosophers, literary critics, and film scholars, is reflective of the post-Zionist enterprise. It contains sections by the "new historians" and critical sociologists, Israeli scholars who reevaluate Zionist historiography; critiques of Zionist ideology and meta-analyses of Israeli history and politics; work by literary and cultural scholars highlighting marginal voices, including Palestinian citizens, Arab Jews, women, and LGBTQ Israelis; and work reevaluating the American Jewish relationship to diaspora and to Israel.

However, critics of post-Zionism as well as some post-Zionist critics have also noted that post-Zionist critiques, in the quest to challenge the Zionist narrative, have ignored the revolutionary and critical aspects of the Zionist project itself. Zionism, at its inception, was a utopian national movement that developed in response to the oppression and disenfranchisement of European Jews. In this context, it was an anti-colonial project advocating for the liberation of an oppressed minority. But as Eran Kaplan has noted, "Post-Zionism has deprived Zionism of its liberating, revolutionary dimension and has described it, by its very nature, as part of the European system of oppression of all non-Europeans."[38] This is in part because the post-Zionist critique also accounts for the colonial aspects of Zionism's political realization, which eventually resulted in the accommodation of a European colonial framework through Jewish settlement, and eventual political sovereignty, in the East. Zionism was both a revolutionary liberation movement and a colonial enterprise, and "the return thus reflects the attempt of a persecuted minority to adopt the consciousness of the majority, albeit through a disengagement from the minority society."[39] Much post-Zionist discourse, in its figuration of Zionism as a colonial movement in the terms of postcolonial critique, does not credit this double-edged understanding of Jewish nationalism but rather views any liberatory possibilities of Zionism as always embedded in or corrupted by its colonialist aspirations.

Recently, some scholars have argued for the emergence of another paradigm beyond post-Zionism. For example, Kaplan's 2015 book is titled *Beyond Post-Zionism*. And Assaf Likhovski has described a "post-post-Zionist" historiography, which relies on a Foucauldian notion of power as dispersed and in which relationships with the state are sometimes described as symbiotic and sometimes as antagonistic, in a more complex representation.[40] Kaplan laments the cultural emphasis of post-Zionism, arguing that it does not offer viable political positions.[41] But Raz-Krakotzkin envisions potential political benefits to this imaginative project, in which a more culturally and historically heterogenous notion of Jewish-Israeli identity creates space for a new ethics and politics.[42]

The literature addressed in this book might be considered part of this post-post-Zionist trend, both in that it refuses simplistic and binary understandings of Jewish nationalism, Zionist tropes, and Israeli identity and in that it concerns itself with opening new spaces for ethical and political critique. It addresses the lacuna between Zionist utopia and the colonialism attached to sovereignty, between powerlessness and power. While it employs some of the techniques of post-Zionist critique, in an attempt to imagine a heterogenous Israeli identity encompassing many forms rather than resorting to the singular image of the New Jew, it is also aware of its position as work that is enabled by the existence of the state of Israel and accounts for the potential that Israeliness makes possible.

It does this through the lens of diaspora, consciously or unconsciously applying Raz-Krakotzkin's notion of exile as a point of critique and possible redemption for Zionist thought. At a time when the Zionist project of the ingathering of exiles has essentially ceased, this literature explores the symbolic function of diaspora for breaking down monolithic notions of Israeli and Jewish identity. While contemporary theories of Jewish diaspora purport to show what diaspora looks like from the diaspora, and to assert its value to the Jewish present, and post-Zionism offers a critique of the idea of homeland from within, diaspora Israeli culture not only explores what Jewish diaspora looks like from Israel but also proposes an Israeli diaspora that exists in relationship to, but does not perfectly overlap with, Jewish diasporic life. Finally, it explores the implications of that Israeli diaspora, as distinct from a preexisting Jewish diaspora, for Zionism and Jewish nationalism more generally.

The image that emerges from Israeli diaspora culture suggests the contingency of accepted narratives of Jewish history, particularly teleological Zionist narratives, reconsidering the inevitability of the state of Israel, the Israeli-Palestinian conflict, and even the Holocaust. It makes space for marginalized or excluded Jewish identities that remain unaccounted for or are elided in the binary between Israel and diaspora. And it is polyphonous, reinscribing languages other than Hebrew, both Jewish and non-Jewish vernaculars, into the corpus of Israeli literature and culture. In its refusal to be one or the other, to accept the dichotomies of center and periphery, homeland and exile, Zion and diaspora, it exposes the fallacy of the authenticity or purity of identity. At a moment when Israeli political culture has increasingly insisted on defining Israeli identity as exclusively Jewish, to the exclusion of non-Jewish citizens of the state, and the Israeli religious establishment has increasingly insisted on defining Jewishness according to rigid interpretations of Jewish law, diaspora has become a way for Israeli writers and artists to reimagine both national and Jewish identity and the relationship between them.

In doing so, diaspora Israeli culture produces new configurations of Jewish and Israeli identity, new understandings of homeland, exile, diaspora, and Israel, that are dependent on, rather than opposed to, each other. This work replaces binary notions of Jewish identity with multivalent conceptions of Jewish nationalism that can include both Israel and diasporic spaces. The texts analyzed in this book use diaspora as a way of excavating hidden, suppressed, or potential histories and identities, ones that for ideological and political reasons have been elided from accepted narratives of both Israeli and Jewish diaspora culture. In doing so, they bridge the gap between Israel and diaspora, a gap that they expose as artificial and imposed by a power structure that has constructed oppositions and dichotomies instead of allowing for the possibility of a rich, plural understanding of the circulation and, yes, migration of culture, language, and community. At a strained moment in diaspora-Israel relations, this art and literature may have something important to convey about how we understand and negotiate coexistent ideas of homeland and diaspora.

Chapter 1 focuses on several works of speculative fiction that take as their starting point the contingencies of Zionist history: namely, proposed Jewish states in locales other than Palestine. Nava Semel's *E-srael* (*Isra Isle*) imagines a world in which Mordecai Manuel Noah's plan to establish a Jewish state in Grand Island, New York, has been realized; Lavie Tidhar's *Unholy Land* and Yoav Avni's *Herzl Amar* (Herzl Said) take as their premise the success of the 1903 Uganda Plan and the establishment of a Jewish state in East Africa. In not taking the outcomes of the Zionist project for granted, these alternative histories suggest the almost accidental nature of homeland. At the same time, they are cognizant of their own grounding in the language, culture, and politics of the modern state of Israel. This duality allows them to inhabit a contingent space between homeland and diaspora, suggesting that the two are not opposed but rather reliant on each other.

The next chapter considers Ruby Namdar's epic novel *Habayit Asher Nekhrav* (*The Ruined House*) alongside Maya Arad's *Hamorah Le'ivrit* (The Hebrew Teacher) within the context of the history of Hebrew in the diaspora and specifically in America. *The Ruined House*, a magic-realist novel, literally brings Zion (in the form of the ancient Temple in Jerusalem) into the world of an American Jewish college professor living in New York. *The Hebrew Teacher*, a satirical novella, brings Israel into a midwestern college town in the form of an academic conflict over Israeli politics and Hebrew instruction. Both works make use of the layered history of Hebrew to create a linguistic pastiche made up of translations, citations, and imports from other languages. In doing so, they create a robust image of Jewish diaspora life as inextricably linked to, and even necessary for, the existence of Israel. At the same time, they make an argument for Israel, and Hebrew, as necessary to the survival of global Jewish culture.

Chapter 3, by contrast, examines translingual Israeli literature, in this case in English. Rela Mazali's hybrid fictional-theoretical work *Maps of Women's Goings and Stayings* provides a framework for reading two recent works of translingual Israeli fiction in English: Shani Boianjiu's *The People of Forever Are Not Afraid* and Ayelet Tsabari's *The Best Place on Earth*. Translingual Israeli literature challenges the exclusive association between Hebrew and Israeli culture, suggesting the possibility of linguistic pluralism in Israeli literature. It looks outward, toward a globalized cultural landscape, but also points inward, offering a critique of Zionist tropes. Again, this work is poised on the brink between diaspora and Israel, insisting on new definitions of Israeli culture that are not moored to place either linguistically or thematically.

Chapters 4 and 5 turn to both literary and nonliterary forms of culture to examine the idea of a "return" of Jewish, Israeli, and Hebrew culture to diasporic spaces. Chapter 4 focuses on *And Europe Will Be Stunned*, a video installation by the Israeli artist Yael Bartana that proposes the idea of a pioneering return of Israeli settlers to Warsaw. The film proposes a utopian community on the very site of the Warsaw ghetto as a corrective to the evils of Israeli nationalism as well as Polish antisemitism and complicity in the Holocaust. The film envisions both the utopian possibilities and the cynical failures of such a movement.

The final chapter, however, describes just such a movement in real time: it explores the community of Israeli writers and artists who have settled in Berlin (including Yael Bartana herself) since the early 2000s. Many of these artists, along with Berlin-based Jewish and non-Jewish colleagues, have self-consciously tried to establish a kind of utopian artistic community in Berlin. This community is embodied in the creation of the Poetic Hafla, a cross-cultural gathering featuring poetry, music, and art. These gatherings, along with other literary and academic projects, attempt to repatriate Hebrew to Europe, its starting point, and contend with one of the fundamental tenets of Zionist ideology: the negation of the diaspora.

Taken together, these varied literary and cultural expressions imagine a variety of what Raz-Krakotzkin has called "possibilities of a new consciousness." They offer an imaginative modality for envisioning a more complex and nuanced politics of diaspora, one that privileges rather than elides marginal and suppressed voices, contends with the realities of power and dispossession, and celebrates the transnational, transcultural, and translingual. The magic of literature and art is that it can open up spaces that are not always accessible to us in the real world and that in turn can allow us to envision and shape a reality that is more like our imaginations. Diaspora Israeli culture's challenge to entrenched conceptions of Jewish identity as rooted in homeland and exile reflects an age in which the ability to travel easily, to communicate over the internet, and to consume global culture online has rendered many boundaries and borders obsolete, even while the power differentials and inequalities that remain create or enforce different types of boundaries. The twenty-first century calls for new modes of visualizing diaspora Jewish and Israeli identity, and the literature, art, and culture depicted in this book offer a contemporary lens for envisioning a shared future that accounts for a dynamic conception of homeland.

1

Zion in the Diaspora

Alternative Histories, Alternative Homelands

Utopian desire is the fire of fiction; utopia realized (or defeated) consumes it by subsuming all alternative worlds.

—Sidra DeKoven Ezrahi[1]

The soul is greater than the soil, and the Jewish soul can create its Palestine anywhere, without necessarily losing the historic aspiration for the Holy Land.

—Israel Zangwill[2]

Although most Zionist historiographies posit a teleological historical evolution that ends inevitably with the creation of the state of Israel, Palestine was never the only proposed location for a Jewish homeland. Indeed, even up to the establishment of the state, other geographical locations were being explored for the solution to the "problem of Jewish homelessness."[3] Many varieties of Zionist and Jewish nationalist thought competed for dominance and for the chance to solve the very real and immediate problems of nineteenth-century European Jews: hunger, privation, and violence. And some Zionists—including, even, the "father" of political Zionism, Theodor Herzl, for a time—posited that the urgency of a solution to the problems facing European Jewry was more important than the specific geography of that solution. From the late nineteenth century to the early twentieth, these territorialists, as they have been called, explored a variety of options for Jewish settlement and political autonomy outside of the biblical land of Israel. But since the creation of the state of Israel, a Zionism that equates homeland with Israel has predominated, and, as Adam Rovner has noted, the ascendance of Zionism as "the chief Jewish nationalist ideology" often renders "past and present alternative visions of nationhood invisible."[4]

These alternative visions, however, have found new expression in a period in which allohistory, or alternative history, is an increasingly common and popular genre, not just in fiction but even in historical scholarship. Gavriel Rosenfeld has suggested that the rise in both popularity and respectability of alternate history is related to a number of factors, including the discrediting of deterministic political ideologies since World War II, postmodernism, and recent scientific and technological trends.[5] Rosenfeld has suggested that "alternate history is inherently presentist. It explores the past less for its own sake than to utilize it instrumentally to comment upon the state of the contemporary world."[6] Literary works that imagine alternate outcomes for important historical events and processes, like World War II and the Holocaust, the assassination of John F. Kennedy, or the collapse of the Soviet Union, do so to explore the fears, hopes, and desires of a contemporary author and audience. Rosenfeld suggests that for this reason, allohistories are useful tools for reflecting on and understanding historical memory.[7] But at the same time this makes them a useful tool for understanding the dominant preoccupations and concerns of the present day. In addition, the what-if scenarios presented by literary allohistories can offer a critique of the past, by pointing to potentially preferable outcomes to alternate historical paths.

Then perhaps it is no surprise that the unsuccessful Jewish homelands of the nineteenth century should become the subject of twenty-first-century alternate histories. After all, since 1948 the utopian imaginaries of Zionism have been put to the test by the realities of the state of Israel and the Israeli-Palestinian conflict. Imagining a different past might allow for a retreat into utopianism untested by reality, offering a way to think our way out of what seem to be intractable problems. Significantly, however, none of the recent Israeli allohistories of alternative homelands indulge in utopia: rather, they paint their alternative histories with a dystopic brush, often reproducing the very problems that allohistory might allow an escape from. In this sense, perhaps, these works also engage with what, in the context of Hebrew literature, Shaul Setter has called "speculative temporality": a type of narrative play with history and time that does not simply rewrite the course of events but in refusing what he calls "the time of state sovereignty" opens a space in which assumptions about both time and historiography, as well as the narrative demands of literature, are challenged.[8] The challenge embedded in the alternative Jewish homelands considered in this chapter is a collapse of simple distinctions between utopia and dystopia, as well as Israel and diaspora, a collapse evident in the ultimately circular relationship that is revealed between history and allohistory.

Three recent Israeli novels take up the question of alternative homelands through the genre of allohistory: Nava Semel's 2005 *E-srael* (*Isra Isle*), Yoav Avni's 2011 *Herzl Amar* (Herzl Said), and Lavie Tidhar's 2018 *Unholy Land* (originally in English).[9] Each takes up an abandoned historical proposition: *Isra Isle*, the 1825 plan of Mordecai Manuel Noah to establish a Jewish homeland, called Ararat, on Grand Island, New York; *Herzl Said* and *Unholy Land*, the rejected 1903 Uganda Plan, in which British colonial authorities offered up a parcel of land in East Africa to the Zionist Congress for Jewish settlement. These novels engage with the realities of Jewish sovereignty by imagining a world in which the Jewish state exists in different places and different forms; they explore the relationship between nation and culture by designing homelands in which different Jewish or non-Jewish languages are privileged as national languages; and they reflect on both the pros and cons of Jewish nationalism from the somewhat safe distance of the fictional page. By doing so, they engage in a critique of Zionism as the only possible form of Jewish nationalism and the state of Israel as its only possible outcome: the alternative homeland imaginatively creates a space for other possibilities for Jewish nationalism, language, culture, and identity.

While they take up different possible homelands in vastly different ways, these novels share in common the use of an alternative history to speculate about the possibilities of Jewish nationalism but without erasing Israel entirely. Rather, they all encode references—nominal, linguistic, historical, political—to the extant state of Israel and allude to, even reproduce in other contexts, the geopolitics of Israel-Palestine and its accompanying conflicts. *Isra Isle* and *Herzl Said*, as novels written in Hebrew, necessarily assert the existence of Israel in their very language, imagining other national Jewish languages in the language of the Israeli state. As Adam Rovner has noted about *Isra Isle*, "The novel's counterfactual story-world is made possible only thanks to the verifiable ontological status of Israel, thus reifying Zionist ideals as transhistorical."[10] These works engage the critical possibilities of allohistory while at the same time insisting on a historical reality outside of it, safely exploring the possibilities as well as the pitfalls inherent in other homelands while inhabiting their own.

ISRA ISLE AND THE LANDSCAPES OF DIASPORA

Nava Semel's 2005 Hebrew novel, *E-srael*, published in English as *Isra Isle*, imagines an alternative Jewish homeland built around an obscure historical proposition: the 1825 plan advanced by Mordecai Manuel Noah to establish a Jewish homeland called Ararat on Grand Island, New York (fig. 3). Semel (1954–2017) was a popular Israeli writer whose work often focused on the "second generation": children of Holocaust survivors, of which she was one. Semel was born into a prominent Israeli family—her father, Yitzhak Artzi, was a politician and member of Knesset, the Israeli parliament; her older brother, Shlomo Artzi, is a beloved pop singer—but her work is also widely known and has been adapted for stage and screen, as well as published abroad. She was the recipient of numerous literary prizes both in Israel and abroad before her early death from cancer.

Through its speculative plot and alternative histories, Semel's *Isra Isle* offers multiple, coexistent notions of nationalism and its place in Jewish life and history, exploring the limits, both ideological and geographic,

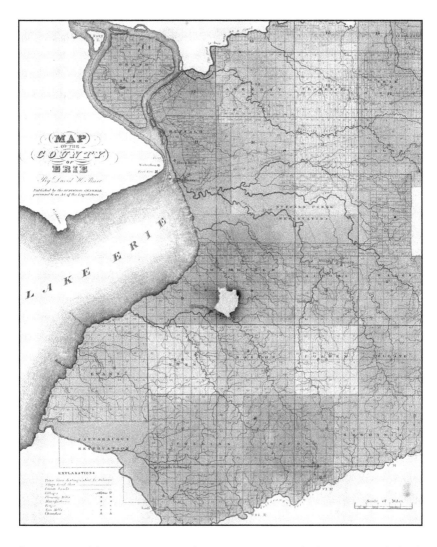

Figure 3. Detail from an 1829 map of Erie County, New York, showing Grand Island. David Rumsey Map Collection, David Rumsey Map Center, Stanford Libraries.

of Zionism. The novel imagines a Jewish identity, even a Jewish national identity, that moves beyond a binary conception of homeland and exile entrenched by Zionism and the establishment of the state of Israel, and yet it does so in Hebrew, carrying the language beyond the confines of its contemporary role as an official state language. At the same time, as a Hebrew novel, *Isra Isle* brings the reality of the contemporary state of Israel to bear within the context of its allohistorical plot both deliberately and necessarily, by virtue of the language in which it's written.

The novel is divided into three parts, loosely connected: the first part is set in September 2001 and tells the fairly straightforward story of a New York City police detective of Native American ancestry, Simon T. Lenox, tasked with searching for a missing Israeli national, Liam Emanuel, who turns out to be a descendant of Mordecai Manuel Noah, the American journalist, diplomat, and visionary who imagined a Jewish state on Grand Island, New York; the second part of the novel, set in September 1825, recounts an alternative history of Noah, in which he travels to Grand Island with a young Native American woman, whose family has been violently driven from their homes there, as his guide; the third part of the novel is pointedly set in an alternative September 2001 and tells the tale of a world in which Isra Isle, a Jewish state on Grand Island and one of the United States, has become the homeland of the Jews and the state of Israel does not exist. This tripartite format indicates the novel's reluctance to rely on one historical narrative or frame, and its use of contiguous timelines challenges any teleological view of historical development. Rather, it puts these histories and homelands in conversation with one another, establishing certain connections between them—names, ancestries, locales—but consciously avoiding any cause and effect relationships.

The primary link between the three sections of the novel is the location of Ararat—Grand Island. This focus on the landscape of Grand Island recalls Hebrew literature's transnational roots by emphasizing diaspora spaces, deconstructing the link between the Zionist subject and the land of Israel. Eric Zakim has detailed the way that Zionism and its adherents articulated an understanding of the modern Jewish subject as tied specifically to the land of Israel and the role that Hebrew literature playcd in framing "political culture's self-understanding through an aesthetic confrontation between this new Jewish subject and the object of nature in Eretz Israel."[11] An integral part of the creation and articulation of this New Jew was Hebrew culture. But *Isra Isle*'s focus on American, and particularly Native American, landscapes and culture challenges this imbrication of Hebrew literature and the Zionist subject with the land and landscapes of Israel.

The novel also presents a recurring metaphor for the idea of home as unfixed through the concept of the *boydem*, which is a feature of the first and last sections, bracketing the narrative. *Boydem* is a Yiddish word referring to an attic or garret. It has entered modern Hebrew to refer to a small storage space in a house or apartment, hidden and extraneous. Interestingly, this term itself reveals the heterogenous, diasporic history of Hebrew. Although Eliezer Ben-Yehuda, one of the main architects of modern vernacular Hebrew, presented the language as linguistically pure and derived from ancient Jewish sources alone, modern Hebrew absorbed many terms, expressions, and grammatical constructions from the languages of Europe.[12] Hebrew is especially indebted to Yiddish, the diaspora "jargon" of the Jews denigrated by early Zionists and Hebraists. Yet the Yiddish *boydem* also becomes, in the story, a powerful image of a shelter that can exist in any place, a moveable refuge that is not itself home but in which home can be kept. As Simon T. Lenox remarks in the first section of the novel, "Maybe Israel is the Jews' *boydem*?"[13] The novel, however, suggests that more than one *boydem* may exist at any one time.

Each section of the novel takes up the question of homeland in its own way, and these multifarious conceptions are loosely connected primarily through the shared locale of Grand Island.[14] Tracing the way that the landscape of the island and America itself operate in the three sections of the novel reveals the way that the concept of the *boydem* is translated into an alternative space, a moveable homeland. The novel uses the landscapes of America—the wilderness and eventual megastate of Grand Island, the landmarks of New York City—as the touchstone for Jewish identity and belonging. Indeed, the novel freely mixes Native American and Jewish mythology, religion, and culture in a way that deeply roots Jewish existence in American soil while also raising the problem of claims to indigeneity. The American setting is also linked to Jewish narratives of messianic and political redemption, producing various models and shifting notions of home that preclude a single definition.

Part 1 of the novel, titled "Grand Island" in a nod to the centrality of that location not only to this section but to the work as a whole, focuses on the search for a missing Israeli national, Liam Emanuel. That the missing person's given name means "my people" embodies the fluctuation of nation and home on which the novel concentrates and again recalls the metaphor of the *boydem*. As it turns out, Liam Emanuel is a descendant of Mordecai Manuel Noah, and he has come with a deed of ownership to claim Grand Island as his patrimony. As the narratives of the detective assigned to the case, Simon T. Lenox, and Emanuel converge, and the two meet at Grand Island, these two modern national narratives also come together.

Lenox wonders, "How can the Native American investigator explain to the Israeli that land is not property and no one can own it? It was given to both the creators and the creatures to guard. We are all temporary guests, and land cannot be inherited" (H 98, E 90). In partial answer to this question, Semel manipulates biblical texts in order to bring the landscape of Grand Island literally into Jewish tradition, rewriting Psalm 137, the iconic song of diasporic lament:

עַל נַהֲרוֹת בָּבֶל / שָׁם יָשַׁבְנוּ /גַּם-בָּכִינוּ / בְּזָכְרֵנוּ אֶת-צִיּוֹן (Ps. 137:1)

By the rivers of Babylon, / there we sat, / sat and wept, / as we thought of Zion.[15]

Semel's version inverts the formula, substituting remembrance for forgetting and the first person for the collective voice:

על נהר הניאגרה, שם ישבתי גם בכיתי, בשוכחי את אררט. (H 108)

By the rivers of Niagara I sat and wept when I forgot Ararat. (E 100)

The text also transposes the iconic warning "אִם אֶשְׁכָּחֵךְ יְרוּשָׁלָיִם" (Ps. 137:5), "if I forget thee Jerusalem," into its opposite, "אם אזכרך ירושלים": "If I remember thee Jerusalem on the Niagara. . . . If I remember thee Tel-Aviv on the Niagara" (H 108, E 100). This mash-up of homelands, holy centers, languages, and foundational texts muddles the boundaries between these spaces both geographically and symbolically, forming a complex web of interconnections rather than a linear series. It also literally imports the landmarks of the diaspora homeland—Niagara, Ararat—into the foundational texts of Jewish tradition and Hebrew literature.

This transformation of the American landscape into an element of Jewish, and Hebrew literary, tradition continues in part 2, "Ararat," titled after the name that Noah gave to the putative Jewish homeland on Grand Island.[16] In this section, a first-person narrative told from the perspective of a young Native American woman, known as Little Dove, whose community on Grand Island was violently expelled by American forces, the landscapes of America are constructed as a touchstone for Jewish identity and belonging. The narrator has been taken in as a servant (although she appears to be treated essentially as a slave) by a white couple on the mainland, and when Mordecai Manuel Noah comes to stay with them she offers to be his guide to the island he has just purchased. As she rows him to the island, she reflects on the concept of homeland and the island itself:

> There are other islands in the world besides this small strip of earth that juts out of the water. . . . Nevertheless, this island is my home. For me it is the whole world. And for the Jewish chief? Nothing. A tiny patch scratched with a nail on the scrolls of paper the white people call "maps." . . . Except that their maps do not show the traces scattered around this land, nor even the downy meadows that turn golden in summer, or the rustling canopy of foliage that comes in winter. The coyotes, the raccoons, the doves, and the ravens all move in their circles with the maple and elm trees. Everything in its place, as though there were no Buffalo, no America, only this island alone. (H 125, E 117–18)

This narrative, centered in between the two contemporary stories, grounds her observations about the American landscape and the Native and Jewish relationship to the island. The admixture of these two cultures and the land itself is literally embodied in the novel when the narrator and Noah have a sexual encounter that, it is implied, impregnates her. The novel treats this connection as the link that binds the other characters in the book both to their Jewish identities and to the American landscape they call home. However, the necessarily coercive nature of the sexual relationship between a white man and an enslaved Native woman raises questions taken up elsewhere in the novel about the nature of Jewish claims to indigeneity and the ties that bind the Jews to the land.

THE SHADOW OF ISRAEL

The presence of Israel as a reality and the questions it raises about Jewish nationalism lurk in the background of the third part of the novel, titled "Isra Isle" after the name of the Jewish homeland that has been established in Grand Island. In this section, whose timeline in the Hebrew is denoted as "September 2001—Parallel Time" (H 174),[17] Isra Isle has been established as a thriving independent metropolis on Grand Island and is one of the United States. A politician from Isra Isle, a female descendant of the founder named Winona Emanuela Noah, has won the nomination of an unspecified political party for the U.S. presidential race. This part of the narrative takes the form of a long diary entry or letter written from a Black American photographer named Simon to his Jewish boyfriend, Jake, who was born on Isra Isle but has lived for many years in self-exile on the mainland.

While the presence of a Jewish homeland in the United States in this timeline has obviated the need for one in the land of Israel, there is a shadowy, sometimes playful hint of the state of Israel in the text. The novel nods to real-life places and events as a way of underscoring the status of Isra Isle as an alternative homeland while at the same time recalling the existence of the state of Israel. For example, there is an area

of Isra Isle known as the West Bank, in this case the west bank of the
Niagara River, an upscale area "with all the yachts docked in the private
marinas" (H 192, E 184). In a more overt comparison to the contested
landscapes of the state of Israel, as well as the Jewish homeland's integration into the American landscape, the narrator, Simon, reflects on
the way that Isra Isle has accommodated its increasing population into a
tiny territory by "pack[ing] them all in vertically, turning Isra Isle into
an imitation of Manhattan. Of course it also emulates Gaza in Grand
Palestine, the most tower-laden metropolis in the world" (H 241, E 231).
In these nods to the disputed spaces of modern-day Israel-Palestine, the
novel gestures at what might have been—a peaceful marina called
the West Bank, ample housing for all of Gaza's residents—while troubling the alternative homeland of the text with a shadow of today's reality. At the same time, it appears to unproblematically incorporate these
contested territories—the West Bank and Gaza—into the Jewish state,
eliding present conflicts.

But perhaps the most interesting reference to the ghost of a sovereign Israel within the world of *Isra Isle* is the name of the neighborhood
where the presidential candidate Winona Emanuela Noah lives: Spring
Hill. The name Spring Hill, which sounds just like what it designates
in the book, an upscale suburban neighborhood, is also a literal translation of "Tel Aviv." Although even in the Hebrew version of the text, it is
written phonetically as "spring hill" (H 211), it cannot be mistaken for
anything other than a reference to the city that is a symbol of Israel's
modernity and cosmopolitanism, a city established by Zionist pioneers as
a sign of Jewish progress and advancement. But in transliterating the name
of the city into Hebrew, the text in this case imports its own alternate
homeland and its language into Hebrew, a language that has been constructed as synonymous with Israel and with Israeli identity and culture.

Most interesting is Simon's reflection on the name, a passage not
fully translated into the English version of the novel. As he watches the
candidate arrive at her estate, he thinks, "Spring Hill. Home. The more I
repeat these words to myself, which were meaningless last night, the
more loaded they sound. A sort of whispered spell *that was intended to*

build the diaspora [galut], but strangles the place to death."[18] Something about the conjunction between the place name, Spring Hill, and the concept of home is suffocating. Given the shadowy presence of Tel Aviv contained within the transliterated English, this suggests the potential danger in calling any one place home. Making a homeland out of diaspora has strangled it, and the implication is that the same might be true for its shadow parallel. The concept of a fixed and immovable center, a singular home, suggests constriction of Jewish life and culture rather than vitality.

The land and landscapes of Israel do make one overt appearance in this section, in a description of the pilgrimage of Simon's boyfriend, Jake, to the territory of Grand Palestine. Jake's journey honors the final wishes of his grandmother to scatter her ashes in the land of Israel. Jake combines the ashes with soil taken from the ruins of the Twin Towers as an homage to Simon, whose flight home from Isra Isle happens to be on one of the planes that crashes into the World Trade Center. This visit to the Holy Land, itself a movement between various possible ideas of home and homeland, ends the book. The ritual described in this coda is not a familiar Jewish one, because Judaism demands burial of the body, and represents, like the mixture of the ashes, another hybrid form of religion and culture. Here, this amalgam is relocated to a homeland unrealized, described as "a desolate place, which has sunken into blessed oblivion" (H 254, E 243). Again, the unbounded movement of the narrative between the locations and landscapes of various homelands, real and imagined, and the imbrication of local and imported cultures suggests a multivalent, dynamic, and transnational conception of home. At the same time, it is a reminder of the modern state of Israel, its own landscapes and language, and the way that its existence makes even imagining an alternate reality possible.

PARALLEL LIVES, PARALLEL LANDS

The particulars of Israel's history and the Israeli-Palestinian conflict are reflected even more precisely in Yoav Avni's *Herzl Said* and Lavie Tidhar's *Unholy Land*. Both of these novels imagine a Jewish homeland (called "Israel" in *Herzl Said* and "Palestina" in *Unholy Land*) roughly in the region proposed to the Zionist Congress for settlement by the British colonial authorities in East Africa.[19] *Herzl Said*'s "Israel" is sandwiched between present-day Uganda, Kenya, and South Sudan, sharing borders with each; Palestina is envisioned as a smaller territory cut mostly from present-day Kenya (figs. 4 and 5). Despite their slightly different geography, however, both of these imagined homelands reproduce Israel's conflicts with its minority populations and its neighbors, describing similar issues, sometimes even in the same language, with the native African populations and nations in the region.

Yoav Avni (b. 1969) is a writer and translator with a background in management and communications whose work has been categorized as science fiction and fantasy. His novels have been nominated for or have won Israel's Geffen Prize, an award for science fiction and fantasy literature, a number of times. His work has not been widely translated or distributed in the foreign press, a phenomenon perhaps attributable to the relative invisibility in Israel, at least until very recently, of certain types of genre fiction. By contrast, Lavie Tidhar's work has had great success and wide distribution because he writes in English. Tidhar (b. 1976) is a prolific writer who has published dozens of novels, novellas, comics, and short stories. He was born and raised on a kibbutz in Israel's north but has traveled extensively, lived mostly outside of Israel since he was a teenager, and currently lives in London. A number of his books touch on World War II and the Holocaust—like Semel, Tidhar comes from a family of Holocaust survivors, and his mother was born in a displaced persons camp after the war.

Like their backgrounds, Avni's and Tidhar's novels are radically different in their narratives and genres, and they are written in different languages. Nonetheless, they both essentially import modern-day

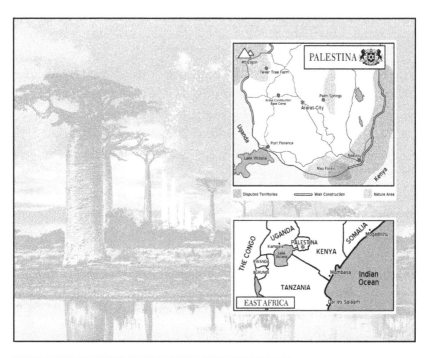

FIGURE 4. Map and detail from *Unholy Land* showing the location of Palestina within contemporary East Africa and the national crest of Palestina. Palestina and East Africa maps created by Elizabeth Story © 2018 by Tachyon Publications. *Unholy Land* crest © 2018 by Sarah Langton.

FIGURE 5. Map of Israel from *Herzl Said* showing its location sandwiched between Kenya and Uganda. Tel Aviv is located on the shores of Lake Victoria. Reprinted by permission of the author, Yoav Avni, http://yoavavni.com.

Israel, with minor differences, into a new locale. Perhaps realistically for any colonial country, both "Israel" and Palestina have strained relationships with their neighboring countries and domestic problems with native local populations that parallel those of present-day Israel. There are land disputes with the Kenyans, including settlements in occupied territories; security barriers and Green Lines; terrorist attacks; and civil rights disputes regarding minority residents. In *Herzl Said*, even the language used to refer to these problems borrows from the language of the Israeli-Palestinian conflict: at the beginning of the novel, "Israel" is in the midst of a withdrawal from an occupied strip of land it intends to return to Kenya, referred to as *haretsua*, just as the Gaza Strip was during the 2005 withdrawal. The transposition of the current conflict to these alternative histories, drawing parallels between the Israeli-Palestinian conflict and the novels' Israeli-African conflicts, seems to suggest that present-day Israel's territorial conflicts are not a special case. However, as these novels progress, it becomes clear that beginning from this point of apparent confluence is actually a technique that points to the perils of sovereignty, wherever it is achieved.

Although Zionism posited a natural or autochthonous Jewish attachment to the land of Israel, one enshrined in Israel's founding documents, in these novels Jews have no less strong an attachment to their homelands in Africa. The opening lines of the Proclamation of the State of Israel declare, "The Land of Israel was the birthplace of the Jewish people. Here their spiritual, religious, and national identity was formed." It ascribes the establishment of a Jewish community, and the declaration of the state, to settlement "impelled by this historic association" between people and land.[20] But in *Unholy Land*, the protagonist Lior Tirosh feels much this same connection to Palestina. Upon arriving at the airport from his home in Germany, "Tirosh took a deep breath, and when he expelled it, it was the old breath of Europe he was expelling, and when he breathed again he felt renewed, much more himself. He was a Palestinian."[21] And others claim precisely the same spiritual link to Palestina that the proclamation insists Jews have with the land of Israel: Bloom, another main character, believes that their parcel of land in Africa "was one given to us by covenant" (UL 145). Kfir and Ari, protagonists of *Herzl Said*, actually travel from "Israel" to Palestine, where they meet a handful of Jewish settlers who never left when "Israel" was established in Africa. Kfir is upset when these settlers refer to them as "the Africans," because he's insulted at their sense of superiority. He reflects resentfully, "as if Israel is somehow similar to the other countries in Africa, and as if there is anything to compare between Israel and their goose yard here."[22] Even the attachment to the land can be transferred; much like *Isra Isle*, these works suggest that it is the attachment, not the land, that is holy.

Finally, both of these novels present an image of a Palestine that is, in the absence of an Israeli state, transnational, polyphonous, and multicultural. *Unholy Land* describes a number of chronologically coexistent historical possibilities and parallel universes; Ursalim, inhabited by one of the main characters, Nur, is a Palestine without borders. In her world one can travel across some of what are, in our world, the most heavily policed boundaries in the world. Nur describes taking "the slow train from Beirut to Jaffa. . . . Here again Hebrew became prevalent in the air, and in Jaffa Harbour you sat at an outdoor fish restaurant run by a man from Syria, where tourists gathered in a cloud of foreign perfumes, a multiplicity of tongues" (UL 95). This world has suffered a catastrophe, called the Small Holocaust, that has destroyed the city of Jerusalem, and the "nature of its destruction and the amount of pain it had caused brought, after a few years, a peace born of shared victimhood, creating in this way a new Middle East that collectively mourned Jerusalem" (UL 105). The porous boundaries of this place are mirrored in the mixing of languages and cultures fostered by the consciously trans- or anti-national Middle East described by it.

Likewise, in *Herzl Said*, although little reference is made to national boundaries, Yaffa, Palestine's main city, is a cosmopolitan, transnational space, inhabited by American soldiers, who seem to be part of an occupying or supervisory force that is never specified; German Templars; local Arabs; and, of course, tourists like the protagonists, who are young Israeli men traveling after their army service. When Kfir and Ari go to Yaffa with their Arab host's family, they stop to eat in a German café, and "from the moment that they crossed the doorstep, they passed into a world entirely decorated with marble and milky glass and with the scent of baked apples all around, and women with short pastel skirts and German words, standing out like cool, hard edges from the warm Arabic" (HA 202). This world within a world is typical of the Yaffa of the novel, mixing cultures, languages, and populations. Although it is a different kind of novel from *Unholy Land*, one that humorously winks at reality in its portrayal of an alternate world, *Herzl Said* nonetheless imagines its Palestine as a similarly transnational space, not utopian by any means but also not subject to colonial hegemony. In both novels, this is in contrast to the Jewish homeland in Africa, which does suffer from the postcolonial conflict that is more familiar to readers with knowledge of the present-day state of Israel.

By simply importing Israel's current problems and transforming the Israeli-Palestinian conflict into the Israeli-Kikuyu conflict or the Palestina-Nandi conflict, these alternate histories suggest, rather than the ways history might have been different "if only," the ways that history is always the same given similar conditions. In their casual transference of allegiance, national identity, and longing to alternate homelands, they indicate that it is narrative and imagination, rather than some assumed autochthony, that make the home into a homeland. In the end, it is the very idea of homeland that appears problematic: conflict follows the nation, and the places untouched by nationalism (or those that have moved beyond it) are the ones without borders.

HYBRIDITY AND COLONIZATION

Another way in which the tragic effects of colonialism as well as postcolonial conflict are made evident in all of these alternate histories is through the elaboration of imaginary hybrid cultures in their respective speculative homelands on Grand Island and in Africa. While hybridity has often been theorized as a site of postcolonial resistance to colonial hegemony, the complex cultural hybridizations and appropriations depicted in these novels also suggest its dangers. Homi K. Bhabha has described the culturally hybrid as articulating an "in-between" space, which functions to "provide the terrain for elaborating strategies of selfhood—singular or communal—that initiate new signs of identity, and innovative sites of collaboration, and contestation, in the act of defining the idea of society itself."[23] In the context of postcolonial theory, these in-between spaces allow for the development of extraterritorial or transnational conceptions of identity. And, indeed, in the early history of Hebrew literature, hybridity served precisely this function for the peripatetic Jewish population of Europe, helping to forge a communal identity across national boundaries. The establishment of the state of Israel and the adoption of Hebrew as a national language with a national culture backed by state power, however, retroactively complicate the transnational origins of Hebrew culture.

The fraught understanding of the hybrid in these alternative homelands mirrors the tangled position of Israeli culture with regard to colonialism and postcoloniality. In imagining Hebrew culture back into the diaspora and diasporic settings, these novels reflect on the possibilities and limits of Hebrew's transnationalism in its national form. This is evident in their treatment of hybrid forms of culture, which exposes the interplay between hybridity and appropriation, postcolonial resistance and colonial power, transnationalism and sovereignty. In their work on diaspora and the return to its sites, Marianne Hirsch and Nancy K. Miller note that they hope to "propose alternatives to the celebration of rootlessness and diasporism by making space for the persistent power of nostalgia, and the magnetism of the idea of belonging."[24] It is this balance between the valorization of diaspora as a site of resistance to state power and the longing for the protection of that power that these novels explore in their approach to hybrid cultural forms.

On Isra Isle, even the most fundamental Jewish practices have been reconfigured to reflect American landscapes, history, and mythology. Isra Islers worship a deity known as "Yehowakan Tanka," a mash-up of the biblical Jehovah (or yud-hay-vav-hay) and Wakan Tanka, the local Native American deity. Even the use of Wakan Tanka in the novel is a conflation of disparate and geographically inappropriate Native American traditions—Wakan Tanka is a Lakota term for the sacred or divine, and the Lakota people, a subculture of the Sioux, were residents of what is now the Midwest and the Dakotas, not the area in which Grand Island is located. This disregard for the specifics of Native culture on the part of the novel is itself a form of appropriation that parallels the practices described on Isra Isle.

Jewish Isra Islers have also adopted or adapted other elements of Native culture, including the longhouse as a meeting space, referred to as the "holiest of holies" in a reference to the Temple in Jerusalem; the sport of javelin throwing, for which Isra Isle is the host of the Snow Snake, the world championship; and various emblems and symbols, like the Noah family crest, which consists of a seven-oared candelabrum and a bow-shaped tomahawk. But perhaps the most significant cultural mixture is represented by Isra Isle's bar mitzvah ritual. Rather than ascending to the *bimah* to read from the Torah, young Jews coming of age on Isra Isle go alone in a canoe to Niagara Falls. Wrapped in a prayer shawl, the young bar mitzvah sails alone for four days and four nights on what is called a "maturation journey" (H 206, E 197).

Isra Isle's focus on Native American culture recalls earlier eras of American Jewish literature, in which Hebrew and Yiddish writers of the early twentieth century appropriated the image of the American Indian as a way of making their own claims to Americanness. American Hebraists of the early twentieth century wrote about Native Americans at least partly as a function of their antimodernism and antiurbanism, finding in Native American life and characters a way to be American writers without embracing elements of contemporary American life that repelled them. These writers saw Native Americans as representative of the "true America" that was belied by the crowded, faceless cities of the early twentieth century.[25] For American Hebraists, "the Indian was therefore a perfect theme, expressing a critique of America even while typifying a more 'authentic' Americanness."[26] It was precisely this "authentic" or "natural" Americanness represented by Native Americans that Yiddish modernists seized on as a way of claiming their own place in American culture. Rachel Rubinstein claims that many Jewish representations of American Indians expressed a conflicted relationship between Jewish tribalism and the liberal, rational ideals of the Enlightenment.[27] Likewise, Semel's representations of a hybrid Native-Jewish culture on Isra Isle, which implicitly claims a kind of indigenous identity for Judaism, reflect a conflicted relationship with sovereignty and parallel arguments regarding Jewish autochthony in Palestine.

However, like the works by American Hebraists and Yiddish modernists, *Isra Isle* also uses the figure of the Native to draw parallels between Jewish and Native American experiences and to suggest other historical connections. Michael Weingrad notes that American Hebraists saw the Indian as a "safe" figure for identification, a victim of both genocide and assimilation yet completely unconnected to the history of antisemitism. At the same time, the plight of Native Americans "foregrounded Zionist passions concerning land and sovereignty."[28] Writing before the establishment of the state of Israel, those Zionist interests had a slightly different register than the one they have in *Isra Isle*, in which the Native characters cannot but stand as a parallel to Palestinians, also the victims of a colonial project that pushed them from their native lands. And while the cultural hybridity depicted in the novel may signal a utopian hope for the possibility of an enriching and peaceful hybrid existence, it is notable that there are no actual Native Americans left on Isra Isle—they were all forcibly and violently expelled before the establishment of the state.[29]

Thus the mixed Native-Jewish culture of *Isra Isle* has the effect of envisioning an expansive Jewish civilization that can adapt without assimilating, taking on the character of its surroundings, in this case America. At the same time as this hybrid construction pushes back against the boundaries of nationalism and national cultures, it also points to the troubling underside of hybridity: cultural appropriation. In particular, this cultural appropriation is the outcome of the American colonial project, whose primary victims were the Native peoples of America, suggesting that the problems of nationalism and colonialism are not new. The reference to American colonialism raises the specter of the Israel-Palestine conflict, visualizing the victimization of Native Americans as parallel to that of Palestinians. At the same time, the example of American colonization of Native American lands, like the African conflicts depicted in *Herzl Said* and *Unholy Land*, shows that national conflict like that in Israel is not unique but rather reflects problems endemic to any national project. As Adam Rovner has suggested, "The paradoxical messages underlying Semel's alternate history help expose a fundamental ambivalence at the root of Zionism itself: the simultaneous desires to be a nation apart and to be a nation like all other nations."[30] The parallel offered in *Isra Isle*'s depiction of Native-Jewish hybrid culture and the Jewish relationship to Native peoples uses the diaspora setting to expose the fundamental historical paradox inherent in Hebrew's nationalization and Jewish sovereign power.

In both of the African homeland novels, the hybridization of Jewish culture with local African cultures is primarily depicted in descriptions of the cuisine and languages of "Israel" and Palestina. In Tidhar's Palestina, Yiddish and Hebrew are still spoken and used, but the national language is Judean, a "mix of Ben-Yehuda's Hebrew with Yiddish and Swahili" (UL 19). In Avni's "Israel," Hebrew is the national language, but the imprint of its geographical context is evident in slang. For example, when the main character, Kfir, is practicing Arabic words and phrases for his upcoming post-army trip to Palestine, he tries out the greeting *ahlan* on his friend Ari. Ari, confused, asks him what it means. Of course, to any Hebrew reader, this common greeting derived from Arabic is immediately recognizable, but in the transplanted context of the book it's unfamiliar to the Israeli characters (HA 66). On the other hand, when Kfir and Ari travel by plane (on El Al, no less) to Palestine, the captain makes announcements in both Hebrew and Swahili (HA 88). In both cases, it is evident that there is no pure, unadulterated Hebrew language or culture—no matter the context, the language is always shaped by geography and the surrounding cultures.

In "Israel," the shaping of Israeli culture by the surrounding African cultures is primarily documented through foodways. When Kfir dines at Ari's family home, the main dish is *ugali*, a cornmeal-based cooked porridge eaten throughout sub-Saharan Africa and known by several regional names. In this "Israel," *ugali* is so integrated into the national culture that it is even served weekly to soldiers in the army. It's clear that the adoption of local food cultures has political implications when Kfir notes that his brother, a staunch Israeli nationalist opposed to the pullout from the occupied Masai territories, does not eat *ugali* because he "refused to touch Mumbo-Jumbo food for nationalist reasons" (HA 45).[31]

In *Unholy Land*, Jewish "Palestinians" eat local cuisine and play African games, but the hybridization of culture is more evident in religious and cultural artifacts. Tirosh, the main character, explains that not only do most Jewish citizens have African curios at home, but "for a time every second mezuzah was hand-carved out of ebony or soapstone, even ivory, which he had seen once" (UL 62). The creation of Jewish ritual objects with traditional African artistic elements both reflects the hybridity of local culture and recalls colonial practices, such as white colonists and travelers coming to Africa to collect hunting trophies or to loot the continent for treasures like ivory. The symbol of the hunting trophy also appears in *Herzl Said*, in the form of a crocodile head mounted on the wall of the colonel who discharges Ari and Kfir from the army. The crocodile had, a year before, bitten off the colonel's leg in an accident, and the trophy is a sign of both the officer's personal revenge and the supremacy of the Israeli military over the African landscape. Thus the hybrid forms of culture reflected in these African Jewish homelands, much as in Semel's *Isra Isle*, participate in sometimes troubling ways in colonial power rather than simply reflecting a decolonial identity particular to diasporic life. At times, these hybrid forms even display a conscious use of sovereign power to appropriate local autochthonous cultures. To various degrees, these novels all draw parallels to the Israeli or Hebrew-language context to which they belong, bringing actual Israeli history and culture and its relationship to sovereign power into the texts.

Unholy Land explicitly links national sovereignty with the temptation of colonialism through a megalomaniacal geopolitical plot for Jewish colonization of the world that is connected to control of the land of Israel. Near the end of the novel, Lior Tirosh's father, known only as General Tirosh, reveals his plan to first conquer all of Africa, moving outward from Palestina, and then more. He tells his son, "'No borders! No walls! A Jewish nation as far as the eye could see, from the Cape to Cairo! And from there...' He approached the map and stabbed his finger at the terminus point of the train and ran it along, into the Holy Land" (UL 238). His plan appropriates the language of transnationalism and diaspora—no walls or borders—for the purposes of colonialism. And despite the diasporic locale of the Jewish homeland, Palestina, this plot makes explicit that control of the land of Israel is nonetheless central to his idea of Jewish world domination. Again, the fraught position of Israeli sovereignty with regard to Jewish diasporic history is made clear through the hyperbole of this plot. The cultural hybridity described in these texts likewise occupies a precarious position between the articulation of a decolonized identity and colonial appropriation, resting on the uncomfortable acknowledgment of Israeli sovereignty and Hebrew cultural hegemony.

TIME, HISTORY, AND CATASTROPHE

A central function of alternate history is to speculate on the consequences of history by reimagining it. If one crucial historical detail is altered, what are the effects on the rest of history as we know it? Karen Hellekson notes that the genre "speculates about such topics as the nature of time and linearity, the past's link to the present, the present's link to the future, and the role of individuals in the history-making process. Alternate histories question the nature of history and of causality; they question accepted notions of time and space; they rupture linear movement; and they make readers rethink their world and how it has become what it is."[32] In speculating about alternative possibilities, allohistory disrupts teleological historical narratives. These novels about alternative Jewish homelands specifically disrupt Zionist narratives that trace the establishment of the state to the abasement of Jewish diaspora life.

In Israeli national discourse, the existence of the state itself is often predicated on the events of World War II and the Holocaust. The Holocaust is used as an example of the reason for the necessity of Israel's existence, as well as a crucial motivator for the United Nations' vote to partition Palestine and create a Jewish state after the end of the British Mandate. Thus, it is no surprise that each of these allohistorical novels about alternative Jewish homelands, homelands established before World War II, also alters Jewish Holocaust history, even the events of the Holocaust itself.[33] This revision of catastrophe serves as a rebuke to both teleological Zionist narratives of Jewish sovereignty and the short-sightedness of early Zionists who fixated on the land of Israel.

One crucial motivating factor in the proposals explored in these novels—Noah's Ararat and the 1903 Uganda Plan—was to alleviate the immediate suffering of European Jewry. Noah's first attempts to buy Grand Island from New York State were partly influenced by the 1819 Hep Hep riots in Prussia; the Zionist Congress's interest in the Uganda Plan was partly linked to anti-Jewish violence in Russia, in particular the 1903 Kishinev pogrom, which loomed large in the Jewish imagination. In each case, the proposed homeland was envisioned as temporary, a place for the Jews to achieve autonomy until they could return to the Holy Land. Max Nordau, Herzl's colleague and second in command, referred to Uganda as a *Nachtasyl*, a "night shelter" for the Jews until more permanent conditions could be achieved.[34]

Thus it is no surprise that these alternative histories imagine a timeline in which these prewar homelands have prevented the worse violence to come. Put in place before World War II, they have altered global Jewish demographics in such a way that there has been no Jewish genocide during the Holocaust (or no Holocaust at all). In *Isra Isle*, the presence of this city of refuge has prevented the Jewish genocide of the Holocaust, although not the Holocaust itself, whose victims have been the disabled, homosexuals, Roma and Sinti, and others; in *Herzl Said*, Hitler was captured and the war ended in 1940, with no Holocaust; in *Unholy Land*, there was no Holocaust and the German Reich still exists, swastika flag and all, although Hitler was assassinated in 1948. This elision of the

Holocaust breaks the association between the establishment of a Jewish state and Jewish tragedy, disconnecting nationalism from catastrophe. It also, perhaps, stands as a rebuke to those early Zionists who, insisting on Jewish sovereignty in the land of Israel, rejected the Uganda Plan and others like it, which, in these alternative worlds, has averted Jewish genocide.

This theme is most prominent in *Unholy Land*, in which a vision or prophecy of the Holocaust is precisely what causes the acceptance of the Uganda Plan, the historical pivot on which the novel's alternative history rests. In 1905 the Zionist Congress sent Nahum Wilbusch (né Wilbus-chewitz) to the territory in East Africa offered by the British for Jewish colonization. He was tasked with surveying the land and reporting on its suitability as a *Nachtasyl*. Ultimately, Wilbusch, who was secretly a sympathizer of the rejectionist camp of Zionists who saw Palestine as the only suitable location for a Jewish homeland, returned an unfavorable report to the congress, and the plan was rejected. But in *Unholy Land*'s alternative history of Wilbusch's expedition, he got lost in what is called an "in-between place" and had some kind of vision. In the world of the novel, this space is imagined as being between two parallel possible realities. In this "in-between place," Wilbusch found a mirror that showed him the future and, afterward, despite hardships suffered on the journey, returned a positive report to the congress that resulted in the acceptance of the plan (UL 51–52). While it is never specified in the novel, oblique references to Wilbusch's vision indicate that what he saw in the mirror was the Holocaust and the genocide of the Jews. In this case, then, it is to avert the Holocaust that a Jewish homeland was established in Africa, rather than as an outcome of the Holocaust. Thus catastrophe—in this case the anticipation of it—is still instrumental in Jewish nation building, but the homeland does its job: the Holocaust is averted in the world of Palestina. Still, it appears that tragedy is instrumental in the shaping of Jewish nationhood.

A more general consideration of the ways that catastrophe and nationalism are intertwined is also evident in these novels in their approach to the events of September 11, 2001. *Isra Isle*, which is partly set in Manhattan, centers its chronology around 9/11, and the attacks play a role in both of the modern sections of the novel. In the first section, as part of Simon T. Lenox's assignment to find Liam Emanuel, his office is relocated to the eighty-fourth floor of the North Tower of the World Trade Center (WTC), where he feels "stuck in a place where he doesn't belong. . . . He has better conditions here, ample space—an office designed to win him over, furnished with an executive leather chair and state-of-the-art laptop. But all these props serve only to underscore how foreign he is in this new domain" (H 9, E 5).

The WTC, particularly for the post-9/11 reader, has become synonymous with American nationalism. As Neil Leach has documented, buildings like the WTC can become points in a symbolic structure that enable the fantasy of national identity through materiality, much as a flag might: "[Buildings] may become the visible embodiment of the invisible, the vehicle through which the fantasy structure of the homeland is represented."[35] After 9/11, American national identity was consolidated around the symbol of the WTC. Lenox's foreignness in this space underscores his marginality as a Native American, even while it relocates him within a space that is metonymous with Americanness.

This simultaneous push and pull of nationalism gestures toward the tragedy at the heart of American nation building through its reference to a contemporary American national tragedy. Lenox's forced move into the WTC building, as well as his sense of otherness there, can be seen as an echo of the genocide and displacement of Native peoples on which the United States was built. Lenox is a reminder that the nation's existence is dependent on the genocide of Native Americans, just as Grand Island's is in the third section of the novel. And, as we have seen, the presence of Native Americans, as well as the co-optation of their culture and tradition in the novel, often functions as a reminder of the position of Palestinians with respect to Jewish nation building in the state of Israel. At the same time, Lenox himself insists on his own American identity, musing, "American—that's what he was. If he were to yield to superstition, he would be undermining the ideal of one nation" (H 46, E 43). This assimilative movement, however, also marks a loss: an erasure of the particularity of his Native culture or its absorption into a universalized American culture that does not mark its origins.

Lenox's office move, then, works both to underscore the history of forced migration and displacement at the heart of American nationalism and, at the same time, to demonstrate the possibilities, as well as the losses, that assimilation into the national idea entails. It also foreshadows the events of 9/11, an event that has not yet occurred in the novel, although it eventually happens twice, in both the first and the third parts of the book. The post-9/11 reader cannot help but reference the WTC as a loss, one that stands at the heart of a tragedy that underscored the crisis of nationalism. Indeed, the fact of the alternative timeline of part 3, labeled carefully in conjunction with the fateful date at the beginning of the section, might lead a reader to conclude that in this utopian allohistory, in which the peaceful Jewish homeland of Isra Isle has prevented some of the tragedy of the Holocaust, 9/11 might also be avoided. But this section, too, ends with 9/11, when the plane Simon is taking home to New York crashes into one of the Twin Towers.

This repetition of catastrophe suggests that in the world of the novel, even the relocation of the Jewish state from the contested land of Israel-Palestine has not obviated ethnonational conflict or the geopolitical processes that led to 9/11. At the same time, it allows for elaboration of the novel's themes of homeland and nationalism through the lens of what became an American national tragedy. The presence of 9/11 as a pivotal event in both the first and last sections of the novel underscores the instability of homeland and a nationalism linked to place that is introduced by Lenox's move to the WTC. The chronological dislocation created by the coexistent but variant timelines of the first and third sections forces, as Richard Gray has suggested, "a continual process of reinterpretation, a process of questioning that, theoretically at least, is without end because it is precisely that, the process of questioning, the performative character of historical truth, that is the point."[36] By focusing these questions on the events of 9/11 and the symbol of the WTC, the novel makes use of one national crisis to explore the questions of Jewish nationalism, homeland, and language that it raises through the construction of the imaginary state of Isra Isle. And it suggests that no matter the timeline, national tragedies, or tragedies of nationalism, are foundational to the nation itself and therefore at some base level cannot be averted. As with the case of the Small Holocaust in *Unholy Land*, *Isra Isle*'s treatment of 9/11 and Native American history indicates that catastrophe inheres in nation building and that national conflict is inevitable. The dystopia of these alternative histories suggests that war, colonialism, and terror are all natural outcomes of nationalism, wherever the nation establishes itself. In this view, Israel and its conflict with the Palestinians is the rule, not the exception, and the presence of the Zionist narrative on the edges of these alternative homelands serves to normalize Israel's history and present through an acknowledgment that the what-if is not so different from what is.

2

American Hebrew

The Transnational Israeli Novel in the Twenty-First Century

Just as the history of Jewish nationalism includes the unrealized dreams of diaspora homelands, the history of Hebrew has its own diasporic past. Modern Hebrew emerged from both a synchronic and a diachronic fusion: synchronically, modern Hebrew grammar and vocabulary were drawn in various ways from European languages as well as Yiddish; diachronically, modern Hebrew grammar and vocabulary were drawn from the many temporal layers of the language, including biblical, rabbinic, and medieval texts. But as Zionism took hold in the prestate Yishuv, ideology began to retroactively shape the image of Hebrew as inextricably linked to Israel and as oppositional to a denigrated diasporic Jewish culture.

Linguistically, the modern Hebrew literary idiom relied on the grammar and vocabulary of other languages, including Yiddish, Russian, and German. When modern Hebrew literature arose in the nineteenth century, Hebrew was not a vernacular language and lacked both the modern vocabulary and the particular syntax necessary to represent dialogue. Uri Nissan Gnessin coined the modern Hebrew word for "consciousness," *hakarah*, by turning to the root for "knowledge," because both German and French derive their words for "consciousness" from "knowledge." And Robert Alter notes that the Hebrew writer Micha Yosef Berdichevsky had a "predisposition to make Hebrew work as though it were a dialectical variation of standard literary European."[1]

At the same time, the long history of the Hebrew language meant that there were many different forms and varieties of the language to draw from to create a modern literary style. S. Y. Abramovitz, who created the definitive *nusakh*, or style, of modern literary Hebrew, drew on various temporal layers of Hebrew from the ancient and medieval periods, the inflections and syntax of Yiddish, and literary influences as varied as Dickens, whom Abramovitz had read in translation, and Gogol.[2]

These writers drew on European literature and language for their influences because, culturally speaking, they were Europeans as much as they were Jewish. Indeed, beginning with the *haskalah*—the Jewish Enlightenment, which began in late eighteenth-century Germany—and continuing through Abramovitz and later generations, Hebrew writers in Europe were invested in demonstrating both their own European-ness and the Europeanness of their literature. Partially as a result of this investment in European culture, and partially as a result of the peripatetic lifestyles of many of the major modern Hebrew writers, their styles were heavily indebted to European modernism. As Shachar Pinsker has shown, "Modernist Hebrew prose fiction, as it emerged from 1900 to 1930, was shaped by the encounter between young Jewish writers attempting to forge a sense-of-self in Hebrew and the shifting terrain of European modernity."[3] Similarly, Allison Schachter has argued that writing in literary languages that had no fixed national borders gave rise to many of the particular modernist techniques employed by modern Hebrew and Yiddish writers and that their very modernism was a way of imagining "alternative forms of literary community" to the dominant national model.[4] In other words, the origins of modern, and modernist, Hebrew fiction lie in the encounter between Jewish writers and the cultural centers of the diaspora, and that literature developed as a specifically transnational phenomenon.

However, since the establishment of the state of Israel in 1948, Hebrew literature has been largely concentrated in Israel and, as Yaron Peleg has noted, the establishment of the state remains the primary marker by which Hebrew literature and culture have been analyzed and categorized by critics like Gershon Shaked and Dan Miron.[5] In recent years, however, the gravitational pull of the state on Hebrew literature has been tested by Hebrew writers living outside of Israel, as illustrated by the controversy over the 2015 Sapir Prize for Hebrew literature. In that year, the Hebrew writer Ruby Namdar, who has lived in New York City for more than a decade, was awarded the Sapir for his novel *Habayit Asher Nekhrav* (*The Ruined House*), making him the first recipient of the award who was not a resident of Israel. Namdar (b. 1964) was born and raised in Jerusalem in a Persian Jewish family. Although they spoke Hebrew at home, his grandmother also taught him Farsi. He began writing fiction after his graduation from the Hebrew University of Jerusalem, but until the publication of *The Ruined House* he had only published one book of short stories and a novella. In 2000, he began splitting his time between New York and Israel and eventually settled in New York, where he lives with his family.

While written in a rich, resonant Hebrew, Namdar's novel takes place in his adopted hometown of New York and focuses on an American Jewish professor, making its setting and themes uniquely diasporic. A few months after Namdar was awarded the Sapir, the prize rules were changed to exclude from eligibility writers who reside outside Israel. Although the prevailing argument of the prize committee for the change was because of the difficult economic conditions for writers living in Israel, it is hard to see the modification of rules as anything other than a response, even a backlash, to Namdar's win.

The controversy over the Sapir Prize points to the power of the Zionist insistence on the connection between language and land, as well as old notions of the diaspora as an improper or inferior place for Jews and Jewish culture. In an age of globalization and expanded opportunities for connection beyond borders, an increasing number of Hebrew writers choose, for various reasons, to make their homes outside of Israel. While the numbers of these writers remain small, their work nonetheless exerts influence on the Israeli cultural landscape, as evidenced by Namdar's prizewinning novel. Likewise, the work of Maya Arad, another Hebrew novelist who has lived in California for decades, is extremely popular in Israel. Arad (b. 1971), raised on kibbutz Nahal Oz as well as in

Rishon Letzion, earned a PhD in linguistics at the University of London and since that time has always lived abroad. Since 2003, when her first novel appeared, she has published eight books of fiction, both novels and novellas, many of them satirical portraits of American academia. Since 2014 she has been a lecturer at the Taube Center for Jewish Studies at Stanford University, where her husband is also a professor.

Despite her long residence in the United States and the focus of her work on American life, Arad is little known to English readers in America, as her work has not been extensively translated. Some of her short stories and samples of her novels have appeared in English translations online, but no American publisher has yet produced a full English edition of one of her works, despite their largely American settings and characters. This demonstrates Peleg's claim that "it is possible to speak of Hebrew works written outside of Israel only in relationship to the sovereign Hebrew state," since those works are published and mostly read by Israelis.[6] At the same time, they can tell us something about the relationship between the American Jewish community and Israel. Omri Asscher, in his study of translation practices between Hebrew and English, notes that "although translation was meant to serve as a bridge to the culture of the source literature, upon close examination it seems to attest above all to the target-language culture—its expectations and concerns and the symbolic boundaries it sought to establish in response to the challenge represented by its Jewish Other."[7] The relative lack of translations of Arad's work offers some insight into the interests and appetites of American Jewish readers, in particular, with regard to Israeli culture.

The complicated relationship of these Hebrew novels and novelists to Israel and America offers a critique of the Israel-diaspora relationship, and even the framing of Israel and diaspora as oppositional, in both their language and their settings. In an article on Hebrew writers who live outside of Israel, Beth Kissileff asks, referring to Cynthia Ozick's claim that the only Jewish literature that has survived in the diaspora is in some way "centrally Jewish," "If something is in Hebrew and written in the Diaspora—and of the Diaspora—does that make it 'centrally Jewish' by language alone? Or is a new definition needed?"[8] Equally, we might ask whether something written in Hebrew is "centrally Israeli" by language alone or whether transporting the language beyond the borders of the land challenges what it means to be Israeli.

Contrary to Peleg's claim that most Hebrew literature written outside of Israel nonetheless chooses Israeli subjects and settings, the work of Maya Arad and Ruby Namdar is largely located in American landscapes and populated with American characters, even when those American characters are originally, or also, Israeli. Namdar's *The Ruined House* and Arad's novella *Hamorah Le'ivrit* (The Hebrew Teacher), in particular, both follow college professors at American universities through personal and professional crises. The colleges, professors, and circumstances—as well as the genre—of these books are radically different, and yet through different routes they take similar approaches to the question of Hebrew in America and diaspora Jewish life. Namdar's novel follows the American Jewish college professor Andrew Cohen, who begins to have visions of the Temple in Jerusalem and its destruction, as he descends into a nervous breakdown of his own. Arad's novella chronicles the Hebrew lecturer Ilana Goldstein, forced into retirement due to declining enrollment in her university Hebrew classes and a conflict over the politics of Hebrew with a newly hired Israeli professor of Hebrew literature.

These books, in their own ways, express a deep identification with American landscapes, cultures, and attitudes even while maintaining a connection to Israel as an (not *the*) anchor of Jewish life. Rather than expressing an alienation from America and American life, these writers explore the ways that Hebrew might live and thrive in America, geographically removed from the state of Israel, as part of the vibrancy, multiculturalism, and multilingualism of diaspora Jewish culture. While their work is not explicitly political, the relocation of Hebrew language and culture to an American setting nonetheless challenges Zionist conceptions of Hebrew culture as a nation-building enterprise. They both recognize Hebrew as an important element of Jewish culture and history, while questioning its status as the primary national language of the Jewish people. In these works, Hebrew does not stand between the characters and their Americanness, nor is it the signal par excellence of their Jewishness, their Zionism, or their Israeliness. Whereas the novels discussed in chapter 1 imagine a world in which the state of Israel does not exist in its present form, Namdar's and Arad's works contend with the coexistence of multiple Jewish homelands, recognizing America as a center of Jewish life equally important to Israel. In their imagining, these multiple centers of Jewish life enrich, rather than diminish, both Jewish and Hebrew culture.

O NEW YORK

In *The Ruined House*, New York is not just the backdrop to the events of the book but, in a sense, a character itself. The Hebrew title of the book, *Habayit Asher Nekhrav*, literally "the house that was destroyed," refers to the destroyed Temple in Jerusalem. In Hebrew, the dual meaning of *bayit*, which can refer both to an everyday home and to the central location for worship in biblical Israelite religion, makes the title a kind of double entendre. Not only does it conjure up the origins of Jewish diaspora, which began with the destruction of the first Temple in 586 BCE, but it also suggests a more quotidian type of ruin, the deterioration of the very idea of home. In contrast to this image of a destroyed home (or homeland), it presents a vital, dynamic portrait of contemporary New York in the months leading up to September 11, a destructive event that becomes a foil to the historical destruction of the Temple.

The terms in which New York is described and discussed in the novel verge on an almost liturgical glorification. The second chapter begins with a lofty homage to the city: "O Manhattan, isle of the gods, home to great happenings of metal, glass, and energy, island of sharp angles, summit of the world! Have not we all—rich and poor, producers and consumers, providers and provided for—been laboring for generations with all our might, under the direction of an unseen Engineer, to build the most magnificent city ever known to humankind?"[9] The passage continues with specific references to the landmarks and landscapes of Manhattan: the Empire State Building, the Hudson River, Wall Street, and the like. It celebrates, with possessive language like "our island," identifying the place as belonging to both speaker and readers, the grand beauty and accomplishments of New York. This focus on New York as a celebrated locale establishes the city not just as a setting for the novel but as a character in it, the place (or at least one place) to which the *bayit* of the title refers.

This apostrophic ode to New York also recalls the work of Walt Whitman, an iconic poet of the landscapes of New York. In his poem "Mannahatta," Whitman writes of "Numberless crowded streets, high growths of iron, slender, strong, light, splendidly uprising toward clear skies" and "The mechanics of the city, the masters, well-form'd, beautiful-faced, looking you straight in the eyes."[10] Namdar's celebration of the landscape describes, like Whitman's, an almost religious admiration for the craft and construction of such a massive city, finding beauty in its buildings and streets. But the beginning and end of Whitman's poem may provide an even clearer reading of the specifically transnational character of Namdar's New York. The first line of "Mannahatta" begins, "I was asking for something specific and perfect for my city, / Whereupon lo! upsprang the aboriginal name." Whitman begins from an acknowledgment of the city's origins as a native space, adopted (or stolen) by those who built it into its current incarnation. After recounting its many wonders, Whitman ends, "City nested in bays! my city!" In the course of the poem, New York has gone from its "aboriginal," native roots to becoming the possession of the poet, the white settler. The original name, that "word from of old," is now "the word of *my* city" (emphasis added). Likewise, Namdar's ode to New York, echoing Whitman's poem in Hebrew, suggests that through the linguistic transformation and appropriation of writing about the city in Hebrew, he, too, takes possession of the place, bringing it into the Hebrew literary tradition, according it the position of a linguistic homeland.

This is a very different attitude toward New York than Hebrew literature written in America historically took. Michael Weingrad has detailed the ways in which New York came to represent, for an early twentieth-century generation of American Hebraists, all of the characteristics that led to their own alienation from American life: urbanism, loneliness, modernism, irreligiosity, exile.[11] Unlike Namdar's embrace of the city, which echoes Whitman's classic of American literature, poets like Shimon Ginzburg used similar language to decry the ills of New York. In his poem "No York," Ginzburg, too, addressed the city apostrophically, but to different ends, predicting its demise: "A day will come—Moloch! City!—when you will be overthrown."[12] Ginzburg, unlike Namdar, rejects New York as a home, comparing it instead to a false god.

Nonetheless, even poets like Ginzburg could not resist the call of the city entirely, and the power of its landscapes and images nonetheless drew them. In another poem, "Behar beit Kolombiyah," Ginzburg, like Namdar, brings the New York landscape into a Jewish geography. The title of the poem, which Weingrad translates as "On the Temple Mount of Columbia," accounting for the dual meaning of the word *bayit* discussed above, recalls, like the title of the novel, the sacred geography of Judaism, in which the Temple Mount is the center and the site of homeland. Here Ginzburg too uses the resonant layers of Hebrew to attach Jewish significance to New York landmarks, in particular Columbia University, a kind of modern-day temple of learning and advancement, as well as potential assimilation.[13] Thus, *The Ruined House*, while revaluing earlier Hebrew literary representations of New York, also follows in a tradition in which the city is inevitably experienced as a center of Jewish life, one that verges on the holy.

"THE REAL AMERICA"

Ilana, the eponymous Hebrew teacher of Arad's novella, echoes some of the American Hebraists' disdain for New York while at the same time expressing affection for America itself. When another professor suggests that a prospective job candidate might not want to take the position because of the location of their university, Ilana thinks, "What's so bad about the Midwest? This is the real America, friendly, welcoming—she would not be able to survive in New York for even a month."[14] Her affection not just for America but also for the heartland—the Midwest—as the "real America," reflects her own sense, after forty-five years in the United States, of deep belonging. Even her personal dislike of New York, and her understanding of it as culturally and geographically distinct from the Midwest, suggests how deeply embedded she is in the American landscape. And her love for the Midwest, her characterization of it as the "real America," also reflects an understanding of the whole of the country, of Americanness itself, as compatible with Jewish life and even with her cultural status as an expatriate Israeli.

Nonetheless, Ilana is deeply identified with Israel and her own Israeliness. Danielle Drori argues that Ilana and her foil, the anti-Zionist Israeli professor of Hebrew literature Yo'ad Bergmann-Harari, are vehicles for Arad's satire of the entrenchment of two binary worldviews: one that envisions Israel as the Jewish homeland and center of Jewish life and culture, which is specifically Hebrew, and one that is determined to decenter Israel as the Jewish homeland and reemphasize the importance of diaspora in Jewish history and contemporary life.[15] Arad's satire, then, also functions to ridicule the very binarism represented by Ilana's and Yo'ad's divergent worldviews. But at the same time, Ilana herself is also represented as far more ambivalent than her association with the state of Israel might suggest.

For example, while Ilana often expresses some disdain or distance from American Jewish life and culture and the diaspora in general, she nonetheless knows that she has, in many ways, become American, maybe more American than she is Israeli. To be collegial, Ilana invites the new professor Yo'ad to her house for a Shabbat dinner with some friends of hers and her American husband, Shelly. Just before he arrives, Ilana has a moment of panic: "Suddenly she was ashamed of it, the house of which she had always been so proud. She imagines what he thinks: a diaspora home. She, diasporic!" (19).[16] At the same time that Ilana experiences a moment of shame for her diaspora lifestyle, through the eyes of Yo'ad, who she mistakenly imagines will judge her for her insufficient Israeliness (he actually judges her for the opposite), she nonetheless also acknowledges that she is, indeed, diasporic, as she puts it.

Likewise, at dinner, Ilana expresses disdain for American Jewish practices while at the same time acknowledging that these have become her own standard modes of identifying as Jewish. As she looks around her Shabbat table, "everyone looked so diasporic to her. Amusing, with their customs. And what is this hypocrisy? Saying *kiddush* and lighting candles but going to synagogue by car? In the meantime she has already assimilated and gotten used to it, it's hard for her already to remember how she felt then, when she had just arrived here" (23). Ilana is still able to look at her very own Shabbat table, her very own standard Jewish practices, as an Israeli outsider, seeing them as somehow inauthentic, while at the same time understanding that these practices make up who she is now.

Although Ilana ostensibly represents a stock Israeli character, one who still feels an uncomplicated affection for the state, with which she literally shares a birthday, it is clear that she is not one or the other, Israeli or American, but an amalgamation of both. When she finds herself thinking of herself as Israeli, she knows this identity is not sufficient to describe her anymore. Speaking to Yo'ad about the local consulate, which he declines to work with, she finds herself getting defensive on Israel's behalf. "We have no other state, she thinks, but doesn't say. Who is she to talk? She's been in America forty-five years already" (55). Ilana's ambivalence, her in-between identity, calls into question the very binary upon which she imagines her identity as an Israeli depends, the opposition of Israel and the diaspora. In many ways, Ilana has become a "real American" while at the same time remaining resolutely Israeli.

RECONCEIVING HOMELAND

In *The Ruined House*, the merging of diaspora and homeland is accomplished not through a human character but through a kind of mystical recasting of New York as the Jerusalem of America. The opening scene of the novel, written in an elevated, precise style, describes how "the gates of heaven were opened above the great city of New York, and behold:

all seven celestial spheres were revealed, right above the West 4th Street subway station, layered one on top of another like the rungs of a ladder reaching skyward from the earth" (H 11, E 3). The Temple in Jerusalem was imagined by the Israelites as the place where the *Shekhinah*, the presence of God, resided, a gateway into heaven much like the one described in the opening of the novel. Here, the same honor is bestowed on a quintessentially New York space, one that defines and maps the city itself and distinguishes it from other American cities: the subway.

The image of the ladder in this scene also recalls the biblical story of Jacob's flight from his own home in the land of Israel, an individual exile and one that also set in motion the origin story of the Jewish people. On his journey, Jacob dreams of "a ladder set up on the earth, and the top of it reached to heaven; and behold the angels of God ascending and descending on it" (Gen. 28:12). The novel borrows language verbatim from this passage, inserting in the middle of the biblical language the passage that locates the event in the middle of Manhattan:

וַיַּחֲלֹם וְהִנֵּה סֻלָּם מֻצָּב אַרְצָה וְרֹאשׁוֹ מַגִּיעַ הַשָּׁמַיְמָה וְהִנֵּה מַלְאֲכֵי אֱלֹהִים עֹלִים וְיֹרְדִים בּוֹ:

. . . שֶׁל סוּלָם הַנִּצָּב אַרְצָה, מַמָּשׁ מֵעַל תַּחֲנַת הָרַכֶּבֶת הַתַּחְתִּית שֶׁל הָרְחוֹב הָרְבִיעִי, וְרֹאשׁוֹ מַגִּיעַ הַשָּׁמַיְמָה.

While Halkin's translation preserves the flow of the sentence, a more literal translation of this passage from the novel that accounts for its biblical prooftext might read: "a ladder planted on the earth, directly above the Fourth Street subway station, with its top reaching the heavens." It makes use of vocabulary deliberately drawn from the biblical passage, in particular the six words *sulam mutzav artza ve'rosho magia hashamayma* (a ladder planted on earth and its top reaching to heaven), which in Namdar's borrowing are interrupted by a clause locating the action in the midst of New York. This kind of word play is typical of the novel's mixed style, which itself recalls the heterogenous roots of Hebrew. And in its dependent middle clause, the text quite literally inserts New York itself into the Hebrew canon by placing the Fourth Street subway station in the middle of Jacob's biblical dream.

This placement also has meaning for the relationship between Israel and diaspora; a *midrash* in Bereshit Rabbah connects the dream metaphorically to the Temple:

> "That there was a ladder": refers to the ramp to the altar. ". . . Set up on the earth": that is the altar, "An altar of dirt you will make for me" (Ex. 20:24). ". . . And the top of it reached to heaven": these are the offerings, for their fragrance goes up to heaven. ". . . And behold, the angels of God": these are the high priests. ". . . Were ascending and descending on it": for they go up and go down on the ramp. "And behold, the Lord stood above it": "I saw the Lord standing by the altar" (Amos 9:1). (Gen. Rabbah 68:12)[17]

In this interpretation, the elements of Jacob's dream represent elements of the Temple and its sacrificial cult. The image of the ladder, here extending from the Fourth Street subway station into the heavens, relocates the center of Jewish life, Jerusalem, squarely in the midst of New York City. Thus not only is New York relocated into the central text of the Hebrew canon, but Jerusalem, and by extension the Jewish homeland, is relocated into the space of the diaspora.

These reconfigurations of space offer a fluid conception of the relationship between center and periphery, homeland and diaspora, that challenges the binarization of these concepts and locations. Likewise, the content of the dream offers a conception of the relationship between homeland and exile as one of exchange rather than separation. In another *midrash*, the rabbis claimed that the angels ascending the ladder—notably, the ascent comes before the descent—were those who accompanied Jacob inside the land and those who descended were a separate set of angels meant to accompany him in exile (Gen. Rabbah 68:12). Again, here we have a dichotomy between the land of Israel and the diaspora, but again that binary is bridged by the image of the ladder and the angels who move from earth to heaven and back. This movement suggests fluid passage rather than a strict boundary, and the association of New York with a direct line to the divine—whether through angelic exchange or access to the Temple—anoints the city as a center, or homeland, much like Jerusalem.

This image of exchange is also consistent with the tradition of transcultural literature to which Namdar's novel and Arad's work belong and serves as a metaphor for the very process of creating Hebrew or Israeli culture outside of Israel. Transcultural literature—including Hebrew literature written outside of Israel and Israeli literature written in languages other than Hebrew—offers a view of cultures as not being "mutually exclusive absolutes as in the past; rather, they are increasingly being perceived as hybridizing organisms in continuous dialogue with one another, fluctuating in the ongoing transmutation of cultural 'permeations,' amalgamations, and confluences."[18] As is evident in the opening scene, in *The Ruined House*, New York becomes the pivot for this dialogic exchange and in this way offers a transcultural reassessment of the definitions of and relationships between homeland and diaspora.

New York's role as coexistent homeland is established through a process of mapping that offers an alternate geographical historiography of the city. This revisionist geography refigures New York as a center of Jewish life on par with Jerusalem, and America with the land of Israel. This is evident, for example, in the novel's description of Yom Kippur in Manhattan. The main character, Professor Andrew Cohen, a secular American Jew, is nonetheless heading to synagogue on the morning of Yom Kippur, the one day of the year that he attends services. The city is described as having a slightly altered character on the holy day: "Broadway was less crowded than usual. Yom Kippur made itself felt all over the city, most of all on the Upper West Side" (H 44, E 34). Like the silent streets of Jerusalem on Yom Kippur, here New York is imagined as a Jewish space, a place where the holiest day on the Jewish calendar makes a noticeable impression.

The novel also makes clear the ways in which center and periphery shift over time, in a fluid exchange reminiscent of the ascent and descent of the angels. As is evident from the passage above, it is not just New

York as a whole but the Upper West Side specifically that functions as
the diasporic center of Jewish life in the novel. But the book also recalls
a recent history in which the center of New York Jewish life was located
elsewhere, on the Lower East Side. Indeed, as Andrew navigates his way
to the synagogue on Yom Kippur, which is nostalgically located in that
historically Jewish neighborhood, he stands in the subway station considering his route:

איך מגיעים ללואר איסט סייד? זה ממש בצד השני של העולם: צריך
יהיה לקחת את הרכבת מספר 1 או 9 לרחוב ארבע-עשרה, לחצות את
המעבר התת-קרקעי אל הרציף של הקווים הכתומים: B, D או F
ולהמשיך משם דרום-מזרחה. צריך להקפיד ולרדת בתחנה הנכונה, בשנה
שעברה הוא שקע בקריאה ומצא את עצמו בברוקלין (46).

How do you get to the Lower East Side? It's on the other side of the
world, really: you would have to take the 1 or 9 train to 14th Street,
cross the underground passage to the platform for the orange lines:
F, B, or D, and continue from there southeast. You have to pay attention
and get off at the right station, last year he was absorbed in reading and
found himself in Brooklyn.[19]

The Lower East Side, of course, is the neighborhood most closely associated with the history of Jewish life in New York and perhaps even in
the United States as a whole. But in this precise and complex catalog of
its actual and practical distance from Andrew's home on the Upper West
Side, it is clear that the Jewish world of New York has shifted away from
this center and now resides elsewhere, perhaps diffused throughout the
city and even the country. This movement suggests that there can be no
fixed center, no perpetual and eternal homeland, existing for eternity in
relationship to a far-flung exile but rather that the human sense and definition of what constitutes a center—and, by extension, what constitutes
exile and how that is valued—shift over time. Homeland and diaspora,
then, are always relative, not just to each other but to time, to history,
and to culture.

Likewise, these multifarious homelands are also permeable and infiltrate and influence each other. Once the heavens above New York have opened, the world of the ancient center, the Temple in Jerusalem, begins to invade contemporary America. This occurs primarily through Andrew, who becomes the conduit for visions and dreams of Jerusalem and the Temple as the date of its destruction approaches. These visions begin rather innocently, with an occasional glimpse of an odd beam of light or white cow walking down a city street, escalating into violent images of rape and murder that seep into his waking world, causing him to become physically ill and even afraid to leave his apartment. Eventually, although the cause and effect relationship is unclear, Andrew begins to have a kind of nervous breakdown.

This breakdown and the permeability of the worlds of ancient and modern, homeland and diaspora, and Jerusalem and New York also suggest the instability of the idea of a fixed and permanent center. The novel, divided into seven books, contains an epigraph at the beginning of each book. The epigraph of the sixth book is a translated excerpt of William Butler Yeats's 1919 poem "The Second Coming," which contains the well-known line "Things fall apart; the center cannot hold." This text signals one of the novel's main themes: the suggestion that no one "center" can, for all eternity, function as the fulcrum for a diverse, rich, heterogeneous Jewish life and culture. By privileging New York as a Jewish homeland, while at the same time acknowledging the historical primacy of Jerusalem, the novel repudiates the binarism of homeland and diaspora that underlies Zionist ideology and, by extension, Israeli culture. And in translating a classic work of English literature into Hebrew, the novel also brings other literary traditions into Hebrew culture. Indeed, translation of foreign literature into Hebrew was, as Adriana Jacobs notes, "a major, indispensable component of modern Hebrew literary production" in the early twentieth century and was crucial to the development of a Hebrew literary idiom in both prose and poetry.[20] The epigraphs, then, affirm the persistence and importance of the diaspora to Jewish life and culture, not just in the past but also in the present.

A GOOD TIME FOR HEBREW

In both *The Hebrew Teacher* and *The Ruined House*, a focus on language is one mode of affirming the physical and geographical mixing of Israel and diaspora represented in other parts of the books. The main character in each of these novels undergoes a major crisis, and while the nature and expression of those crises are very different, in both they at least partially stem from a collision of an Israel and a diaspora assumed to be diametrically opposed but revealed to be deeply intertwined. The crises themselves, then, arise from the artificiality of the dichotomy between Israel and diaspora, and whatever resolution is achieved comes about from the new understandings of diaspora as home that are hinted at above. Another primary way this effect is achieved is through the use of Hebrew in the novels. Indeed, both books, as Hebrew novels written in and about America by Israeli authors living permanently in the United States, exist as artifacts, in a sense, of the challenge to the dichotomization of Israel and diaspora. They are examples in themselves of Hebrew in America, of the existence and flourishing of a diaspora Hebrew culture even after the adoption of Hebrew as a state language by Israel.

Likewise, their translation history reveals something about the relationship between Israeli Hebrew culture and American Jewish culture: Namdar's book, the recipient of a major Israeli prize that carries with it an award that includes an English translation, was published in the United States by a major American publisher (HarperCollins) and positively reviewed in the *New York Times*; Arad has hardly been translated into English at all, and while her work has been the recipient of critical accolades and smaller awards, she has not received the kind of state-sponsored approval that attends to a prize like the Sapir. Asscher catalogs the ways Israeli literature translated into English was historically chosen for translation because the subject matter accorded with what American Jewish audiences expected or wanted representations of Israel to be.[21] While *The Ruined House* is, in many ways, as focused on Jerusalem and Judaism (both ancient and modern) as it is on its American landscapes and American Jewish life, Arad's novels tend to be focused on American academia, academics and writers, and families, sometimes without much reference to Jewish life or Israel. Nonetheless, the way both Arad and Namdar examine and use Hebrew consciously deconstructs the dichotomy between Israel and America reflected in this translation history and reconstructs a new, multivalent understanding of diaspora and its relationship to Israel and, especially, the state.

In a way, these works recapture an earlier period in American Hebraism, when the writers of the *tarbut ivrit* movement imagined the United States as a potential center of Hebrew culture.[22] The establishment of the state of Israel foreclosed that possibility, but, in an age of globalization and migration, not only America but other cultural centers that were once the laboratories of Hebrew literature, like Berlin, have again become the sites of Hebrew cultural production. As Namdar has said, "Hebrew is my real homeland."[23] Much like George Steiner's notion of text as homeland, this idea of Hebrew as mobile, as creating a cultural space in the diaspora, establishes its value outside of Zionist ideology and its association with state power, although, unlike Steiner's claim, not necessarily in opposition to it.

The very first line of Arad's novella works to begin this deconstructive project. Although the novella is written almost entirely in Hebrew, the very first line is in English: "It wasn't a very good time for Hebrew" (4). Opening the story with English, especially an English line describing Hebrew in crisis, immediately signals that language is contingent and, perhaps, arbitrary, suggesting that both the memoir Ilana is writing and the novella itself could easily be composed in either language. Adam Rovner writes that Arad's novella "glories in its multilingualism and flaunts a lack of fealty to national borders," in which even the Hebrew itself is inflected with American English.[24] This is reflected in the transliterations of common English phrases and place names, as well as English idioms in English, that pepper the text. A particular American Jewish flavor is also imparted to the Hebrew through the introduction of common Yiddishisms used by the American characters, including Ilana's husband, Shelly, when he calls the new professor Ilana has a conflict with a "putz," and her former department chair, when he uses the affectionate term "meydele." This use of Yiddish also reconstructs an elided history of Hebrew as part of what Benjamin Harshav, borrowing a term from Itamar Even-Zohar, called the linguistic "polysystem" of Ashkenazi Jewish culture.[25]

This polysystem is made explicitly evident in *The Ruined House* as a deliberate technique to expose the synthetic nature of modern Hebrew and peels away the layers of its diaspora history, destabilizing the Zionist narrative that associates Hebrew with Israel and Israel with Hebrew. Several methods employed in the novel call attention to Hebrew's diverse and complicated origins, as well as its polyphonous history: the long sections of a partially invented sacrificial service that end each section of the book; the epigraphs that appear at the beginning of each book; the incorporation of translated popular songs into the text; and the translation and transliteration of place names. Many of these techniques also have a parallel, even if executed on a smaller scale, within Arad's novella.

In Namdar's novel, the first layer of this linguistic pastiche lies in a text that appears in sections, a few pages at a time, inserted into the novel at the end of each book, which function as parts of the larger narrative. This text is the *seder ha'avodah*, or the "Order of the Ritual" for the sacrificial service, that details the process of the high priest preparing himself, performing the sacrifices, and entering the Holy of Holies on Yom Kippur. However, the text that appears in the book is not the text that appears in the High Holiday liturgy but rather one of Namdar's own creation, cobbled together from both existing sources and the imagination. The text details the sacrificial rite through the long *piyyut*, or devotional poem, written in alphabetical order, composed by the eleventh-century poet Meshullam ben Kalonymous;[26] excerpts from the Mishnah and Talmud that describe the Yom Kippur sacrifice; parts of the sixteenth-century kabbalistic text *Sha'ar Hagilgulim*, by Rabbi Chaim Vital, a disciple of the kabbalist Yitzhak Luria; the third-person narrative of the priest's activities drawn from standard liturgies; and a long narrative of Namdar's own creation detailing these events through the experience of a common priest observing and participating in the ritual (fig. 6).

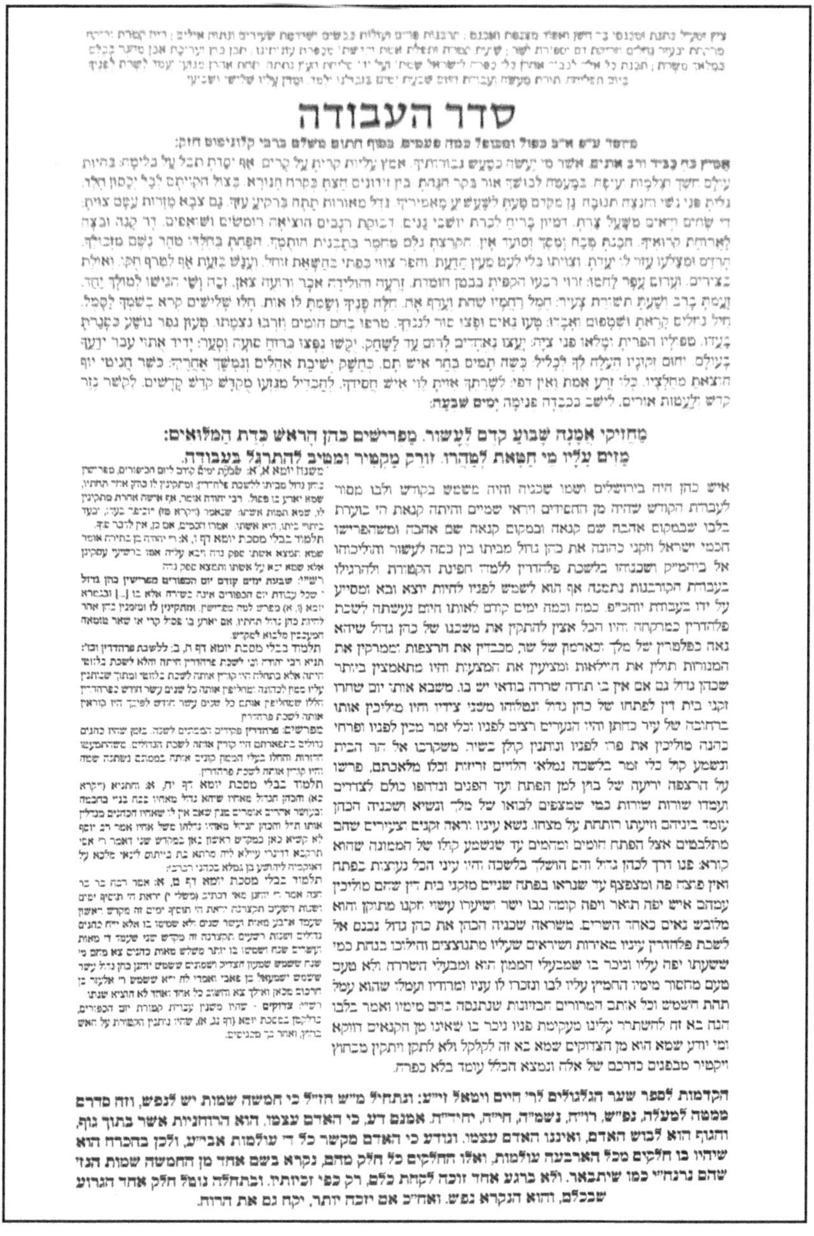

סדר העבודה

מַחֲזִיקֵי אֱמָנָה שְׁבוּעַ קֹדֶם לֶעָשׂוֹר. מַפְרִישִׁים כֹּהֵן הָרֹאשׁ כְּדַת הַמִּלּוּאִים:

מַיִם עָלָיו מִי חַטָּאת לְטַהֲרוֹ. זוֹרֵק מַקְטִיר וּמֵטִיב לְהִתְרַגֵּל בָּעֲבוֹדָה.

FIGURE 6. An image of the first page of the *seder ha'avodah* from *Habayit Asher Nekhrav*, showing the organization of the various texts and layers of Hebrew on the page.

Setting aside the links this invented text has with the rest of the novel and its function in relationship to the plot, it highlights certain elements of language that relate specifically to the diasporic context and theme of the novel. Crucial to this unusual makeup of texts is that it represents the many temporal layers of Hebrew language, from the biblical through the modern period, as well as the varieties of religious expression for which Hebrew has been used throughout its history. But most importantly, even in a text focused on Jerusalem as the center of Jewish life and the origin of Jewish ritual worship—and, even further, on the central point of the central point of that worship, the Holy of Holies in the Temple—this synthetic *seder ha'avodah*, in its composition and language, calls attention to the diasporic history of Judaism and, by extension, of Hebrew.

It does so first through the choice of texts. Arrayed on the edges of each page are selections from both the Mishnah and the Babylonian Talmud related to the sacrificial rite. The central text governing Jewish religious life after the destruction of the Temple, perhaps the very text that established rabbinic Judaism as a religion, was not composed in Israel, the focal point around which the text itself pivots, but rather in the diaspora communities of Babylon. The *piyyut* that forms the bulk of the *seder ha'avodah* in modern Ashkenazi liturgies and is quoted in sections on each page of Namdar's invented text was composed by an Italian poet and Talmudist who later settled in Germany. And the excerpts from *Sha'ar Hagilgulim* about the reincarnation of souls, portions of which appear at the bottom of each page of this contemporary *seder ha'avodah*, were written by a kabbalist born in Tzfat who later lived in Egypt and Ottoman Syria and was the head of the Damascus Jewish community, where he died. Finally, there are the unattributed texts on the page, which also chronicle the sacrificial rite, although with the addition of marginal characters and including very modern, novelistic documentation of the actions, feelings, and reactions of both priests and the community. These texts, although written in a classical idiom, are contemporary, written by the author of the novel specifically for the purpose of the book. And, like the rest of the novel, we know that these texts were written in New York, by a Hebrew writer who lives, even now, in a Jewish, and Hebrew, diaspora.

Thus, the very choice of texts for this synthetic liturgy purposefully reflects a long history of Hebrew language, and Jewish culture, in the diaspora. This diasporic history of Hebrew is also revealed through language, specifically through the use of mostly Greek loan words common in rabbinic Hebrew. All of the texts use common classical Hebrew vocabulary derived from Greek, words like *palhedrin* (also *parhedrin*), which refers to the counselors to the high priest; *istnis*, Greek for "delicate," used to describe the high priest's constitution; and the adaptation *hediyot*, a layperson or a lay priest, derived from the Greek *idiotes*, or "commoner" (and also, of course, the source of the English word "idiot"). The use of these etymologically Greek words in the Hebrew of the description of the holiest service in Jewish religious tradition indicates the extent to which Hebrew, at its very core, has always been influenced, and even constructed, by its contact with non-Jewish diasporic cultures. The fact that these Greek words were used to describe a specifically Jewish rite shows that even the most vital Jewish religious and cultural elements—like the priesthood or the sacrificial rite—cannot be described except through language derived and adapted from the surrounding culture. In other words, diaspora is not just incidental to the development of Hebrew as a Jewish language but actually necessary to it.

The literal flip side to the device of the fabricated *seder ha'avodah* are the epigraphs that appear (in the Hebrew edition only) at the beginning of each book, as the seven major sections of the novel are called. While the *seder ha'avodah* appears at the end of each book (with one exception in which a section appears in the middle of the first book), the epigraphs appear on the other side of the page (or the next one). These epigraphs are chosen from a variety of sources, including Hebrew poets, the German psychoanalyst Carl Jung, and American and British poets. Again, this choice of sources reveals the fundamentally absorptive nature of Hebrew and its dependence on outside influences, Jewish and non-Jewish, for its vitality. In addition, the epigraphs and their authors reflect not only on the subject matter of the individual books and the novel as a whole but also on the history of Hebrew language and literature.

However, that these epigraphs appear only in the Hebrew edition of the novel also speaks to issues of cultural translation between Israeli and American audiences. The English-language poems represented in the epigraphs, appearing in English, would of course not have the same effect as they do in the Hebrew version, where, again, they speak to the absorptive history of Hebrew and its dependence on foreign translation for its development. Like the *piyyut*, the medieval acrostic devotional poem, in the *seder ha'avodah*, the Hebrew and Yiddish writer Uri Tzvi Greenberg's poetry is both practically and culturally difficult to translate. While a *piyyut* would be familiar to the American Jewish reader, as they are common elements of the liturgy, it would have little significance to a broader English-language audience, and the alphabetical acrostic would have been difficult to preserve. Greenberg is often labeled "untranslatable" because of his neologisms and expressionist aesthetics, and Namdar felt there was "no need to add yet another layer of alienation between the novel and the American reader," who would have had no touchstone for understanding Greenberg's work in the context of the history of Hebrew literature.[27] However, Greenberg's extreme right-wing politics as well as his sometimes unflattering portrayals of non-Jews might also make his work unpalatable to American readers. Indeed, the epigraph preceding book 4 contains the line "There are two kinds of men in the world: circumcised—uncircumcised" (191), a declaration that might not sit well with the American reader. Asscher has documented many instances in the history of Hebrew translation into English in which the Hebrew version was modified or redacted for essentially political reasons, either because it did not accord with American ideas about Zionism and its morality or because it offered antagonistic portrayals of diaspora Jews.[28] The decision not to translate these epigraphs, then, highlights the complexities of attempting to illustrate the multivalent layers of Hebrew language across cultures.

Nonetheless, the choice of Hebrew poets reflected in these epigraphs points to the diasporic and multilingual history of Hebrew literature. Two of them (book 1 and book 4) are excerpts from poems by Greenberg, from a late work of his Hebrew poetry, *Rehovot Hanahar* (Streets

of the River). Although later in life Greenberg was adopted as a giant of
the Hebrew literary world, he began his career as an avant-garde Yiddish
poet in Europe, editor of the Yiddish journal *Albatros*, and one of the
primary members of the Yiddish Expressionist poetic group Di khalyas-
tre (The Gang). After he immigrated to Palestine in 1924 and began to
publish his Hebrew poetry there, he was still long considered a marginal, outlying figure in the world of Hebrew letters. The Yiddish poet
Avrum Sutzkever described Greenberg as an example of the *aleynflier*,
literally "one who flies alone," noting, "He was not born to fit in. Such
was and remains still in great measure the fate of loners or solo flyers in
world poetry."[29] Even as late as the 1950s, according to Meir Wieseltier,
Greenberg was the "exiled king" of Hebrew poetry, a status that hints at
Greenberg's reputation and influence while still insisting on his marginal
status.[30] Chana Kronfeld has commented that Wieseltier's characterization suggests "a poet who is marginalized by an internal (ideological)
exile within the territorial Zionist modernism."[31] This ideological exile
was twofold: Greenberg's political association with the right-wing Revi-
sionists, whose views were more extreme than those of the mainstream
political Zionists, placed him at the margins of Jewish nationalist political discourse; and his dual association with both a uniquely European
modernism and the Yiddish language, which refused to be territorialized
and nationalized by Zionism, marked him as an outsider in the world of
Hebrew letters. The choice of Greenberg for two of the book's epigraphs
nods to the expansive geography and peripatetic history of Hebrew literature, one in which the diaspora was a common, even necessary, element
of a writer's literary origins.

Another of the writers quoted in an epigraph is Gabriel Preil, an
American Hebrew poet who bridged three languages and cultures. Yael
Feldman has noted that to write in Hebrew Preil "had to cross two language barriers: Yiddish, his European mother tongue, which continued
to be the language spoken at home throughout his life, and English, the
language he acquired in his new home-country and which soon became a
rich literary source for young Preil."[32] Again, Preil's presence here recalls
the multifarious history of Hebrew literature as both an Israeli and a

diaspora phenomenon, as well as an American one. In addition, his proximity to Yiddish and his incorporation of English literary influences suggest, like the composite faux liturgical texts, the extent to which Hebrew is not a purely Jewish or solely Israeli language but has always been dependent on other cultural and linguistic influences. Preil often wrote about New York in his poetry, and this reference to him establishes a literary legacy for writers like Namdar, writing in Hebrew in diaspora locales about diaspora landscapes. At the same time, the poem itself, "At This Time, In This Place," suggests the contingency of the idea of home, dependent on circumstance and time, much like the alternate geographies of New York detailed in the novel.

These Hebrew epigraphs function as "paratexts," which can serve "as a means of directing our attention to the very processes by which we understand and interpret the past through textuality."[33] In this case the paratexts work to recall Hebrew's transnational history and to deterritorialize it, decoupling Hebrew from any exclusive association with the land of Israel. The epigraphs also reference the poetry of John Berryman and William Butler Yeats, who wrote in English, as well as a psychoanalytic text of Carl Jung, originally in German. The inclusion of these texts, like the linguistic mixing of the *seder ha'avodah*, underlines the notion of Hebrew language and culture as dependent on non-Jewish and non-Hebrew influences for its dynamism.

The paratexts of Arad's work appear in the form of the literary influences that inform the genre of many of her novels. Drori notes that despite Arad's declared attachment to Hebrew and to Hebrew-language literature, much of her literary inspiration comes from non-Hebrew sources and other literary canons.[34] She places *The Hebrew Teacher*, along with some of Arad's other work, into the genre of the academic satire, a genre she associates primarily with the English novels of Barbara Pym. Likewise, Arad's very first novel, *Makom acher ve'ir zara* (Another Place, a Foreign City), whose title itself hints at Arad's own position as an expatriate Hebrew writer, was inspired by a novel by Vikram Seth, *The Golden Gate*, and written in the form of Pushkin sonnets, which were developed by the Russian poet Aleksandr Pushkin for his nineteenth-century narrative poem *Yevgeny Onegin*. Reading Seth's novel led Arad to examine Avraham Shlonsky's Hebrew translation of *Onegin* and then to engage in her own literary experiment with the Pushkin sonnet.[35] As Adriana Jacobs notes of this novel,

> By creating a literary text that so explicitly engages translation, multilingualism, and intertextuality, Arad acknowledges the heterogeneity of Israeli literature, the continued presence of "outside ideas" and marginalized "inside ideas" at work in Israeli culture, and the transnational and diasporic future of Hebrew literature. To the extent that Arad's work addresses these questions, it also interrogates the very notion of a "national canon" in a world where authors and texts circulate in—and are translated into—increasingly global and transnational networks.[36]

The varied layers of Arad's own Hebrew and generic experiments point, like Namdar's *seder haʿavodah*, to the complex and multilingual origins of both historical and contemporary Hebrew texts.

Ilana's own autobiographical text, which she is beginning to write at the outset of the novella and from which the ironic English line "It wasn't a very good time for Hebrew" is drawn, likewise suggests the way that Hebrew literature is imbricated with world literature and specifically with American English and American Jewish culture. Drori describes Ilana as an "ethnographer" of her environment, and her autobiography becomes "meta-poetic exploration of the act of writing Hebrew outside Israel."[37] The results of this exploration are somewhat ambivalent, and Ilana spends much of the novella trying to decide which language to use. "She debated which language to write in: directly in English, or first in Hebrew, and then to translate with Shelly's help? Her English is not good enough, but her Hebrew suddenly feels stiff. . . . Forty-five years outside of Israel, and she has no language" (43). Ultimately, Ilana decides to begin in English, although the text in which Ilana is writing in English is itself in Hebrew. This comically complex rendering, with texts and languages nestled within each other like Russian nesting dolls, suggests the impossibility of extracting any "pure," unadulterated version of Hebrew language or literature untouched by other languages and cultural influences.

Both the absorptive quality of Hebrew and its influence by other cultures and languages are also reflected in the use of translation and citation in *The Ruined House*. One example is the use of popular American songs to evoke particular moods or periods. For example, one afternoon Andrew takes his young daughter to visit his elderly mother, who is now confined to a nursing home. As they sit with her, Andrew has a powerful memory of his mother when she was much younger, singing to his older daughter when she was a baby, twenty-five years earlier. The song Andrew remembers, not identified by name in the text, is "I've Told Ev'ry Little Star," from the 1932 musical *Music in the Air*, with music by Jerome Kern and lyrics by Oscar Hammerstein II. In the text of the novel, part of the song is reproduced in a Hebrew translation that is faithful to the meaning of the song without perfectly preserving the rhyme scheme.

I've told ev'ry little star	סִפַּרְתִּי לַכּוֹכָבִים וְגַם לַיָּרֵחַ
Just how sweet I think you are	כַּמָּה אַתְּ נֶהֱדֶרֶת
Why haven't I told you	סִפַּרְתִּי לְכָל הָעוֹלָם
(H 185, E 181)	לָמָּה לֹא סִפַּרְתִּי לָךְ?

So, what is preserved in the text is a popular American song from the generation of Andrew's mother, Ethel, which Andrew is remembering in English, translated into Hebrew, in a novel about an American Jew in New York written by an Israeli expatriate.

In this case, the translation demonstrates almost in real time the way that Hebrew can and does absorb, as well as appropriate, not just linguistic but cultural influences from surrounding societies, much like Arad's work. While the *seder ha'avodah* is an ancient text that refers to the absorptive history of Hebrew, this song and other instances of translation in the text claim this process also as a contemporary one. It is no accident that the song is written by a famous American Jewish songwriting team that deeply influenced an era of American popular culture.[38] Hana Wirth-Nesher has written of the tendency among American Jewish writers to expunge traces of Jewish languages or accents from their writing in order to assimilate.[39] Here we have a contemporary inversion of this theme, in which English is elided from an Israeli Hebrew representation of American Jewish life. In a sense, the novel "claims" this popular American song (an American Jewish song, if we consider its authorship) for Jewish culture through its Hebraization. At the same time, the novel legitimates American culture as a site of Hebrew culture or acculturation, linking Hebrew with both America the place and a specifically American culture. By assimilating a certain kind of American Jewish culture into Hebrew, this translation and appropriation creates a particularly diasporic hybrid Hebrew culture detached from Israel as a location and a cultural reference point.

Considered in conjunction with the pseudo-historical texts detailing the sacrificial rites, the cultural and linguistic translation of this contemporary material also continues what can be seen as a tradition of Jewish borrowing from dominant cultures. However, in the instance of the contemporary narrative, the valence of this borrowing is altered by the presence, however marginal in the context of the novel, of the state of Israel. While the Greek in the *seder ha'avodah* recalls a period of Roman occupation and political hegemony over the Jews of Judea, the translation of the American song into Hebrew occurs in the context of a coexistent Jewish sovereignty that links nationalism to Hebrew language and literature. Historically, this meant a unitary association between Hebrew and Israel, as Benjamin Harshav notes: "Nation-state ideology promoted the ideal: 'One nation, one land, one language.' . . . Forces of power and/or cultural authority worked to enforce this unity, identifying the ethnic and political boundaries with language borders."[40] This use of translation challenges that association between land and language by recontextualizing Hebrew in a location outside of Israel and importing into it a different culture. Rather than simply deterritorializing Hebrew, it reconnects Hebrew with the other places of its use and development, recalling its history as a diaspora language and suggesting that this history did not end with the establishment of the state of Israel as a putative linguistic home.

Namdar's claim that Hebrew is his homeland is reflected in Arad's work as well. The epigraph to her 2006 novel, *Sheva Midot Ra'ot* (Seven Moral Failings), is a quote from the Hebrew novelist Y. H. Brenner:

> How many times, when I hear one writer from among our friends say to another: Is your new work about life in the Land of Israel? It awakens such a feeling of incredulity in me: as if writing is an external thing, so to speak, and one writes of the life of Jews in Lodz, the life of Galicians, the life of the Karaites, the life of the Spaniards, the life of the Land of Israel, the life of Petach-Tikva . . . and not an internal thing, discovering the internal life and its nature within relationships and shades of a known time and known surroundings. (4)[41]

Brenner's text suggests that the context in which Hebrew is used is irrelevant, that, like all language, its goal is to reveal something essential and internal about the people and society of any time and place. Arad's placement of this epigraph at the start of a sprawling novel about the complicated social and professional politics of a college campus and academia in general, one that includes Israeli, American, Jewish, and other immigrant characters, suggests that Hebrew is adequate to represent any subject, any place, and any moment.

The Ruined House deliberately takes up the task of placing Hebrew in a diasporic locale as if to prove Brenner's point, using place names as one technique. Of necessity, a number of street and place names are recorded in transliterated form in the novel: Broadway, Hudson, Houston, Delancey. But many of the place names that are translatable are actually rendered in Hebrew translation rather than in transliteration, particularly numbered streets. So, for example, on the very first page of the novel, our attention is directed to the subway station (itself called "תחנת הרכבת התחתית") at "הרחוב הרביעי"—Fourth Street. However, there are, of course, a number of place names that fall in between these two poles, which could be translated or partially translated but are simply transliterated in the text. For example, locations like Washington Square Park or the Upper West Side are rendered in transliteration rather than in full or partial translation (Washington Square Park, for example, could have been פארק ככר וושינגטון סקוור or even הפארק בוושינגטון or even פארק ככר וושינגטון). The effect of this mingling of English and Hebraized place names leads to a hybridized language of place, one in which both languages infiltrate each other. Rather than one language overpowering or colonizing the other, English and Hebrew names operate symbiotically, neither fully assimilating the other, each borrowing something from each. Wirth-Nesher has observed that American Jewish immigrant literature "underscored the centrality of Hebrew textuality as itself constituting a Jewish homeland."[42] But the mutual linguistic borrowing in *The Ruined House* decenters the language of home, appropriating diasporic places and spaces for Hebrew but at the same time marking the Hebrew in which they are written as hybrid or foreign.

This symbiotic relationship resembles the process described by Jacques Derrida with regard to translation, in which "a translation espouses the original when the two adjoined fragments, as different as they can be, complete each other so as to form a larger tongue in the course of a sur-vival that changes them both."[43] This view of translation and its role as a universalizing, rather than a particularizing, force is in stark contrast to Zionist notions of language and culture. As we have seen, the notion of "Hebrewism" or Hebrew culture arose specifically as a mode of constructing a particularly Israeli Jewish identity. The use of translation as a way of universalizing Hebrew culture unravels the tight knot between Hebrew and Israeli culture imposed by a hegemonic Zionist cultural narrative.

The process by which Zionist translation norms established an exclusive relationship between Hebrew and Israeli Jewish identity is illustrated by Ilana's musings on her own name in *The Hebrew Teacher*. Yo'ad, whose last name is the hyphenated German-Hebrew synonym Bergmann-Harari, explains to Ilana that he added his grandfather's Germanic surname to his given Hebrew surname (of which it is a translation) "because of the negation of the negation of exile" (10). In his semi-ridiculous attempt to reclaim diaspora Jewish history, Yo'ad has retranslated his name into its diasporic original but kept both versions,

revealing a certain ambivalence but also exposing the Zionist translational practices that attempted to elide or erase diaspora Jewish history and identity. This revelation spurs Ilana to reflect on her own,
very Hebrew, name: "And this was her great pride: she was Ilana—in a
generation when most girls were still Batya and Tsipi and Penina, Ilana
Drori—in a class full of Druckman and Lipstadt and Shmuckler—and
when she married she felt a real pinch when she transformed suddenly
into Ilana Goldstein" (10). Not only has Ilana's move to America complicated her Israeli Jewish identity, but it has forced her to acknowledge,
and perhaps reluctantly reclaim, her own diaspora Jewish history, one
overwritten by Hebrew even in her own name.

The conscious exposure of the diasporic beneath the Hebrew is
evident in moments in *The Ruined House* like the one, for example, in
which Andrew, walking east down "harekhov hameah ve'eser" (110th
Street), encounters a number of Jewish families heading to the river for
Tashlikh, a ceremony performed on the Jewish New Year in which Jews
throw bread into a flowing body of water as a way of symbolically casting off the previous year's sins, in order to begin the year anew. "*Tashlikh*, Andrew told himself, smiling fondly with sudden understanding.
It was Rosh Hashanah (the word came to him in its old East European
pronunciation, a relic of his distant Sunday School days) and *tashlikh* at
the Hudson, with its colorfully symbolic casting of sins into the water,
was an entertaining annual ritual that the Upper West Side was known
for" (H 35, E 25). Again, here we have the linguistic and cultural mixing
characteristic of the novel, in which certain street names, like 110th, are
rendered in translation but locations like the Upper West Side appear
transliterated. In addition, we have a description of Jewish religious
observance described as a typically New York scene. And finally, in
Andrew's mind, as he thinks the Hebrew name of the holiday, we are
consciously alerted to the fact that he thinks it not in the modern Hebrew
accent with which most readers of this book would pronounce it—Rosh
HashaNAH—but rather in the Ashkenazi Hebrew accent of his diaspora
Jewish education—Rosh HaSHOneh. The European accent in Hebrew
was deliberately discarded and overwritten by the creators of modern

vernacular Hebrew, like Eliezer Ben-Yehuda, in accordance with their understanding of diaspora Jewish culture as degraded and weak. This aside calls attention again to the temporal and cultural layers of Hebrew, reminding us of the diversity of Hebrew's history and background and of its long life in the diaspora, a life it still lives for many diaspora Jews, like Andrew. In describing this quintessentially New York scene in Hebrew, one that, the text reminds us, has a diaspora flavor rather than an Israeli one, the novel reinscribes that accent—in this case, an Ashkenazi one—on the language.

The settings, linguistic experimentation, and cultural mixing on display in Namdar's and Arad's work are all a reminder of Hebrew's history at the same time as they, like the speculative homelands of chapter 1, remind us of the existence of Israel and the status of these novels as part of a national literature. As Drori notes of the underlying politics around Hebrew language in *The Hebrew Teacher*, Arad "bring[s] her reader to see that there is no neutral understanding of Hebrew in academic and non-academic contexts. Those who insist on Hebrew's inextricable ties to Israel . . . and those who search for evidence of Hebrew's 'post-national return to the diaspora' . . . cannot deny the dominance of Israel in any contemporary, cultural, and political discourse around Jewish literature in general and around Hebrew literature in particular."[44] While the characters of *The Ruined House* and *The Hebrew Teacher* are in and of the diaspora, Israel, like Andrew's visions of the Jerusalem Temple in the midst of New York, occupies a space in that diaspora that cannot be elided or denied.

Nonetheless, these works also function to recall and reinscribe Hebrew's diaspora past within its continuing present. This literature is not nostalgic and does not claim the mantle of authenticity. Instead, it challenges a prevailing Zionist historiography of Hebrew language and literature by reconsidering questions of homeland and diaspora in a time of globalization and exchange. In discussing the consequences of transcultural literature, Arianna Dagnino notes that it has the tendency to transcend the "the borders of a single culture and nation, but . . . also promote and engage with a wider global and literary perspective and, possibly, a new way of imagining and living identity."[45] At one time

Jewish literature itself was defined by its transculturality, as "a literature of migration, the literature of a transplanted nation," as Benjamin
Harshav has called it.[46] However, Harshav represents a Zionist notion of
Israel, and Israeli Hebrew culture, as the teleological end point of this
migration and transplantation when he goes on to note: "Because of that
centrifugal movement away from the source, it could not survive in the
long run, except in the state of Israel. Yet it left a great, highly complex and contextually bound literature in our libraries."[47] This sense of
diaspora Jewish literature and diaspora Hebrew culture as having been
completed with the establishment of the state of Israel is precisely the
idea that Namdar and Arad work against. In the words of Haim Weiss,
who helped to edit the original Hebrew edition of *The Ruined House*,
"The isolation of a language, and the self-isolation of a culture, is a death
sentence. Such a culture will wither and become devoid of meaning."[48]

The Hebrew Teacher itself, from its first English sentence, warns,
in its way, against that outcome. In the end, Ilana decides to write her
memoir in English, because "she wants to remind people of things, after
all, not just reminisce. Who will read it if she writes in Hebrew?" (66).
And yet, these words appear on the page in a Hebrew that invites us to
consider, that reminds us, like Ilana, of the flexibility and power of the
language even in, or perhaps because of, its unfamiliar setting. In a 2015
interview, Maya Arad was asked about recurring images that appear in
her work and noted that one of these was "maybe an old woman peddler
with merchandise nobody wants that appears like a cameo in all kinds
of books. A metaphor for the situation of the Hebrew woman writer
in the diaspora?"[49] Beyond this self-deprecating comment, however, we
can see this peddler also as a metaphor for the persistence and adaptation
of Hebrew in the diaspora, moving from place to place, without a fixed
home, in search of the right audience.

3

Hebrew in English

Translingual Israeli Literature

While novels like *The Ruined House* have raised questions about the suitability and admissibility of contemporary diaspora Hebrew literature into the Israeli canon, contemporary Israeli writers who use English as their literary language have approached the tension between homeland and diaspora from the other direction. As we have seen, the historiography of Hebrew literature as inextricably linked to the diaspora has been relatively unexplored, largely because, as we saw in the last chapters, the origins of Hebrew literature are generally linked to the Zionist narrative and the land of Israel.[1] At the same time, with the rise of vernacular Hebrew and the establishment of the state of Israel in 1948, the new nation consciously undertook a project of both Hebraizing Israeli literature and Israelizing Hebrew literature. As Yael Chaver has shown in her study of Yiddish in Palestine, this process had its roots in the Yishuv, the prestate Jewish settlement in Palestine, which began to "construct a mainstream narrative that could not concede the existence of an alternative culture—or even a subculture—marked by language because such an admission would cast doubt on the total success of the project."[2] This meant the official elevation of Hebrew as both a vernacular and literary language at the expense of Yiddish, Ladino, Judeo-Arabic, and other diasporic influences. Hebrew was constructed as the only authentic language of Israeli literature.

As Chaver demonstrates with regard to the Yishuv, the attempt to cleanse nascent Israeli culture of anything but Hebrew was always complicated by the continued persistence of literature in, cultural references to, and linguistic remnants from other languages. Specifically referring to the tension inherent in Zionism and its attendant Hebraism originating as a diasporic phenomenon, Chaver writes, "Far from being resolved by the gradual realization of the Zionist dream, this tension continued to lie at the core of the yishuv throughout its formative stages and *exists perhaps even in the Israel of today*."[3] Evidence of the continued subaltern multilingualism of Israeli literature can be found in the prominence of certain Israeli writers who do not conform to the Hebraist-Zionist model: Karen Alkalay-Gut, an American-born Israeli poet who publishes in English; Ida Fink, the celebrated Polish-language author of stories with Holocaust-related themes; and Yosl Birstein, the son of the eminent poet Melekh Ravitsh who became a kibbutz shepherd and a Yiddish storyteller. Since 1980, the Israel Association of Writers in English has provided an organizational umbrella for Israeli writers of literature in English.[4] These writers challenge the dominant view of Israeli literature as monolithically Hebraist and complicate the cultural equation between Zionism, Hebrew, and Israeliness.

Israeli literature in English falls into the category of what Steven Kellman calls translingualism; that is, it is authored by writers who have consciously chosen to write in a language other than their native one. As Kellman notes, by "refusing to be constrained by the structures of any single language, translinguals seem both to acknowledge and to defy the claims of linguistic determinism."[5] This linguistic fluidity denies the unitary identification of language with a particular state or territory and rather produces a transcultural model for literary production and consumption.[6] For Israeli writers, this is a particularly fraught movement across boundaries because of the conscious territorializing of Hebrew and its exclusive identification with the land (and later state) of Israel in Zionist ideology and historiography that has been described as "Hebrewism."[7]

The linkage of Hebrew with Israel deliberately elided the diaspora history of modern Hebrew and modern Hebrew's inherent "impurity"—that is, its dependence on the vernacular languages of Europe for its development. In addition, the Zionist emphasis on Hebrewism led to an exclusion of other Jewish and non-Jewish languages as authentic expressions of Israeli culture, relegating these to the denigrated realm of the diaspora. According to Liora Halperin, multilingualism in the prestate period "evoked for denizens of the Yishuv (the prestate Jewish community in Palestine) a long history of Jewish exile that, despite Zionist rhetoric, was not entirely effaced in the homeland."[8] Translingual Israeli writers, then, recover this history of Jewish multilingualism and in doing so challenge the relationship between Hebrew and national culture and the link between language and homeland. They also recalibrate the opposition between Israel and diaspora, between homeland and exile, on which Zionist Hebrew culture has been dependent.

MAPPING TRANSLINGUALISM

The challenge to monolingualism presented by translingual Israeli literature is very clearly outlined by the writer and activist Rela Mazali in her unusual 2001 English-language novel/autobiography/manifesto *Maps of Women's Goings and Stayings*. Mazali (b. 1948), who is known primarily as a political activist, is the founder of the Israeli feminist organization New Profile, which works to demilitarize Israeli society, and Gun Free Kitchen Tables, which aims to increase gun control and reduce the number of firearms in Israel and the occupied territories. *Maps of Women's Goings and Stayings* confronts the connections between genre, language, and the question of homeland and diaspora in its exploration of movement and travel, deterritorialization, and transcultural exploration. Mazali notes the importance of language to her project from the outset: "All those who come to the talking house understand and speak English. No coincidence; it's the most commonly used world map, almost obligatory for travel."[9] However, Mazali constantly calls attention to the artificiality and choice involved in her language of composition. Even the title reflects a certain awkward English syntax that draws attention to itself as a possible "bad" translation from another language. At the same time, the title's awkward syntax privileges the act of going rather than staying; that is, it expresses no loyalty to the here of the homeland, to nation or national language.

A similar effect is created by the strange and sometimes awkward prose of the book, part of which records verbatim—including, as Mazali writes, "all the stutters, all the tangled sentences sidetracked along the way and left unending, all the uhms, the I means, the you knows" (34)—conversations with actual *and* fictional women about their travel experiences. This has the effect, she notes, of making the prose foreign and contrived, "a visible veil through which you're aware, on and off, that you're peering, as you piece together a recounted reality, palpably non-real" (34). Thus Mazali preserves a sense even within English of the Hebrew and other languages that lie behind her language of composition and the artificiality of language itself. She calls attention to her translations from Hebrew to English and back again, writing of one of her transcriptions, "This section of the notes is written in my Hebrew. Maria was speaking her excellent Swedish English and I was taking it in and recording it in Hebrew, which I write quicker than English. Now, in the absence of her exact words on tape, I'm translating back into English" (194). Mazali draws back the curtain on the wizard of language, revealing the utilitarian mechanisms behind it and demystifying its connection to identity and home.

Mikhail Bakhtin recognized the power of what he called "linguistic consciousness," the self-consciousness of language that Mazali refers to here, in demystifying the connections between language and nation. In a cultural realm in which this self-consciousness does not yet exist, "the objects and themes are born and grow to maturity in this language, and in the national myth and national tradition that permeate this language." But through linguistic consciousness, the ability to see language from outside of the monolithic linguistic framework that formed it, "language is transformed from the absolute dogma it had been within the narrow framework of a sealed off and impermeable monoglossia into a working hypothesis for comprehending and expressing reality." Crucially, he notes, it is "polyglossia," the presence of other languages of speech or composition within the culture, that "fully frees consciousness from the tyranny of its own language and its own myth of language."[10] The poly-glossia of translingual literature thus has the function of deconstructing monoglossic links between language and national myth.

Jacques Derrida has explored the connections between the "mono-lingualism imposed by the other" and the cultural hegemony of nation-alism and colonial power through the lens of his own experience as a Francophone North African Jew, once stripped of his citizenship yet still inculcated into the language and culture of the nation from which he was forcibly expelled. His assertion that "my language, the only one I hear myself speak and agree to speak, is the language of the other"[11] comes from his understanding of himself as located not fully within any of the cultures available to him, cut off from Arabic or Berber by virtue of both his background and the French colonial order, from French by vir-tue of his Jewishness and his origins in North Africa, and from Jewish languages, cultures, and traditions no longer adequately preserved in his community such that they were his own. Here he laments the deprivation of the polyglossia of other languages that might allow for a resistance to the "monoculturalist homo-hegemony" he describes, one connected to nationalism and colonialism.[12]

The challenge that translingual Israeli literature in English presents to Israeli nationalism and military occupation is complicated by its ren-dering in the tongue of another hegemonic power, one that occupies other societies not only with physical force but also with the soft power of a homogenizing globalized culture. Yet as the literature examined in this chapter shows, it is nonetheless representative of what Yasemin Yildiz has called "the postmonolingual condition": "a field of tension in which the monolingual paradigm continues to assert itself and multi-lingual practices persist or reemerge."[13] This "field of tension" reflects the push and pull between nationalism, Zionism, and Hebrew monolingual-ism and "the utopian promise of a 'language without soil'" made possible by translingual and multilingual literatures.[14] While Israeli translingual literature does not entirely escape these colonial pressures, it nonetheless creates a space in which those tensions are made evident and brought to bear against Derrida's "monoculturalist homo-hegemony."

HEBREW IN ENGLISH

In the last decade, several works of fiction in English written and published by Israelis have engaged in a demystification of language that challenges the naturalized link between Hebrew and Israeliness both by claiming the mantle of Israeli literature in English and by complicating the oppositional relationship between homeland and diaspora as it has been reinforced through language. Two contemporary Israeli writers, Shani Boianjiu and Ayelet Tsabari, have consciously inserted themselves into this literary discourse on Zionism, Hebraism, and Israeli identity with recent prose fiction written in English. Unlike many other Israeli writers of languages other than Hebrew—like Alkalay-Gut and Fink—these authors were born and raised in Israel, and Hebrew is their native language. Boianjiu (b. 1987) grew up in the Galilee and later attended part of high school and college in the United States, at Phillips Exeter Academy and Harvard University, respectively. Her writing has appeared in a number of high-profile English-language newspapers and literary magazines, including the *New York Times* and the *New Yorker*, and in 2011 she was named one of the National Book Foundation's "5 under 35," becoming the youngest writer to receive the honor. Tsabari (b. 1973) was raised in Petach Tikva, and like many young Israelis she spent time after her military service traveling the world, eventually settling in Vancouver, Canada. From the time she was a teenager, she wrote in Hebrew for Israeli magazines but had largely stopped writing in adulthood until her partner asked her to write him a story as a birthday present. Shortly after, she enrolled in a creative writing program in English, eventually earning a master of fine arts. Since her first book of stories was published, she has published a memoir, *The Art of Leaving*, also in English. In 2019 she moved back to Israel with her family and has continued to write in both Hebrew and English.

As we have seen, Hebrew literature itself was formed at least partially in and by the diaspora, and there has always been a diasporic undercurrent in Israeli literature, but these recent works reflect a new era in Israeli literature that is heir to the transnational diasporic origins of Hebrew literature at the same time that it is indebted to the Americanization and globalization of Israeli culture. From a position in the global center, but on the Israeli margins, these works offer a critique of national culture and complicate historically Zionist claims to an authentic Hebrew Israeli literature. Through both language and thematics, these works place themselves in a global rather than a national context, linking Israel and Hebrew literature to a larger global cultural narrative. Paul Jay has written that "globalization emerges as something like a discourse for redescribing the entire history of colonization, decolonization, and postcoloniality."[15] Globalization offers a mode for describing the weakening of the bonds and borders of the nation-state and nationalism. In these works, the postcolonial critique offered by the use of English and other elements of global popular culture is complex and at times paradoxical. English, of course, is historically a colonizing language but in this context also operates as a deterritorializing force; Hebrew, officially the national language of the state of Israel, has, since the 1967 occupation of the West Bank, also become the language of a colonizing force, not only in the occupied territories but increasingly within the state itself. In 2018 the Knesset enshrined the hegemony of Hebrew into law. That year Israel's legislative body passed a new Basic Law—in the absence of a constitution, basic rights and national principles in Israel are enumerated in the Basic Laws—titled "Israel as the Nation-State of the Jewish People." The law downgraded Arabic, which until 2018 had the status of an official language of the state, to a "special status" and declared Hebrew to be *the* official language of the state. This complex interplay of language and power engages with Derrida's "monolingualism of the other" in its exposure of the multiple sites and vectors of power through which language operates.

Shani Boianjiu's 2012 novel-in-stories *The People of Forever Are Not Afraid* and Ayelet Tsabari's 2013 book of short stories *The Best Place on Earth* explore the nature of Israeli nationalism and nationality both thematically and through innovative uses of language itself. By writing in an English inflected with Hebrew, these works consciously invert Hebrew's traditional relationship to the languages of the Jewish diaspora, while at the same time challenging the hegemony of Hebrew and its equation with Israeliness and even Jewishness. At the same time, through the exploration of marginal characters—women, Mizrahim, foreign workers—and themes—pacifism, misogyny, female sexuality—in Israeli culture, they challenge some of the foundational myths and popular understandings of what it means to be Israeli. It is not an accident that the literature examined in this chapter is written by women and that it focuses, at least in part, on gender. The challenge and critique embedded in the translingualism of these works are connected to a larger reevaluation of Zionist ideology and Israeli social norms, particularly with regard to gender.

Like Mazali, these works of "Hebrew in English" defamiliarize English to remind us of their consciously translingual character. Boianjiu, for example, often uses awkward constructions that sound like poor translations, even when they do not actually refer back to a Hebrew original. One character explains that for breakfast "my mother *organizes* a tomato and tea for me," and another "lives *in* Jerusalem Street 3."[16] This could be a kind of direct translation of a Hebrew idiom—for example, the deliberate choice of a slightly awkward pronoun to translate the Hebrew prefix *be-*, which could mean either "in" or, in more idiomatic English, "on"—or it may simply be an inflection of the English of the novel with a nonspecific foreignness. In another story Boianjiu uses the phrase "machine automatic gun," which seems to be a reference to rules of Hebrew syntax, in which the adjective follows the noun. But in this case it amounts to mere confusion, because it simply reverses the two adjectives modifying "gun" rather than placing them both after it. At the same time, it is clear that this awkward phrase does not actually refer back to any Hebrew original because in Hebrew "machine gun" is rendered as a single word, *maklea*. In effect, Boianjiu creates her own nonstandard English, inflected by a general foreignness that seems both connected to and disconnected from Hebrew at the same time, calling into question the very notion of an authentic original source language.

Tsabari uses a slightly different linguistic technique to mark her English as something other than standard, by frequently importing Hebrew (and occasionally Arabic) words into the text, often translating them simultaneously. This tactic has the effect of locating her English outside of Hebrew, a place into which Hebrew must be imported and in which it is always slightly artificial, requiring translation and explanation. In stories that are focused largely on Israel and Israeli characters, this denaturalizes and deterritorializes Hebrew. In just the first few pages of the first story in this collection, we encounter "dossit," slang for a religious woman; "ir lelo hafsaka," the city that never sleeps, to describe Tel Aviv; and "pigua," the word for a terrorist bombing (the story is set during the second intifada).[17] These Hebrew terms are translated within the narrative, either directly or indirectly, a recognition of their illegibility in the context of the English text. The main character in "Tikkun," the first story, tells us that he "had been dreaming about getting away, wishing [he] could afford a flight somewhere" (10). Many of the characters in Tsabari's stories are trying to escape through drugs and alcohol, sex, travel, or immigration—which parallels the book's own attempt to escape, in its way, through English. The escape effected through language may also signal an escape from the strictures of Hebrew literary convention. Hebrew writers of the Statehood Generation and beyond were often preoccupied with national concerns, creating male protagonists whose stories were universalized as the Israeli experience. Literary works that did not conform to these models of the national often received negative critical reception. But, as Esther Fuchs points out, "The problem is that the 'national' and 'universal' concerns addressed by most Hebrew critics hinge on male protagonists, just as their critical theories are grounded in all male authored models."[18] Although Israeli criticism has evolved in recent years, the decision to write in English removes these works from the realm of Hebrew literary criticism, built on gendered, nationalist terms that, as I will show, these works challenge in many ways.

THE ESPERANTO OF GLOBALIZATION

The use of English in Hebrew literature also has its precedents in the fiction of the 1990s, which reflected the beginnings of contemporary globalization through references to the Americanization of Israeli culture generally. This literature often used Hebraized forms of English words, English words in Hebrew transliteration, or Latinate spellings of Hebrew in order to comment on Americanization and globalization. Miri Kubovy writes of the literature of this period, "The detachment from the past denies the uniqueness of the Hebrew language, and English words, transliterated or printed in Latin characters, are integrated into the text as part of the contemporary, meta-linguistic, trendy way of expression."[19] While she argues that in the 1990s, this use of English was intentionally superficial in order to echo the perceived superficiality of global Americanized culture, Boianjiu and Tsabari invert this process, adopting English as their medium for reflecting on deeper national and global themes and critiquing Israeli culture not only for its superficiality but for its very Israeliness. Karen Grumberg has written of the way that Orly Castel-Bloom uses English words and phrases within her Hebrew texts in order to ridicule "the notion of the Hebrew language as the crowning jewel of Israeli unity. In doing so, she collapses the very foundation of the myth of Israeliness."[20] This process is also indebted to earlier Hebrew writers like Yosef Chaim Brenner, who wrote in a Hebrew inflected with Yiddish and Russian in order to "produce a tense, awkward Hebrew that is inflected by translation" that deliberately recalled the diaspora.[21] Here, it is English that is "inflected by translation" from Hebrew, producing a two-way reflection on Hebrew and its imbrication with both the languages of the Jewish diaspora and the language of a non-Jewish global culture.

English, however, is not the only "foreign" language in these Israeli books. Both of them speak the Esperanto of a globalized popular culture that is nominally non-Israeli but also integral to Israeli, and Hebrew, culture. *The People of Forever* contains frequent references to a contemporary transnational culture that is the currency of the young protagonists. The characters' lives are shaped and delineated by a wide variety of media from various places, mentioning, among many others, *Chiquititas*, a children's telenovela from Argentina; *Dawson's Creek*, an American teen television drama; and *Mean Girls*, an American movie featuring contemporary celebrities like Lindsay Lohan and Tina Fey. The three main characters of the novel—Lea, Avishag, and Yael—even literally speak in this global pop-cultural language, as when Lea, steeling herself for something awful, says, "Do or do not. There is no try," and Avishag replies, "May the force be with you" (306). These quotes from the classic American movies *Star Wars* and *The Empire Strikes Back*, which are likely well known to any contemporary reader in any language, become a mode of communication for the characters that substitutes for their own speech.

Indeed, the main characters in *The People of Forever*—Avishag, Lea, and Yael—are themselves defined by their own participation in this global mash-up. And their careers, such as they are, are not only dependent on this global language but also expose the way in which transculturality fundamentally transforms national identity. After they finish their army service and enter the world of adulthood, all of them insert themselves in some way into this global culture: Avishag spends her free time writing fan fiction about an American comic book character named Emily the Strange; Yael travels the world, "translating works she found in China, Romania, Zimbabwe, India, and putting them up online for free. And she wr[ites] music. In all languages" (284–85). Yael's seemingly fantastical ability to write in any language is possible on a planet in which all culture is held in common and globalization is everyone's language.

Lea's post-army work, even more than the other two, comments on the way that the globalization and commercialization of culture deconstruct national mythology. Although she "was living in Tel Aviv and smoking her days away in cafes," Lea writes pornographic novels that, despite the fact that some of them are about "Nazis fucking the life out of Jews in showers," are "well received globally" (284). Rather than depicting the Holocaust as the singular tragedy in the history of the Jewish diaspora and a foundational event in the establishment of the state of Israel, Lea's work universalizes it by placing it within the context of a global capitalist culture that values its ability to sell over its content. The Holocaust in this context, rather than symbolizing the unique specificity of Jewish or Israeli history, is merely the backdrop for a commercially successful, globally popular enterprise. At the same time, Lea's work functions as a parody of Jewish history by transforming a crucial historical event into the low-culture genre of pornography. Lea's novels also recall the history of the *stalagim*, pulp novels that featured erotic domination of American or British prisoners of war by female Nazi guards, which began to appear in the years following the Eichmann trial in 1961. These novels, like Lea's, challenged Israeli cultural norms as well as literary conventions about the formation of the Israeli subject.[22] Unlike Lea's novels, the *stalagim* concealed themselves with English pseudonyms and false translation histories to appear foreign; the openness and global popularity of Lea's work suggest that the repression, erotic and national, illustrated by the history of the *stalagim* has shifted in a globalized world.

The fluidity of global culture and its ability to challenge national myth is also central to *The Best Place on Earth*, in its focus on immigrants and expatriates, airports and travel, and changing conceptions of home.[23] Even the title is an ironic inversion of the lofty place to which Israel has historically been assigned in Jewish consciousness. Moving to Israel is referred to as *aliyah*, or "going up," as if Israel were the pinnacle of the planet, perhaps literally the best place on earth. But in the title story in Tsabari's collection, "The Best Place on Earth" is a slogan on a bumper sticker referring to "Beautiful British Columbia," seen by an Israeli character visiting her expatriate sister in Canada (211).[24] The notion that somewhere other than Israel might be the best place on earth challenges the Zionist conception of Israel as higher on the ladder of Jewish life and culture than the diaspora.

Indeed, Tsabari's book deliberately places itself in opposition to this Israel-centric narrative, locating itself instead in a global space. Many of the characters are Israeli expatriates, immigrants to Israel, or world travelers, and they come from Israel, Canada, Yemen, Russia, India, the Philippines, and elsewhere. Even the stories that take place within Israel often locate themselves in other spaces or the space of the Other. In "Tikkun," a Jewish Israeli character seeking solace climbs up to the Church of the Visitation in the Ein Kerem neighborhood of Jerusalem. He is "drawn to the sound of voices singing in some language [he] can't make out." As worshippers begin to leave the church, he lowers his head, "afraid they can see through [him], know [he doesn't] belong" (16). The idea that there are places in Israel in which a Jew, and the Hebrew language itself, might be a foreigner who does not belong destabilizes the conception of Israel as the Jewish homeland, the place for all Jews and a wholly Jewish place.

EXILES IN THE HOMELAND

Many of the characters and situations described in both *The People of Forever* and *The Best Place on Earth* destabilize the notion of Israel as the homeland of the Jews and its mythological function as the place of ingathering of the exiles. The challenge to the idea of the Zionist dream is accomplished through the introduction of marginal characters, many of whom exist on the edges, if they exist at all, of Israeli society. Both books are populated by stories of those who do not fit into the Zionist image of the place of ingathering, either because the ingathering fails or because certain exiles are excluded from the category of those who deserve to be gathered in. They are of Mizrahi ancestry—a term describing Jews whose roots lie outside of Europe; illegal immigrants and refugees; Israeli expatriates living abroad; LGBTQ; or Jewish immigrants who never acculturate—and their presence in these narratives complicates simple notions of Israeliness.

Tsabari's story "Say It Again, Say Something Else" explores the complexity of language and identity in Israel. The protagonist is a teenage girl, Lily, raised largely in Canada by an Israeli expatriate mother of Yemeni descent, who returns to Israel to live with her aunt after her mother's death. There, she meets a neighbor, Lana, an immigrant from Belarus, on whom she quickly develops a romantic crush. Lily's mother, a pacifist, left Israel so her daughter wouldn't have to join the army, and when Lily expresses her political views to her Israeli cousin, "Talia stare[s] at her in shock." And Talia, writes Tsabari, has "been calling her 'Little Arafat' ever since" (32). Lily's nascent sexuality, her pacifism, and her Yemeni heritage all place her outside the normative construction of Israeli iden-tity. Although Israel is "where her mother was born, where she grew up and lived before she moved to Canada," and despite the fact that "Lily even looks the part," she still "feels like a stranger, a tourist" (23–24).

The story also explores the nuances of Israeli identity through both Lily's and Lana's dual (or multiple) national and ethnic identifications. Explaining her ethnic background to Lana, Lily tells her, "My grandpar-ents came from Yemen, so we are Arabs in a way, Arab Jews" (35). Lily, herself at the intersection of multiple marginal identifications—lesbian, pacifist, immigrant, Yemeni—is able to reconcile two elements of her identity that, in contemporary Israeli discourse, are seen as opposi-tional and mutually exclusive. Paradoxically, Lana, an immigrant her-self, retorts, "No, that's impossible. You're either an Arab or a Jew" (35). When Lily suggests that Lana also inhabits two identities simultaneously, as Belarusian and Jewish, Lana represents the Zionist position when she says, "I'm Israeli now. . . . And so are you" (35). Here, Tsabari reflects the way in which Zionist discourse erases or elides the historical specificity of Jewish cultures, particularly those from the east or Arab lands, in its movement toward a monolithic and uniform Israeli identity.

The complications presented by challenges to a monolithic Jewish, Ashkenazi-dominated, Israeli identity are also apparent in the contem-porary challenges of the global economy, which has brought hundreds of thousands of foreign workers, many of them living and working illegally in the country, to Israel. In "Invisible," Tsabari explores these challenges from the perspective of one of these foreign workers, a marginalized and mostly ignored population within Israeli culture and society. Although Rosalynn has left her own family, including her daughter, behind in the Philippines in order to earn money to support them in Israel, she is con-flicted about where she belongs. After eight years in Israel, although she is not a citizen and is not Jewish, Rosalynn feels attached to the place and alienated from her Filipino roots. Walking back to her employer's home, where she works as a caretaker for an elderly woman, Rosalynn reflects that "the thought of leaving filled her with an ache similar to the one she had felt when she left the Philippines" (125). After so long away from "home," "sometimes Israel and the Philippines would blend in her head, overlap" (125). In the Zionist imagination, the state of Israel is constructed as the original, authentic homeland of the Jewish people. But what does it mean if the contemporary nation-state of Israel can also feel like "home" to non-Jews? This revaluing of the conception of Israel as homeland, not just to Jews but to economic and political refugees drawn to its freedom and opportunity, works to challenge dominant Israeli and Zionist conceptions of the meaning of, in Theodor Herzl's formulation, the "Jews' state." The many layers of belonging—to language, to nation, to place—inherent in the voicing of a Filipina noncitizen by an Israeli citizen, herself part of an internal Israeli minority group, living abroad and writing in English, expose the multiple and intersecting complexities of homeland.

In addition to complicating the notion of the Jewish homeland, the reinscription of these marginal characters exposes the way in which the construction of Israel as the Jewish state has made invisible those who do not fit into this model. In *The People of Forever*, the exclusion of those who do not meet the state's criteria for acceptance, and are there-fore left outside of the narrative of ingathering, is exposed through the stories of two of these invisible characters: one West Bank Palestinian and one African refugee. As part of her army service, Lea is assigned to a checkpoint on the border between Israel and the occupied West Bank. Her job is to check the papers of workers passing through the checkpoint each day: Palestinians who live in the occupied territories, citizens of no country, and work inside Israel. Of these workers Lea muses, "We needed them, but we were also a little afraid they'd kill us, or even worse, stay forever" (60). Here, in the inverse of ingathering, the state wants to ensure the exclusion of Palestinians from the land. This exclusion reveals the dual function of the border and Lea's job as border patrol: it keeps out as well as keeps in, relying on exclusion in order to establish its own legitimacy. The checkpoint exposes the way that Israel, in order to be homeland to some, must be kept off-limits to others.

Just as Lea describes Israeli fears about the infiltration of Pales-tinians from the occupied territories into Israel, Mazali has noted the inverse fear of Israeli activists like her who enter Gaza. She is conscious of the way her crossing into Gaza is dependent on the very people who are the source of the fear: "In fact going into Gaza isn't my going. I move in the fearzone by leave of Palestinians who live there and consent to have us. . . . South of Erez we are by courtesy of our hosts" (168). The boundary, the checkpoint, becomes the site of erasure: of language, of citizenship, of identity. It is as if the border between nation and occupied land, between homeland and no-man's-land, has the power to actualize and de-actualize the self. On the one hand, it has the mythological power to bring into being the image of a new identity, the New Jew, the ingathered exile, while at the same time erasing the very existence of those who remain outside or are excluded.

This erasure is also apparent in Lea's encounter with a particular Palestinian worker named Fadi who crosses each day into Israel through her checkpoint. Lea notices him because, although he is in many ways indistinguishable from the crowd of men trying to pass through the checkpoint, "he stood with urgency. He did not want to be there. He was almost not there, but he was" (67). Eventually, Fadi, whose increasing anger and disaffection is described by Lea, kills one of the other soldiers and is taken to prison. At the end of the story, Lea, who has been imagining Fadi's home life, including a fictional wife named Nur, begins to imagine what she is doing: "I thought of Nur; I thought that she must have showered and that she was already working on getting Fadi out of the Israeli jail, and that she was a strong woman, and then I remembered that I had created her, had invented her, and that I was a soldier and she was not real" (84). Fadi and Nur, excluded from citizenship and dispossessed of homeland, are themselves not "real" or "almost not there" with regard to the Israeli national narrative.

The chapter about Fadi and Nur is immediately followed by a chapter titled "People That Don't Exist," which considers those excluded from the idea of homeland from another angle: the refugee. The title refers directly to a game the bored Avishag, a border guard in the Israeli Army, plays as she watches her computer monitor for illegal crossings. Lonely, she imagines the green pixels are people, the "people who don't exist," for company. But, of course, there are also real people who appear on the monitor, refugees from Africa trying to cross the border into Israel, and the title also indicates the extent to which these refugees are not a part of the conception of homeland on which the state is built. Rather, like Fadi and Nur, they "do not exist" in the context of the Israeli state, which only recognizes as citizens under the Law of Return those with Jewish ancestry.

The story is narrated in alternating first-person sections, labeled "Person A" and "Person B," underscoring the common humanity of the two speakers, who otherwise have little in common except their relative anonymity and powerlessness in the face of state institutions: one, a female soldier in the Israeli Army; the other, a Sudanese refugee trying to cross the Egyptian border into Israel. In her sections, the Sudanese refugee narrates the story of her escape to Israel. She begins, "You'd want to think I don't exist, but I do" (90). And, indeed, the narrative supports this assertion from the Israeli perspective, when Nadav, Avishag's superior officer, tells her, "We can't shoot the Sudanese because that would look bad, but we also don't want them here because then we would have to give them jobs, and they bring diseases, and they lower the Jewish rates" (98). The narration of the refugee's story confirms her existence despite the fact that in the eyes of the state she not only does not but cannot exist, because in her very existence she poses a threat to the Jewishness of the Israeli homeland.

But the novel makes the refugee character visible and gives her a voice, by narrating her story in the first person and alternating it with the first-person story of the soldier Avishag's chemical abortion. As with Tsabari's narration of Rosalynn, however, the voice given to the refugee is, of course, determined by the Israeli writer behind the story, a reminder of the power given to confer or deny existence. Within the story, the two women—soldier and refugee—are mystically connected, sharing an exchange that transcends both real and imagined boundaries and validates their mutual existence. In the course of the narrative, the Sudanese refugee character finally arrives at the border, but just before the group she is with can get to the border fence, Egyptian soldiers open fire, and she is shot. She takes shelter under a tree, where Avishag notices her on the monitor. Looking for her "people who don't exist," she sees a real person this time, the refugee, "curled up like an alien" (102). Avishag reaches out her hand, despite the fact that "we get in trouble if we touch the screen because it gets scratched, but I don't care. I am thinking about someone who isn't me. I reach and touch the green monitor—it is cold and far and real. I pretend to touch the child I'll never meet. I pretend I don't exist. For that while only, it gets to be only her" (102). Avishag's self-effacement in acknowledgment of the worth of the refugee's life appears to forge a magical connection between them, and in the next section, the refugee recounts, "I could feel someone touching me. I felt someone's hand on my shoulder for a very long time. . . . What happened was that someone was there but then was not, and then I, I got up and I ran to the fence made of little knives and I jumped it. Only me" (102–3). Avishag's recognition of the reality of the refugee's existence not only symbolically calls her into being but actually saves her life. In doing so, the refugee does make it across the seemingly impassible border into what she calls "the little country" that means an end to her flight, a refuge if not a homeland.

IMMIGRANTS AND EMIGRANTS

These novels also focus on another type of marginal character that reveals the limits of homeland: the immigrant or emigrant. Many of Tsabari's Israeli characters are voluntary exiles, who feel more at home outside of Israel than in their "homeland." In "Brit Milah," Reuma comes to visit her daughter Ofra in Toronto and to see her new grandson. She thinks of her daughter's sojourn outside of Israel as temporary and assumes that eventually she will come back. As the visit wears on, Reuma realizes that Ofra "felt at home in this cold, strange country" (60). Maya, a young woman just out of the army, goes to India to travel but, instead of returning to Israel after a few months, decides that "India feels like my home" (162) and stays for three years. And Naomi, visiting her sister

Tamar in Vancouver in "The Best Place on Earth," notices that "there was nothing Israeli or Jewish about" her sister's house (214). Tamar remembers her last visit to Israel as an unpleasant experience: "She had missed Jerusalem so much when she was in Canada, but having finally made it there, she couldn't wait to go back to BC. For the first time, she saw the city through a foreigner's eyes: the chaos, the traffic, the aggression, what Israelis loved calling 'passion.' It was as if the city was stuffing itself into your throat. She no longer belonged" (218). As Robert Alter has noted, "The figure of the expatriate is used to put to the test some of the fundamental assumptions of the Israeli national enterprise."[25] These characters reverse the terms *aliyah* and *yeridah*, immigration and emigration, ascribing value to the diaspora and to diasporic Jewish, and non-Jewish, life and suggesting a broader view of contemporary Israeli and Jewish identity.

Inversely, Boianjiu devotes one chapter of her novel to a story of a character who, although Israel is supposed to be his natural home, fails to fit in or fully belong, complicating the idea of Israel as Jewish homeland from within. In "Once We Could Pretend We Were Something Very Else," the main characters of the novel, who all grew up in the same village, have a neighbor whose family immigrated to Israel from England. The neighbor, Miller, has a troubled relationship with the other members of the town, at least partly because of his own racism—he is Ashkenazi, or of European descent, while many inhabitants of the town are of Mizrahi descent, or non-European. Although he himself is technically the foreigner, he calls the protagonists "monkey girls" "because [their] grandparents weren't from Europe" (209). Miller's racism and sense of superiority as an Ashkenazi Jew and a European immigrant underline the extent to which certain members of Israeli society, certain native-born citizens, remain marginal. This marginality represents a kind of continuing exile even within the homeland for some of its citizens.

Perhaps paradoxically, though, the girls like this racist epithet and embrace it. Avishag says, "We once really liked thinking we were animals" (209). Although Miller intends it as an insult, the girls' enthusiastic acceptance of his description indicates their understanding of their outsider status. This embrace of their difference and the knowledge of their exclusion to the margins of Israeli society demonstrate the novel's challenge to monolithic conceptions of Israeli identity. It also points again to the disconnect between dream and reality, national mythology and individual experience, as it becomes clear that Israel has not been successful at integrating all its citizens into this monolithic national identity. Miller himself illustrates the failure of the Zionist dream of integration through his own experience. He, too, does not fit into Israeli society, despite the fact that he has made *aliyah*, an attempt to fulfill the Zionist dream of the ingathering of exiles. Nonetheless, other members of the town view him as an outsider, and Lea's mother tells the girls, "You have to understand . . . these people are not originally from here, so they don't understand" (213). Lea's mother recounts how the Millers had a bar mitzvah party for their son on the communal property of the olive grove, "even though it was not their property and they had no right. They brought in all of their relatives from England and made pita from scratch on an authentic taboon, while marveling over the pastoral and holistic nature of their lives on the Holy Land's border. In loud voices" (213). The Millers, in culture, social mores, and, crucially, language—in the form of their loud voices, presumably speaking English—announce their inability to integrate into Israeli society. Their imitation of local customs and consumption of local foods are revealed to be artificial adoptions out of sync with their true identities as foreigners and outsiders.

When she returns from the army, Lea decides that Miller has killed one of the olive trees on this same communal property and that she has to punish him. It is not insignificant that Lea accuses Miller of killing an olive tree, and one that was the communal property of the town. The long-lived olive tree is a symbol not just of peace but of the Jewish connection to the land. In Avishag's words, "It is highly against the law to kill an olive tree. You are not even allowed to uproot one" (211). Eric Zakim has written of the way that Zionist ideology created a "synesthetic dialectic of 'to build and be built'—of seeing the fate of the land and the people tied together, of linking the invention of the 'new Jew' to the rejuvenation of this devastated landscape."[26] In contrast, here it is the dead olive tree that represents destruction and the arrest or interruption of this Zionist dialectic of the land. When Avishag looks out at the dead tree, she sees "a dark end. A clear beginning of something that had no middle. Its stem broke off in such an abrupt place, I bet that even if someone never knew there used to be more of it, if someone had never seen an olive tree or even any kind of tree before in his life, he could still tell something was missing" (213). What is missing here is the connection between land and national culture, a connection that the insufficiently acculturated immigrant Miller is represented as undoing through the destruction of the landscape, through the death of a tree literally connected to and drawing sustenance from the land itself. However, Miller's family also unravels Israel's claims to be the natural homeland of all Jews through the reversal of their *aliyah*. This, too, is not unexpected within the context of the novel: Avishag notes, "My mom always says that she bets the Miller kids will leave for England without being drafted, and I agree with her" (214). And indeed, when Lea and Avishag go to confront and punish Miller, they find that his wife has taken their children and left the country to return to England. Miller tells them of his wife, "She couldn't take it anymore, wanted to go back to England. . . . 'We can't have something happen to the little ones,' he added in English, imitating the voice of his wife. 'This was all your crazy idea to move here'" (225). The act of *yeridah*, going down, the ideologically backward motion of leaving Israel for the diaspora, is here mocked through the derisive use of English to imitate Miller's wife. But the joke is a double-edged one because, of course, the entire text of the novel, including Miller's ostensibly Hebrew speech and Avishag and Lea's dialogue, is rendered in English.

The abandonment of the Zionist project is looked on with suspicion by the other characters, despite their own marginality within Israeli society. In the same chapter, Avishag, who is getting ready to take up a position as an airport security officer, muses about travelers at the airport: "It is always suspicious when someone leaves. I'll never leave myself. After my shift is over, I'll take the train to Tel Aviv and sleep alone. Then I'll come back the next day. So that I can do the opposite of leaving again" (220). This endless imaginative cycle of returning to Israel both mimics and mocks, again, the notion of the ingathering of the exiles. Avishag's claim that she will "never leave" represents the idea of Zionist *aliyah* taken to its extreme: once here, immigrants (like Avishag's parents) are trapped in an ideological conundrum. It is the failure of the ideology of ingathering to predict its consequences—whether entrapment or its opposite, failure to entrap—that is made ridiculous through Miller's mocking imitation of his wife's English and Avishag's endless circle to the airport and back. In both cases, the homeland is represented as oppressive rather than liberating, an imperfect or impossible alternative to diaspora. In this formulation, the homeland becomes a cage or a prison to the freedom of exile.

DECONSTRUCTING THE NEW HEBREW MAN

As noted before, these books are not incidentally focused on gender and, in particular, the centrality of a certain construction of masculinity to the establishment of a unique Israeli national subject. Just as these books challenge normative notions of a monolithic Israeli identity and the construction of Israel as a homeland for all Jews, they also challenge one of the central pillars of early Zionist discourse: the construct of the New Hebrew Man, the masculine ideal of the physically strong and socially dominant Israeli Jew who would redeem the image of the weak, scholarly, emasculated Jewish man of the diaspora. Daniel Boyarin has shown that Zionism was at least partially a reaction to certain European anti-Semitic constructions of the Jewish man as feminized, homosexual, impotent, and diseased.[27] Zionist discourse proposed a corrective to this perception: the New Hebrew Man, an idea indebted to Max Nordau, an early proponent of Zionism and a colleague of Theodor Herzl. Nordau, a physician, advocated the creation of *Muskeljudentum*, or a "Jewry of Muscle," transforming the Jews from fearful, cloistered students into, as he wrote, "deep-chested, sturdy, sharp-eyed men." These new muscle Jews would be the heirs of Jewish heroes like Bar Kochba and the Maccabees, whom Nordau saw as "the last embodiment in world history of a bellicose, militant Jewry."[28] Nordau's intention was to create

Jewish gymnastic clubs for the development of Jewish physical fitness, but his message resonated with Zionist critics of diasporic Jewish life, who saw the archetype of the traditional, scholarly Jewish man as emasculated and feminine.

In what seems like a direct response to this Zionist proscription for manhood, Ayelet Tsabari's male Israeli characters struggle with and suffer from the expectations associated with the image of the New Hebrew Man. "The Poets in the Kitchen Window" follows a boy named Uri during the first Gulf War in 1990. He is a sensitive boy and an aspiring poet but finds that his literary interests do not conform to masculine expectations. In elementary school, a poem he wrote—paradoxically, about the Yom Kippur War—won an award and was published in the school paper, earning him "a month of mockery from the boys in his grade, who recited parts of it with a lisp and substituted the word fag every time war appeared in the poem" (64). In response, he decides to "find a more manly vocation" and dreams of becoming an officer in an elite army unit (71). This dream is also related to the fact that Uri is Iraqi and "he had never heard of a Yemeni or Iraqi poet, or any Mizrahi poet for that matter" (70), and therefore cannot imagine poetry as a path that is open to him. His dream of becoming an elite soldier is thus a path for him to imagine a way to be an Israeli man, a category from which both poets and Mizrahim are excluded or circumscribed. Later, Uri's sister gives him a book of poems by the Baghdad-born poet Ronny Someck, reinscribing the possibility of both man-as-poet and Mizrahi-as-poet. These two poles—either poet or soldier—correspond roughly to the discursive construction of Israeli masculinity as martial and tough in opposition to a scholarly, weak diasporic Jewish man. The story confounds this dichotomy by suggesting that both can exist simultaneously, as when Uri realizes—during one of his regular bouts of the exercise he hopes will toughen him up into a sufficiently masculine adult—that "it was during these times, skating or running up the stairs to Monkey Park, that some of his best poems were born" (71).

These stories also confront the centrality of the military and militarism to constructions of gender in Israel, exposing the cracks in the facade of the New Hebrew Man. In Tsabari's "Below Sea Level," David, an Israeli expatriate living in Montreal, takes his non-Jewish girlfriend to visit his father, a career army officer. David, unlike most Israeli citizens, never joined the army, and this is a major tension in his relationship with his father, who represents the Israeli masculine ideal: "His Ray-Bans made him look like he was still in the army, though he'd retired a few years ago. He was fit and tanned. The Marlboro Man" (139).[29] David, on the other hand, is described as "into arts, a theatre buff, a Dungeons and Dragons enthusiast, a comics fan" who hated sports and physical activities as a child, much to his father's disappointment (137). But the crucial fact of David's masculinity as it relates to his status as Israeli man is that he never served in the Israel Defense Forces (IDF). His girlfriend, a peace activist herself, assumes that he was a *refusenik*, choosing not to serve for ideological reasons. But this is not exactly the case. "The truth was, his not going to the army had nothing to do with ideology. He was terrified" (146). David recognizes that his evasion of army service by faking depression and crying suggests that he does not conform to gender expectations. His father makes this explicit: "He told David he would have no future in Israel, this would be a stain on his record forever, nobody would ever hire him. He told him he was not a man, would never be a man, called him a coward, worse than those Orthodox yeshiva students" (146). Military service is equated with masculinity and specifically Israeli masculinity. The Orthodox yeshiva students, exempted from military service, represent the premodern, pre-Zionist traditional Jewish life that Zionist discourse constructed as weak and feminine.

Boianjiu addresses the other side of the connection between masculinity and militarism through her portrayal of episodes from the army service of the three main characters, all young women. Although Israel has universal conscription and most Israelis—both men and women—serve in the army, Boianjiu exposes the ways in which the army constructs female soldiers as objects and victims precisely in the service of the masculine warrior image of the New Hebrew Man. Women, like Avishag in *The People of Forever*, even serve in certain limited combat positions, but their presence in these typically male-dominated roles serves in a way to confirm rather than challenge their token presence in the military hierarchy. The chapter titled "The Sound of All Girls Screaming," which chronicles Avishag's military training for a combat infantry unit, begins with an image that seems to mockingly describe the simultaneous presence and powerlessness of women in the military: "We, the boot-camp girls, stand in a perfect square that lacks one of its four sides" (23). The image of military perfection, the square made up of perfectly aligned female soldiers, is here revealed as a myth, even an impossibility. The image of this incomplete geometry, described as "perfect," suggests the incompatibility of Israeli military culture with women soldiers, one that is further explored in the series of stories about Avishag.

"The Sound of All Girls Screaming" connects the tacit imperfection of a platoon of women to the silencing of women's voices and to their tokenization within the military. The sociologist Dafna Izraeli has remarked, "I have witnessed how the token woman is silenced without anyone even having to tell her to be silent."[30] Avishag's military training is a literalization of this precept. She is repeatedly reprimanded for either not talking when she is supposed to—as when she fails to respond to a commander's query with a shouted "No, commander!"—or talking when she is not authorized to do so—as when she tries to comfort a fellow soldier nervous about giving blood. Finally, in a chemical warfare simulation in which the soldiers have to respond to questions in a tent full of tear gas, she takes off her gas mask, saying, "And I talk. I have been waiting for so long. This is my chance. As long as I am choking, I am allowed. . . . My talking serves a purpose. My talking, my tears, are a matter of national security. A part of our training" (30). This episode exposes the connection between the silencing of women in the military hierarchy, their tokenization within the IDF, and national concerns. It is clear that the female soldier, if she opens her mouth to assert her difference, poses a challenge to national conceptions of Israel as a land of masculine warrior-citizens. This challenge is compounded by the reality that the language in which the characters are speaking is English rather than the Hebrew of the New Hebrew Man.

This image is further complicated in a series of chapters about Avishag chronicling her military service, in which we see that although she has been trained as a combat infantry soldier, she is actually serving as a border guard. At her base, Avishag carries on a relationship with her commanding officer, Nadav. Avishag points to the abuses inherent in this relationship when she notes, "Nadav gets to say a lot of things to me, and I let him, because he is my first boyfriend, or because he is an officer" (89) and "no matter what he says he still tells me to show up every night at his tent" (100). From the way Avishag characterizes their relationship, it is not clear to what extent she is able to refuse his advances, both because he is older and more experienced than she and because he has power over her within the military hierarchy. Susan Sered has chronicled the ways in which the Israeli military itself constructs female soldiers as sexual objects for male soldiers, a construction that has larger implications for women both inside and outside the IDF.[31] Rela Mazali, in her activist role, has pointed out some of the consequences of the centrality of the "fighter" image to Israeli masculinity, especially violence against women and sexual harassment.[32] Nadav's seemingly inappropriate relationship with Avishag reveals the way in which the military hierarchy itself is complicit in the victimization of women.

The complicity of the military and its conceptions of masculinity and misogyny come to the fore in the chapter "The Diplomatic Incident," which focuses on Avishag and Nadav's border unit. In this section Avishag and another female soldier check a truck crossing the border and find it full of young women who they know are being trafficked into sex slavery. The narrative makes clear that Avishag's identification as female has been effaced by her identification as soldier, which carries with it connotations of masculinity. When addressed by the trafficker driving the truck as "dude," "Avishag wondered if she really did look like a man from this angle, her gun aiming forward and her hair all covered inside the helmet. Or maybe it was just that somewhere along the line, someplace along the line, it had become understood that everyone was a dude of some sort, and she was the only one who had missed it" (149). The homogenizing masculinization of the military renders all soldiers connotatively male;

the sign of this homogenization is the uniform and accessories of military service, which cause Avishag, and other female soldiers, to look like "everyone," where "everyone" is assumed to be a man.

Avishag and her female colleague want to detain the truck, but their male commander allows it to cross the border since the drivers' papers and passports (and those of their cargo of women and girls) are in order. Avishag, who clearly identifies with the trafficked women far more than with her military uniform, retreats to a guard tower for a shift watching the border. There, she begins to feel like her skin is burning and realizes that "it was the uniform. The stupid uniform underneath the M-16 and the ammunition vest and the bulletproof vest, underneath it was the green uniform all along" (154–55). In response, she strips naked and lies down on the floor of the tower, and her fellow officer does the same. When the Egyptian border guards across from them see the two naked soldiers in the Israeli guard tower, a series of events leads to the "diplomatic incident" of the title, which amounts to an outraged call from the Egyptian military to the Israeli military. Significantly, it is Avishag's decision to remove the sign of her membership in the military, her uniform, to expose the difference of her female body that causes the "incident." Despite the minor character of that incident, what ensues from the women's nakedness indicates that the exposure of the female body concealed by the military uniform—in other words, making visible the conjunction of woman and soldier, two poles that are assumed to be dichotomous and mutually exclusive within the context of the national narrative—literally has the power to affect the nation, by destabilizing the peaceful but tense relationship with Egypt.

Susan Sered has noted the way in which the female body is constructed as incompatible with the image of the masculine warrior-soldier in Israeli society: "The female body is understood to be the antithesis of the warrior's body; it is erratic and undependable, conceptualizations well rooted in traditional Jewish culture. These are traits that do not fit well with military culture."[33] While historically this has resulted in women's virtual exclusion from combat and the top ranks of the IDF, leading to a parallel exclusion from many top positions in civilian society,

Boianjiu reverses the values of the equation between masculinity and military might. Avishag uses her body, in full knowledge of its incompatibility with the Israeli image of the soldier, to retain power and assert agency even in the face of a command from her superior officer. But by exposing the female body concealed in a masculinist conception of military might, she also muddles the oppositional relationship between femininity and power at the heart of the national narrative. At the end of the story, Avishag suggests a revaluation of the equation between militarism, masculinity, and nationalism when another truck full of trafficked women arrives at the border and the driver again addresses her as "dude." "'I am not a dude,' Avishag said to the driver, and she took off her helmet, and her dark hair fell down all the way below her shoulders. 'I am not,' she said" (163). Again, Avishag's assertion of her gender identity is accompanied by the removal of a sign of her membership in the military, and again that removal results in the exposure of part of her body—in this case, her hair—that marks her as female. But in this case, Avishag retains her uniform at the same time as she exposes herself as a woman and insists on inhabiting both roles and both identities simultaneously. Importantly, Avishag here claims her place within the mechanisms of state power at the same time that she refuses it—through her insistence on the compatibility of her female body with the image of the soldier, through her insubordination to male commanders in asserting her gender identity, and through her precipitation of the "diplomatic incident" of the title.

Perhaps the most chilling chapter of Boianjiu's book, "The After War," takes some of the premises of the Zionist equation between masculinity and militarism to their logical conclusion, with horrifying results. This section also challenges some of the fundamental premises of the military itself and of women's service in the IDF, making specific use of language to expose the potential for violence and abuse inherent in that service. One example of the many ways that this chapter plays with language, and with English specifically, to expose and counter Zionist myth-making is a sign in the supply caravan of the army base where the story is set. It reads, "IF YOU WILL IT, WE DON'T HAVE ANY OF IT" (283). The phrase is a sarcastic manipulation of Theodor Herzl's apocryphal

Zionist dictum about the establishment of a Jewish homeland, "Im tirtzu, ain zo agadah"—if you will it, it is no dream. The translation of this aphorism is a reminder that Herzl himself would not have spoken this line in Hebrew, as he was a native German speaker and wrote only in German. It also subverts Herzl's idealistic intentions, mocking the aspiration to homeland as an impossible dream and a utopia as something that the actual state of Israel is not.

In "The After War," the three main characters arrange to serve their reserve duty together on Yael's old base during a near-future speculative war with Syria. The chapter explicitly connects the war with the abasement and abuse of women in its very first line: "And when the boy soldiers returned from the war they tortured the girl soldiers who waited for them" (281). Susan Sered notes that military discourse constructs a category of "women and children" that it is designed to protect.[34] But to the contrary, "The After War" implies that the violence of war is causally linked to the very type of victimization it claims to protect against and suggests that this violence is the undoing, ultimately, of the very self—individual or collective—for which the war is fought.

Even the title of this chapter, "The After War," has multiple interpretations linked to the ways in which it exposes the latent connections between the militarization of Israeli society and violence against women. There is a literal "after war," a war between Israel and Syria that occurs after the protagonists have finished their military service and also after our own timeline. And there is the "after war" that occurs in the novel after this war has been fought, the internal war between abusive male combat soldiers and the women support soldiers. Finally, the "after" of the title also indicates a time perpetually subsequent to our own, a moment that never occurs and never stops occurring, marking it not as a specific experience but as a condition. Esther Fuchs has pointed out the way in which earlier Israeli Hebrew fiction by male authors "reveals an androcentric myth presenting wars as experiences which are likely to emasculate the 'strong sex' and to empower the 'weak sex.'"[35] "The After War" turns that pattern inside out, revealing the ways in which war is inherently connected to the victimization of women.

The sexual abuse that comprises the "after war" begins as the result of what seems to be the kind of casually sexist teasing the women are used to after their military service. "They teased Yael. . . . The boys said if Yael was going to do just one tiny thing to earn her reserve stipend, that thing would be the fattest guy in the group. That's Zionism right there" (297). The men perform their national duties through their military service in wartime; but for the women, their national duty is explicitly linked to their sexuality, and only insofar as it is controlled by men. This formulation embodies Sered's description of the "war society": " 'War societies' such as Israel are characterized by the normalization of violence, the ubiquitous presence of weapons (almost always in the hands of men), and unquestioned conceptualizations of women as victims or potential victims."[36] In this case the victimization of women is revealed to be written into Zionist expectations of gender.

Here the connection between nationalism, war, and misogyny is pushed to its logical conclusion. After Yael refuses to "pity-fuck Baruch," the soldiers take the women to a hill on the base and demand that they spell out, in large letters, with stones, "We Are Whores." In response, Yael says, "We are not writing nothing," another locution that seems translated directly from Hebrew, in which a double negative is standard for expressing negation, while in English the double negative means precisely the opposite. However, she then quotes a Rihanna lyric from the song "S&M" that makes her intention clear: "Nah, nah, nah. Come on" (299). Lea backs her up, saying, "I am a professional writer and I won't even write it in stones. Stones are so permanent" (299). The awkwardness of Yael's initial response in the English coupled with both the quotation and Lea's firm declaration places these events not only in the liminal temporal space of "after" but also in a space in between languages and cultures.

The violence that follows and its resolution are also connected to the ways that the women speak, and speak in a language that is not Hebrew yet inflected by it. After Yael's refusal, the male soldiers imprison them for four days, raping them almost continuously. The text does not directly describe the violence but only refers obliquely to the before and after of it, placing the violence itself into the same type of temporal void described by the "after" of the chapter title. During their times alone, the women speculate about possible resistance or compliance. Lea notes that they are in a supply caravan full of guns and ammunition and implies that they could fight their way out. Yael rejects this idea, claiming, "We cannot. They hold our future in their bodies and heads" (304). This refusal reprises the Zionist image of the New Hebrew Man as the very embodiment of the state itself and suggests that to resist the soldiers would be to resist the state itself and thus their own national identity. When Avishag suggests that they just write "We Are Whores" as the soldiers have commanded, Yael objects, reprising Lea's argument, playing on the English idiom "written in stone," that "Nothing is as written as much as a thing written in stones" (305). She follows this up with a short rant about the reality of their situation that ends, "Either this is the Jewish state or it is not" (305). This conclusion again suggests that the women are bound by their national identity to preserve the integrity of the state, which demands that they resolve the violence being committed against them in a way that both preserves their own agency and subjectivity and also does not dismantle the systems that have allowed or demanded that violence.

Finally, recognizing that the violence against them is linked to their Israeli identity as well as to their speech—or in this case, their refusal to speak, to call themselves whores—Yael comes up with an ingenious solution. In the sense that, as Lea notes, "all Americans always say the opposite of what they mean," Yael tells them, "We have to become a little American. We have to be the opposite of what we are" (308). This solution has two primary metaphorical consequences: first, it deconstructs the link between Zionism, Israel, military, masculinity, and violence; second, it exposes the way in which those connections are their own undoing, as the violence of war transforms into violence against women and that violence slowly destroys the sense of self—personal and national—of all involved.

In suggesting that they "become a little American," Yael intends to unravel the web of national and gender identity that has precipitated the violence against them, the specifically Zionist understanding of women's role in the national narrative as one of sexual servants to the heroic male soldier-citizen. Only by escaping their Israeliness can they remove themselves from the prescribed story in which their rape is a national sacrifice demanded by the state as the price of their citizenship. But there is also a metanarrative at work here about language, because this episode, like the book itself, is already "a little American": written in English, published by an American company. This suggests that the novel's narration of these events, in a sense, is only possible because the book is acting out the same refusal of the national narrative that its protagonists are: to "be the opposite of what we are." The violence at the heart of this episode, a violence on which many of the fundamental assumptions of Israeli society rest, can only be voiced in an Israeli literature that is not Hebrew. Esther Fuchs has shown how in Israeli war-themed fiction of the 1960s and 1970s, Israeli women were depicted as sacrificial victims as a way of bolstering the national narrative.[37] This story, by contrast, exposes the way that the victimization of women and a "war society" built on gender inequality cause the national narrative, and even the national literature, to crumble. As Boianjiu writes in a short section set off by itself: "The boys came and the boys took and the boys came and the women were what they were not. It was very hard to do" (310).

BEING WHAT YOU'RE NOT

The work of being what they are not, of creating a new or alternate narrative of Israeli identity and culture, is a metaphor for the work done by translingual Israeli literature. It is what it is not, and as such creates a new space for challenging and rewriting the Israeli national narrative. In Mazali's formulation, the alternative to the trap of the mythology and ideology of homeland is travel and impermanence. Her work takes place inside an imaginary space, what she calls a "talking house," which is everywhere and nowhere at once. Her real and imagined women come to the talking house,

of and for our talking, our word-made world. Life accommodat-
ing, it doesn't confine us. Its walls are moving, shifted like a preg-
nancy from secret inner places, imperceptibly growing. Mapping
us moving. . . . Use an imaginary "we" where the real we has never
met, never ever convened all at once at any one house. Would proba-
bly never choose to. And actually couldn't—not physically—because
some of us are fictions. "We," then, are here, wherever you place this
moving "here" for the moment, studying our ability to move. To
purposely relocate. (128)

As opposed to the strictly limited borders of the nation-state, which
bound identity as well as geographical place, Mazali's talking house is
constantly shifting, as is the "we" that makes up its populace, both real
and fictional.

Like the *boydem*, Mazali's talking house displaces the concept of
home, deterritorializing it as an imaginative space constructed solely
of language—not one language but a multiplicity of them. It is a space
that is created out of individual authenticity rather than a place super-
imposed on the ideal of the collective, and it is necessarily translingual.
She writes of the idea of this house: "Itself a traveller, this house is not
back home to any of us. We only dwell here in a manner of speaking, discursively, here and gone. Brought by our stories. But it is, to
the extent that talking houses can ever be, a site of self, of truth, of no
pretensions of affectation. It does try to have that meaning of home"
(20–21). It defies borders, the dichotomization of space into inside
and out, of people into us and them, that is demanded by nationalism.
Likewise, Mazali creates series of maps of what she calls "visits," which
chart the "goings and stayings" of the title (fig. 7). Mazali's maps are a
purposeful challenge to political maps that chart the rigid borders and
national-cultural boundaries demanded by nationalism. Rather, they
point to the artificiality of such borders and their danger. Through her
imaginative maps, Mazali attempts to unmask the effaced hybridity
that is allowed, even encouraged, to emerge in the talking house. Her
maps diagram the women who populate the book, the places with which

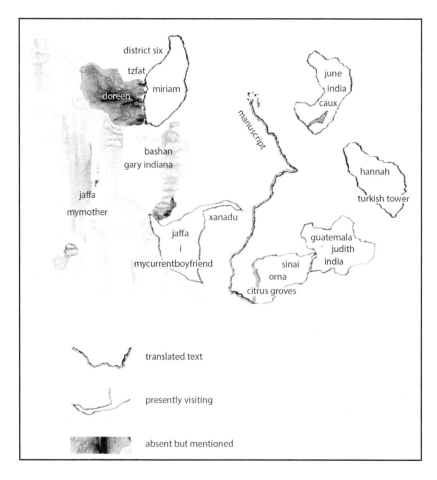

FIGURE 7. Map of the "first visit" from Rela Mazali's *Maps of Women's Goings and Stayings* © 2001 Stanford University Press.

they are associated, and elements of their stories, as well as natural features and a translated medieval manuscript from which Mazali quotes throughout the text. By drawing maps of their stories, Mazali illustrates the alternative mode of organizing space through language taken up by translingual Israeli literature in English. Like Mazali's maps, this work offers a model for permeability and transcultural identity by exposing and challenging national narratives and mythologies that continue to define Israeli culture and society.

4

Haunted Dreams

Exile and Return in the Work of Yael Bartana

Between 2007 and 2011, the Israeli artist Yael Bartana, working in Poland, made a three-part series of video installations titled *And Europe Will Be Stunned*.[1] The series chronicles a fictional Polish political movement called the Jewish Renaissance Movement in Poland (JRMiP), the arrival of a group of Israeli Jewish pioneers who build a kibbutz in central Warsaw, and the assassination and funeral of the JRMiP's leader. In 2011, the video trilogy was chosen to represent Poland at the 54th International Art Exhibition in Venice, the first time a non-Polish artist represented Poland at the Biennale. The same year, Bartana and two collaborators, who also curated her show, Galit Eilat and Sebastian Cichocki, published *A Cookbook for Political Imagination* to accompany the exhibition. The volume aimed to be something more than a catalog, describing itself as "a manual of political instructions/recipes, covering a broad spectrum of themes—constitutions, legal solutions, elements of visual identity, food recipes, social advice, and guidance for members of the movement."[2] And in 2012, in conjunction with the 7th Berlin Biennale, Bartana convened a JRMiP Congress, ostensibly to formulate a future agenda for the group, whose stated purpose was to encourage "the return of 3,300,000 Jews to Poland to symbolize the possibility of our collective imagination—to right the wrongs history has imposed and to reclaim the promise of a utopian future that all citizens deserve."[3] In chronicling the "return" of the Jews—and specifically Israeli Jews—to Poland, *And Europe Will Be Stunned* subverts some of the basic tenets of Zionist ideology, reversing the loci of exile and return. Bartana deploys both the language and the conceptual geography of Zionism against itself, revaluing the central ideas of diaspora and homeland. At the same time, she problematizes the very idea of return, complicating both past and future utopias.

And Europe Will Be Stunned is more than simply a video installation but rather part of a broader multimedia project that works to create a dynamic process rather than functioning as a static representation. The multiple elements of the project—the video trilogy, the book, the staged congress, the JRMiP and its platform (which has its own website)—interact as part of the greater project of *And Europe Will Be Stunned*, which engages with the Jewish past in Europe and the Holocaust, Zionism and settlement as a utopian project, diaspora and homeland, and the problematics of return. The scope of the project is in many ways characteristic of Bartana's art, which is clear from her description in the artist's biography on her website as a "pre-enactor," suggesting an element of prophecy and of activism in her work.[4] Bartana (b. 1970), who works in various audio and visual media, has been exploring many of the topics seen in *And Europe Will Be Stunned* in her work of the last several decades: memory, national identity, forced displacement, and trauma. Taken together, *And Europe Will Be Stunned* and its accompanying projects defy simple interpretations of memory and memorialization, complicate monolithic historical and political narratives, and raise questions about nationalism and its relationship to victimization.

THE NEGATION OF THE NEGATION OF EXILE

As noted in this volume's introduction, Zionist ideology, from its inception in the late nineteenth century, was premised on the notion of the "negation of exile" and the privileging of the land of Israel as *the* (not *a*) Jewish homeland. One of the earliest Russian Zionist organizations, the Bilu, which arose in the wake of the wave of antisemitic pogroms in 1881–82, declared in its manifesto, "Hopeless is your state in the West; the star of your future is gleaming in the East."[5] The notion that Jewish life in the diaspora was hopeless was reiterated in the foundational work of political Zionism, Theodor Herzl's 1897 *Der Judenstaat* (The Jews' State). Herzl wrote of the historical plight of diaspora Jews:

> We have honestly endeavored everywhere to merge ourselves in the social life of surrounding communities and to preserve the faith of our fathers. We are not permitted to do so. In vain are we loyal patriots, our loyalty in some places running to extremes; in vain do we make the same sacrifices of life and property as our fellow-citizens; in vain do we strive to increase the fame of our native land in science and art, or her wealth by trade and commerce. In countries where we have lived for centuries we are still cried down as strangers.[6]

Herzl's vision of a Jewish state was premised on the notion that Jews would never be fully accepted into diaspora social or political life and therefore should reject the prospect entirely.

Zionism was predicated on not only a political rejection of the diaspora but also a cultural rejection of diaspora Jewish life. Zionist thinkers, including Herzl and his contemporaries, created an opposition between the prospect of a "healthy" Jewish national life in their own state and an "unhealthy" or "abnormal" Jewish life in the diaspora. Herzl himself touched on this in *Der Judenstaat* when he claimed that, in the new sovereign state, "we shall give up using those miserable stunted jargons, those Ghetto languages which we still employ, for these were the stealthy tongues of prisoners."[7] Likewise, his colleague Max Nordau, vice president of the Zionist Congress, declared that the Zionist movement "has as its sole purpose the desire to normalize a people which is living and suffering under abnormal conditions."[8] The language that early Zionist ideologues applied to Jewish diaspora life was the vocabulary of degradation.

Early Israeli politicians absorbed this notion and continued to propagate it before and after the establishment of the state. At an address to the youth section of his party in 1944, David Ben-Gurion, later Israel's first prime minister, said, "Exile is one with utter dependence—in material things, in politics and culture, in ethics and intellect, and they must be dependent who are an alien minority, who have no Homeland and are separated from their origins, from the soil and labor, from economic creativity."[9] It is clear from Ben-Gurion's remarks that he is referring not only to a literal exile, to the history and life of Jews in diaspora, but also to a metaphorical state. It is this idea of diaspora as a condition—here, of "utter dependence"—as opposed to life in the homeland, Israel, that is at the core of Zionist ideology and became one of the foundations of Israeli self-conception.

Even long after the establishment of the state, the notion of negation of the diaspora remains central to Israeli ideology. In 2011, the Israeli Ministry of Immigrant Absorption produced a series of advertisements aimed at Israelis living abroad to encourage them to move back to Israel. The ads were created in response to a series of articles detailing the *yeridah*, or emigration, of scores of young Israelis, many for economic reasons, to Europe and the United States. In one of these ads, a young couple comes home from a night out to a dark apartment lit by a single candle, immediately recognizable as a *yahrtzeit*, or memorial, candle. The woman goes to her computer, where the word *yizkor* (remember) appears, and it becomes clear that it is Memorial Day, the Israeli holiday for remembering fallen soldiers. Her boyfriend mistakes the scene for an attempt at romance, and a voiceover intones, in Hebrew, with accompanying text on-screen, "They will always remain Israeli. Their partners may not always understand what that means."[10] In another, an older couple Skypes with their young granddaughter, a lit *hanukkiah* in the background, indicating that it's Hanukkah. They ask her if she knows what holiday it is today, and she responds, enthusiastically and in English, "Christmas!" Again, the voiceover and the text on-screen reads, "They will always remain Israeli. Their children will not"[11] (fig. 8). The clear implication of both of these videos is that the diaspora is ultimately dangerous, a place where Jewish culture is not understood or appreciated, and should be physically rejected by returning to Israel.

And Europe Will Be Stunned challenges this Zionist principle of "negation of exile" by imagining a voluntary and welcomed colonization of the diaspora—Warsaw, specifically—using certain Zionist tropes and

FIGURE 8. The final shot of the Israeli Ministry of Immigrant Absorption advertisement, reading, "They will always remain Israeli. Their children will not."

images. These tropes—of the Israeli pioneer, the kibbutz, and collective labor, among others—are inverted in their transposition to a place that historically was the site of both Jewish victimization and Zionist contempt. This inversion of the center and periphery and the concomitant revaluation of these spheres offer a rejoinder to a Jewish nationalism conceived as inextricably linked to a particular place. At the same time, the settlement of diaspora spaces echoes Zionist settlement of Palestine and raises the question of whether settlement necessitates occupation and conquest. Bartana complicates narratives privileging diaspora Jewish identity by pointing to the problematics of constructing Jewish history and culture as a monolithic or teleological process.

THE JEWISH RENAISSANCE MOVEMENT
IN POLAND (JRMIP)

In place of the Zionist "negation of exile," *And Europe Will Be Stunned* offers an alternate ideology, embodied in the political movement that is the center of the films and its associated projects. The political program of the JRMiP is introduced in the first film in the series, *Mary Koszmary* (Nightmares), which chronicles the debut of the JRMiP in the form of an inaugural speech by the movement's leader, Sławomir Sierakowski.[12] In real life, Sierakowski is a leftist intellectual and journalist in Warsaw, and he plays a slightly altered version of himself in the films. Standing in the Stadion Dziesięciolecia Manifestu Lipcowego, also known as the Tenth Anniversary Stadium, which was constructed partially with rubble from the destruction of the 1944 Warsaw Uprising, Sierakowski proceeds to give a rousing speech outlining some of the key principles of the JRMiP, particularly the return of three million Jews to Poland, roughly the number of Polish Jews murdered in the Holocaust (fig. 9).

Mary Koszmary is essentially an extended political advertisement for the JRMiP, in which Sierakowski expounds on the platform of the new party in terms both political and poetic. The practical element of the political program, which itself is clearly utopian and unrealizable—the return of three million Jews to Poland—is, in some ways, only an

FIGURE 9. Sierakowski standing in the abandoned and overgrown stadium. Yael Bartana, *Mary Koszmary* (Nightmares), 2007, video still, courtesy Annet Gelink Gallery, Amsterdam, and Foksal Gallery Foundation, Warsaw.

instrumental element of Sierakowski's speech and the platform of the JRMiP as developed throughout the video series and the book, articles, and manifestos circulated along with it. The ideological purposes behind this return are, like the visual cues of the films, intertwined with the legacy of the Holocaust in Poland as well as the history of the state of Israel.

The JRMiP's platform, as articulated both in the films and in the accompanying text, suggests a more universal project than the idea of repatriation might suggest. Written in the first-person plural of the typical manifesto, the document indicates that the dream of return voiced by Sierakowski applies widely: "We direct our appeal not only to Jews. We accept into our ranks all those for whom there is no place in their homelands—the expelled and the persecuted. There will be no discrimination in our movement. We shall not ask about your life stories, check your residence cards or question your refugee status."[13] This aspect of the platform marks the JRMiP not as a specifically Jewish national movement but rather as a challenge to chauvinist nationalisms. Instead, it styles itself as an inter- or transnational movement, whose Jewish return functions metaphorically as a general exilic repatriation.

This metaphorical function is evident in the closing lines of the manifesto, which ends with the poetic exhortation:

> With one religion, we cannot listen.
> With one color, we cannot see.
> With one culture, we cannot feel.
> Without you, we cannot even remember.
> Join us, and Europe will be stunned![14]

This proclamation bookends the video trilogy: initially voiced by Sierakowski in *Mary Koszmary*, it is finally declaimed in English by representatives of the JRMiP at his funeral after his assassination in the third film, *Zamach* (Assassination). This mantra of sorts is thus advanced as the central idea underpinning the repatriation plan.

On first glance the manifesto appears to advance a utopian, transnational, universalist message intended to foster understanding and peace, and indeed it is presented as such by JRMiP representatives in the film. But on closer inspection the position of the Jew—or rather the figure of the Jew, the metaphorical Jew—suggests something more troubling under the surface. In *Mary Koszmary*, Sierakowski's recitation of this mantra is accompanied by the exhortation "Heal our wounds, and we will heal yours." This emotional appeal, the idea that Jewish repatriation will heal—or perhaps absolve?—Poland of its Holocaust and Communist past, raises questions about the JRMiP's universalism. As Sara Ahmed has pointed out with regard to the use of emotion and emotional appeals as a tool for healing national wounds, "The question of who is doing the healing and who is being healed is a troubling one."[15] When the healing of the nation is made dependent on the victimized other, "the national body takes the place of the indigenous bodies; it claims their pain as its own. . . . To hear the other's pain as my pain, and to empathise with the other in order to heal the body (in this case, the body of the nation), involves violence."[16] The choice of senses in the JRMiP slogan as the apposite terms for racial and religious categories seems consistent with the emotional appeal for Jewish return as healing Poland, repairing its Holocaust history. But it also raises the specter of responsibility (what Ahmed might call "violence" in this context): rather than acknowledging Polish complicity in or responsibility for the absence of Jews, this political platform transfers responsibility to those Jews to help Poland listen, see, feel, and remember—in short, to be human.

This responsibility for the reconstruction of Polish humanity points to the other troubling (in the dual sense of that word) aspect of the JRMiP slogan, the essentializing of Jewishness as a trope for an ethics of universal humanism. Sarah Hammerschlag has traced a similar type of "revalorization of the rootless Jew" in postwar French philosophy.[17] As she has noted, "The position of outsider allocated to the Jew represented an alternative to the structures of allegiance put in place by both the universalist and the particularist models of French identity. As a product of the racialized ideology of German and French fascism, the Jews came to represent 'destabilization itself.'"[18] In this case, we see the figure of the Jew employed in the service of a universalist notion of a postcolonial ethical nationalism.

Although Sierakowski specifically calls for the return of 3.3 million Jews to Poland, the broader ideology of the JRMiP is directed to all of the "expelled and the persecuted," as the manifesto indicates. Thus the appeal for a Jewish return to Poland is not precisely dependent on the immigration of actual Jews, from Israel or elsewhere. This distillation of the deracinated Jew into a figure or trope, as Hammerschlag notes, allows for "the use of Judaism as an emblem for victim and outsider, an emblem whose content is easily transferable."[19] But paradoxically, while this makes the Jew into a trope for a deracinated universal humanism, it also suggests that Jews as flesh-and-blood humans are irrelevant. Rather, Jews simply become conduits of memory ("Without you, we cannot remember"), ciphers for the past. The seeming contradiction built into the very framework of *And Europe Will Be Stunned*—the conflict between the universalism of the JRMiP's ideology and its political platform of specifically Jewish repatriation—challenges the notion of a simple, transnational solution to the historical problems of nations and nationalism.

SETTLEMENT AND COLONIALISM

Those historical problems are made evident through the film's use of visual allusion to draw parallels between Zionist settlement of Palestine and the "settlement" featured in the second film in the trilogy, *Mur I Wieża* (Wall and Tower). Though this film again presents a challenge to the Zionist principle of "negation of exile" by imagining a voluntary and welcomed colonization of the diaspora—Warsaw, specifically—the fate of that settlement troubles its utopian premise. In *Mur I Wieża*, a group of Israeli Jewish pioneers arrives in Warsaw, constructs a settlement in Muranow Square, and establishes a kibbutz, or a collective intentional community, in the settlement.

This film recalls certain elements of Zionist propaganda films of the prestate period, especially Helmar Lerski's 1935 *Avodah* (Labor). In particular, the section of Lerski's film titled "Building in the Colony" depicts Jewish pioneers in Palestine engaged in cooperative building projects, with workers handing off bricks to each other, carrying large construction items together, and finally completing by hand a building with a large Star of David adorning the top.[20] In 2007, Bartana created a video installation in which Lerski's film was projected alongside her own video, titled *Summer Camp/Awodah*, which depicted the Israeli Committee Against House Demolitions (ICAHD) rebuilding the home of a Palestinian family near Jerusalem that had been destroyed by the Israeli government in 2005.[21] Bartana's film of ICAHD's activities employs the same tropes as those in Lerski's film, and by projecting the two together she makes a connection between the utopian promise of building a Jewish settlement in Palestine with the later displacement by the state of Israel of its original Palestinian inhabitants.

Similarly, the images of workers, of collective labor, and even of the building and star that make appearances in some form in *Mur I Wieża* mark a pole in the triangulated narrative of Israel, diaspora, and Palestinian displacement that is explored in *And Europe Will Be Stunned*. The film is built around a long scene in which a truck carrying wood and building materials rolls into central Warsaw accompanied by Israeli "pioneers," who are dressed much like the workers in *Avodah*: white button-down shirts, khaki shorts or pants, hats, and neckerchiefs. Likewise, these pioneers proceed to build what turns out to be a kibbutz in the traditional "wall and tower" structure of certain prestate Zionist settlements. The allusion to Zionist propaganda films of the 1930s, like *Avodah*, associates this Polish resettlement project with the utopian era of Jewish nationalism (figs. 10 and 11).

However, despite the evocation of Zionist images of the pioneer and the kibbutz, these pioneers march into Warsaw to the strains of the Polish national anthem. The anthem is a reminder of the European location of this Jewish nationalist project, detaching Zionist tropes from their association with Israel and Israeli national symbols and reassociating them with diasporic spaces in which other nationalisms prevail (or coexist, in a utopian interpretation). In a similar fashion, the hybrid flag of the JRMiP,

FIGURES 10 AND 11. Shots of the Israeli pioneers entering Warsaw and building the kibbutz. Yael Bartana, *Mur I Wieża* (Wall and Tower), 2009, video still, courtesy Annet Gelink Gallery, Amsterdam, and Sommer Contemporary Art, Tel Aviv.

a Polish eagle topped by a Star of David, melds Jewish national identity to Polish national symbols (fig. 12). The name of the star (or shield) of David recalls an ancient period of Jewish sovereignty in the land of Israel, the time of kings, but the symbol itself was only widely adopted in the modern period and is a central image on the Israeli flag. The Polish eagle, likewise, dates to the beginnings of Polish ethnic consolidation when Lech, the legendary founder of Poland, saw a white eagle's nest while hunting. This muddling of national images and symbols breaks any singular association of Jewish nationalism with the land or state of Israel, deterritorializing Jewish national symbols like the Star of David and suggesting the potential for their mobility and hybridization. And the combination with Polish national symbols suggests the potential for the reestablishment of a transnational Jewish identity.

Language also plays a role in this hybridized neo-diasporic identity. While the Polish national anthem continues to play in the background, the leader of the group of pioneers begins to instruct the group in modern Hebrew. As in many of the examples of diasporic Israeli

FIGURE 12. The flag of the JRMiP, depicting the hybrid symbol of the Polish eagle topped by a Star of David. Yael Bartana, *Zamach* (Assassination), 2011, video still, courtesy Annet Gelink Gallery, Amsterdam, and Sommer Contemporary Art, Tel Aviv.

culture we have seen, transplanting Hebrew to Warsaw, one of its sites of origin, recalls the transnational roots of the language and decouples it from an exclusive association with the land of Israel. Hebrew again appears after the kibbutz has been built, when the sound of language lessons plays in the background with shots of the pioneers planting, building, and studying. First, we hear "adama zeh ziemia," a Hebrew phrase translating the word for "land" from Hebrew to Polish, while we watch a pioneer plant some flowers. Land is one central element at stake in imagining settlement and questioning homeland, and it was also central to early Zionist ideology, in which agrarian culture and working the land were crucial to the image (if not the reality) of the Zionist pioneer of the first and second *aliyot*. Here the symbolic valence of the land is associated through the image of planting with the space of the Polish kibbutz rather than the land of Israel. Nonetheless, this new land is linked to both Hebrew and Polish through the audio track of the language lessons, again mixing national symbols and territory in unexpected, ahistorical ways.

The second component of the language lesson is "chofesh zeh wolność," a phrase translating "freedom" from Hebrew to Polish, this time accompanied by an image of the pioneers affixing barbed wire to the top of the fence surrounding the kibbutz (fig. 13). This time the introduction of hybrid language and national symbols is not imagined as utopian but rather as potentially menacing, revealing the dark flip side to any project of settlement or repatriation. The barbed wire and fencing surrounding the kibbutz suggest anything but the freedom referenced in the language lesson. Rather, it points to an isolation that is not incidental but tied to the very history of the "wall and tower" settlement referred to in the Polish title of the film (in yet another instance of importation of a specifically Hebrew expression into Polish). *Homa u'migdal* (wall and tower) was a style of construction of Jewish settlements in Palestine during the period of the Arab Revolt (1936–39). These wall and tower settlements were designed to take control of land that had been purchased by the Jewish National Fund but could not be settled because of existing Bedouin encampments or concerns about security. Much like the kibbutz

"Freedom" is "Wolność"

FIGURE 13. The audio of the pioneers' language lesson overlaid on an image of the barbed wire protecting the kibbutz. Yael Bartana, *Mur I Wieża* (Wall and Tower), 2009, video still, courtesy Annet Gelink Gallery, Amsterdam, and Sommer Contemporary Art, Tel Aviv.

in *Mur I Wieża*, which is built in exactly this style, with a hastily constructed prefabricated outer wall and wooden observation tower, the *homa u'migdal* settlements were intended to stake out territory for colonial expansion. But as Sharon Rotbard points out, "In total contrast to its ambitions of expansion, the tactical and strategic solution offered by *Homa Umigdal* served in fact to perpetuate the ghetto mentality and the impulse of enclosure."[22] Likewise, in the film, the isolation of the kibbutz is at odds with the JRMiP project of Jewish repatriation and inclusion.

This isolation, too, recalls the imagery of the Zionist propaganda of *Avodah*, or rather its lacunae. While in that film, as in *Mur I Wieża*, we see settlers and settlement, there are very few images of the already existing population of Arabs in Palestine. Aside from a couple of shots in which Bedouins with camels and donkeys appear marginally, as background to the central focus on the pioneers and their work, *Avodah* omits any visual mention of the Arabs living in Palestine. Similarly, *And Europe Will Be Stunned* contains few images of an already existing Polish population.

In *Mur I Wieża*, a few confused residents of Warsaw wander around the walls of the kibbutz uncertainly; one woman approaches the entrance, adorned with a "Welcome" sign in Hebrew, peeks in, and turns away. Finally, an overhead shot emphasizes the way that the self-contained settlement stands alone, quiet and still, on the square before the film ends (fig. 14). This separation from the community and self-contained isolation belies any utopian vision of healing or mutuality. Other than these minor interactions, the pioneers and movement activists seem to be repopulating Poland in a vacuum. Little attention is paid to the consequences or problems inherent in the resettlement of millions of people in a populous nation. And other than grand semireligious claims of its redemptive value, there is no indication of the benefit of this Jewish resettlement to Poland. If anything, the kibbutz is actually a nuisance, located in the middle of a heavily trafficked public square. The conspicuous absence of actual Poles seems to underscore a potential dark side to this utopian settlement and to suggest that historical redemption comes at a cost.

FIGURE 14. Overhead shot of the kibbutz, silent and isolated on Muranow Square. Yael Bartana, *Mur I Wieża* (Wall and Tower), 2009, video still, courtesy Annet Gelink Gallery, Amsterdam, and Sommer Contemporary Art, Tel Aviv.

In this way, *Mur I Wieża* both celebrates the utopian possibilities of diasporic repatriation and at the same time warns against the glorification of any monolithic solution or definition of identity. Looming in the margins of the film are the Israeli-Palestinian conflict and the questions that the occupation of the West Bank raises not only for anti-occupation activists but also for Israelis and liberal Zionists. As Gish Amit writes in the companion volume to the video installation, *A Cookbook for Political Imagination*, "There is another, equally pressing and crucial question: should the Israelis ask the Palestinians: will you be willing to forgive us for our crimes? Will you be willing to live with us? Will you be willing, you, who are capable of changing our lives?"[23] On the one hand, the movement from Zion to diaspora imagined by *And Europe Will Be Stunned* offers a hopeful vision in answer to this question. As Avi Pitchon writes in *A Cookbook*, "The return to Europe is not the abandonment of the Zionist ethos; it is in fact the next step in its history, a step that goes beyond it, and heals it."[24] But on the other hand, as is evident from the somewhat menacing juxtaposition of images of freedom and isolation, settlement and imprisonment, *Mur I Wieża* also warns against the possible pitfalls of the glorification of diaspora, transnationalism, and utopian solutions.

This embedded critique of both nationalism and blind faith in the transnational, both Zionism and diasporic community, challenges the notion of easy historical interpretations or political solutions that privilege a monolithic notion of Jewish identity or peoplehood. In a 1985 article that addressed the question of homeland in Jewish culture and history, George Steiner wrote, "The locus of truth is always extraterritorial; its diffusion is made clandestine by the barbed wire and watch-towers of national dogma."[25] His thesis hinges on the idea of the text as a moveable homeland, which for most of Jewish history has been carried throughout the diaspora, forming Jewish identity and community around the very idea of transnationalism and extraterritoriality. But his phrasing makes clear that his aim is explicitly political: the image of barbed wire, like its appearance in *Mur I Wieża*, is meant to conjure the violence and isolation inherent in a territorialized nationalism.

And Europe Will Be Stunned makes explicit that the location of that territorialized nationalism is the state of Israel, but at the same time the film offers a challenge to the celebration of diasporism championed by George Steiner, Daniel Boyarin and Jonathan Boyarin, Judith Butler, and others. It does so through a double-edged critique, in which the problematics of settlement and nationalism in general are made evident even in the diaspora setting of the film. In *Mur I Wieża*, these ideas are brought together in a scene in which the flag of the JRMiP—the one that mixes Jewish and Polish national symbols in a seemingly perfect hybridization—is hung from the tower of the kibbutz. Sławomir Sierakowski, the leader of the JRMiP, enters the kibbutz and hands the pioneers a red flag on which the eagle/star symbol is printed in white, which they proceed to hang from the tower, using a handoff technique borrowed explicitly from Lerski's *Avodah*, to applause from the pioneers. Behind this scene, vaguely familiar music plays, a tune that is actually "Hatikvah," the Israeli national anthem, played backward.

While the inversion of the national anthem suggests that this diaspora kibbutz, with its hybridized national symbols, unravels some of the problematics of Zionism and Israeli sovereignty, it also stands as a reminder of the existence of the state of Israel as a historical reality. This raises the specter of the potential for violence and domination inherent in sovereignty, and the solemn ceremony of flag hoisting begs the question of how this particular settlement or variety of Jewish nationalism is different than any other, whether in the diaspora or in Israel. Again, immediately after this scene, which scans over the rapturous faces of the settlers as they watch the flag unfurl, the camera cuts to a shot of pioneers hammering barbed wire into the fence surrounding the kibbutz, a stark reminder of the costs of settlement and territoriality, no matter what place is claimed as homeland.

THE PROBLEMATICS OF RETURN

Another challenge to the notion of an uncomplicated return is expressed through the figure of Rivka, a ghost, a victim of the Holocaust who does not speak but whose voice we hear in the third film, *Zamach* (Assassination). This film opens after Sierakowski's assassination and focuses on his wake and funeral, which is staged as a kind of rally in which eulogists offer competing visions of the JRMiP platform and ideology. Rivka, the ghost, is the very last visitor at Sierakowski's wake, who intones, in voice-over, that she was "murdered and buried anew, who was disinherited, who was moved, breathless, from the mass graves of Auschwitz, Babi-Yar, Treblinka, Majdanek, Sobibor, to the shrine of memory, to the mausoleum of architecture of the sublime in Jerusalem." Rivka is an amalgam, the figural survivor. While she speaks, the camera ranges over the scene of an odd hybrid event, one that recalls both a funeral and a political rally but does not conform to the norms of either. First we see a line of police in riot gear, as well as young pioneers and other civilians with signs and armbands as if at a protest or rally. As Rivka connects Polish Holocaust history to the same narrative that reads the state of Israel as the natural outcome and redemption of victimization, we see the menacing image of state power, this time in a peaceful capacity as protectors of the funeral. In fact, as the scene progresses, it is not clear if the police are there to protect the crowd or to participate in the rally. As she blends into the crowd, Rivka continues, "I can be found everywhere. I am the ghost of return. Return returning to herself." This return is visualized in her turn into and movement toward the group, and with this image the narrative of her movement from Europe to Israel, from victim to victor, is reversed, complicating the unidirectional historical narrative she references.

The rally-funeral itself also presents a number of complicating perspectives of Rivka's story of victimization, return, and repatriation. Five speakers eulogize Sierakowski, himself now a victim of political violence: his widow, an Israeli woman who speaks in Hebrew; the Polish art historian and curator Anda Rottenberg, the daughter of a mixed marriage, speaking in Polish; the Israeli writer and Holocaust survivor Alona

Frankel, also speaking in Polish; the Israeli journalist and television personality Yaron London, speaking in Hebrew; and young representatives of the JRMiP, speaking in English. The self-identification of the speakers, the languages they speak in, and the content of their speeches represent a broad spectrum of possibilities for conceptualizing Polish Holocaust history in relationship to Zionism and the state of Israel. In fact, the entire rally-funeral recalls Michael Rothberg's conception of "multidirectional memory" as encouraging us "to think of the public sphere as a malleable discursive space in which groups do not simply articulate established positions but actually come into being through their dialogical interactions with others; both the subjects and spaces of the public are open to continual reconstruction."[26] It is the very multidirectionality of memory that challenges the monolithic historical narrative of victimization and triumph that forms the subtext of the video series.

Dana Sierakowski, the widow, represents a personal example of the repatriation of Jews to Poland; she notes that she "exchanged one homeland for another." However, she delivers her eulogy in Hebrew rather than in Polish, indicating that the exchange has been less than total and suggesting that national identity is not necessarily simple and unitary. This idea is echoed in her narration of Sierakowski's last moments, which also draw connections between Jewish history, Holocaust memory in Poland, and national identity. In her telling, she and her husband were attending the opening of an exhibit called "Chosen" at the Zachęta National Gallery. They were looking at a Bruno Schultz painting when she heard three shots ring out and Sierakowski fell. Before he died, he pressed a piece of paper into her hands with his last message, which she reads aloud. Sierakowski's message is in English and ends with the admonition, "There are no chosen people." The correlation established between chosenness and Schultz, an emblematic Polish-Jewish victim of the Holocaust, along with Sierakowski's rejection of the very concept of chosenness, suggests the imbrication of this idea, central to Jewish nationalism and national self-conception, with the history of Polish-Jewish victimization during the Holocaust. In rejecting chosenness, Sierakowski rejects a unidirectional nationalism and implicates that nationalism in Polish Holocaust history.

That his Israeli-Polish wife delivers this message, partially in Hebrew, both makes her a representative of the type of national self-conception hinted at in Sierakowski's speech in *Mary Koszmary* and at the same time reflects a certain ambivalence about the utopian notion of Jewish return.

Her speech also points to the somewhat problematic nature of the JRMiP platform of Jewish return to Poland as a mode of healing, discussed above. Right before her remark about having exchanged homelands, which seems to imply an equal trade without regret, she notes, "For you I left everything: my country, my homeland, my parents' house." This repetition of her loss—of home, of family—is a reminder that there is also a cost involved in return, and although it is a voluntary forfeiture it is nonetheless a counterpoint to the redemptive power attributed to Polish-Jewish repatriation by Sierakowski. The emotional or spiritual healing that Sierakowski refers to in *Mary Koszmary*, a central aspect of the JRMiP platform, also necessitates a material loss of the space or place demarcated by the concept of "home," as in Dana Sierakowski's formulation. It is here that the image of the Jew as trope rather than reality, the figure of the Jew as a healing presence, runs up against actual Jews, who have parents and houses and other homelands. In a sense, the memory of the Jew—Rivka, the ghost of the Jewish Holocaust victim—is demonstrably incompatible with real Jews.

The speeches that follow offer a variety of representations of Polish-Jewish history and the Jewish present that reveal the symbolic problematics of Jewish return. Anda Rottenberg, a Polish art historian and curator whose father was a Polish Holocaust survivor, centers her eulogy on the multicultural history of Poland, suggesting that Sierakowski's message and the JRMiP platform are actually an attempt to restore Poland to the ideal of its founders as a multicultural nation. Immediately after her, the Israeli writer and illustrator Alona Frankel, a Holocaust survivor herself, speaking in Polish as if to establish her own legitimate claim to a Polish identity despite her Israeliness and Jewishness, offers a very different portrait of Poland and the purpose of the JRMiP. Rather than a healing process or a return to an ostensibly more authentic Polish history, Frankel characterizes the notion of return as payback for the Holocaust. She says, "I will not live among you. . . . Israel is my country but restoration of citizenship rights a historical injustice." Rottenberg and Frankel essentially offer mirroring perspectives. Their positions bookend the question of return: the one need not return to Poland because she never left; the other refuses to return but demands that Poland acknowledge her right to do so.

The fourth speaker, Yaron London, an Israeli journalist and television personality, delivers his speech in Hebrew and offers a kind of anti-JRMiP perspective. He represents a teleological interpretation of contemporary Jewish history, the notion that a degraded Jewish diasporic existence was redeemed after the Holocaust by the emergence of the state of Israel. "Only utter fools [t'mimim, which can also be translated as 'innocents'] can long for a utopian world in which centuries of riots [*pogroms*] and hatred are erased," he says. And while he claims that Rivka, as a representative of Polish Jewry and Holocaust victimhood, has departed, never to return to Poland, we know that she is, in fact, in the crowd listening. The shot shifts as he speaks, so that we can see as Rivka moves forward through the crowd, carrying a suitcase, to stop right in front of the stage where London stands, facing him (fig. 15).

FIGURE 15. Rivka and London facing each other. Yael Bartana, *Zamach* (Assassination), 2011, video still, courtesy Annet Gelink Gallery, Amsterdam, and Sommer Contemporary Art, Tel Aviv.

He does not notice her. As he intones his final remarks, "The Jewish Diaspora, ladies and gentlemen, ended in Auschwitz," the camera moves to focus on Rivka, who looks into it plaintively. Her presence actively counters London's insistence on the teleological view in which Jewish history ends in the establishment of the state of Israel, precluding any further developments.

HAUNTED DREAMS

This historical teleology, in which Zionism is the answer to Jewish victimization in the diaspora and Israel redeems the degradations of the Holocaust, is at the heart of Bartana's critique. The title of the first film, *Mary Koszmary* (Nightmares), reflects the paradox explored in *And Europe Will Be Stunned*: the way in which the past and the present continue to haunt the utopian Zionist dream. While critiquing the Zionist "negation of exile" and offering up the utopian possibility of a Jewish return to the diaspora, the videos simultaneously reference the problematics of settlement and return. These problems are reflexively presented through allusions to Zionist propaganda about Israeli pioneers and explicit and implicit comparisons to the Israeli-Palestinian conflict.

And Europe Will Be Stunned also references another haunting, one that complicates London's teleological Zionist narrative: the memory of the Holocaust. Primarily, Holocaust memory is evoked through visual references to the Monument to the Ghetto Heroes, featured in the second film, *Mur I Wieża*. This monument is a memorial to the Warsaw Ghetto Uprising designed by Nathan Rapoport and installed in 1948 in an area of Warsaw that was formerly part of the ghetto. *Mur I Wieża* begins with a point of view shot from what we eventually understand to be the wall of the newly built kibbutz across from the monument. In this opening shot, we catch a glimpse of the monument, which continues to appear through the course of the film, as one of the kibbutzniks walks toward the camera with the memorial in the background, spray-painting on the camera, which is contiguous with the wall of the kibbutz, the symbol of the JRMiP (fig. 16). The framing of the shot, early in the video, suggests that the monument and the newly fashioned kibbutz being built across from it represent two poles or stages of Jewish history. Just as the kibbutznik moves from one to the other, the video installation moves between each of these poles—the Holocaust, represented by the monument, and the rebuilding of the diaspora, as represented by the kibbutz in central Warsaw—in order to reinterpret the prevailing teleological model of Jewish post-Holocaust history.

The history and design of the memorial itself are also relevant to the role of the monument in complicating this model. One side of the monument, which faces Muranow Square (and faces the camera in *Mur I Wieża*), depicts a relief of the heroes of the uprising, dedicated "to the Jewish people—Its Heroes and Martyrs." But the other side, what James Young calls the "dark" side, in which images recede into the stone,

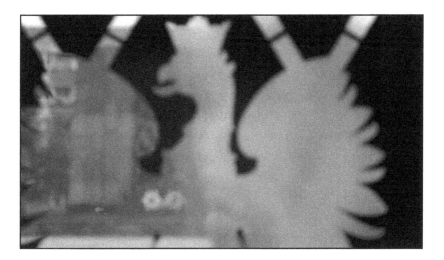

FIGURE 16. Opening shot of *Mur I Wieża*, in which a pioneer spray-paints the JRMiP symbol while the viewer looks out at the Monument to the Ghetto Heroes behind him. Yael Bartana, *Mur I Wieża* (Wall and Tower), 2009, video still, courtesy Annet Gelink Gallery, Amsterdam, and Sommer Contemporary Art, Tel Aviv.

depicts twelve stooped figures fleeing (figs. 17 and 18). These figures represent the twelve tribes of Israel, and this suggests that the whole of Jewish history, up to the moment of redemption depicted on the other side, has been one of rootlessness and victimization. As Young notes, "In this movement between sides, the ancient type seems to pass into the shaded wall only to emerge triumphantly out of the other side into the western light: one type is literally recessive, the other emergent."[27] In other words, the monument itself presents a triumphalist view of Jewish history in which exile and wandering is redeemed through resistance and martyrdom.[28]

Likewise, the monument's structure itself has a dual meaning that creates an implied historical trajectory. The relief emerges from a giant wall, eleven meters tall, which according to Rapoport was meant to evoke both the walls of the ghetto and the Western Wall in Jerusalem.[29] Just as with the sculpture itself, the symbolic value of the wall as background suggests a nationalist historical narrative of return, from a victimized exile to a triumphant Jerusalem, which connects Holocaust memory to Zionism and the establishment of the state of Israel. The massive size and repetitive symbolics of the monument, while focusing attention on the memory of the ghetto, the uprising, and the trajectory of Jewish history, also lend themselves to the ossification of that memory. James Young has written of monuments in general that they "have long sought to provide a naturalizing locus for memory, in which a state's triumphs and martyrs, its ideals and founding myths are cast as naturally true as the landscape in which they stand. These are the monument's sustaining illusions, the principles of its seeming longevity and power."[30] The danger of this longevity, however, is that it can also reify history, preserving one particular narrative at the expense of a multivalent, complex, and contextual conception of both past and present.

This is precisely the problem that *And Europe Will Be Stunned* not only grapples with but also provides one possible solution to, in the form of the artwork itself. It does so in the content and format of the videos themselves but also through the corollaries to the video project: the companion book, *A Cookbook for Political Imagination*; a website for the JRMiP; and a congress of the JRMiP convened in conjunction with

Figures 17 and 18. The two sides of the Monument to the Ghetto Heroes. Photographs courtesy of Melissa Weininger and Wikimedia Commons.

the Berlin Biennale in 2012. The centrality of the image of the Monument to the Ghetto Heroes in *Mur I Wieża* suggests that *And Europe Will Be Stunned* is aware of its role in complicating the narratives of historical memory. Through its imaginative reversal of the process of Zionist settlement and its complex representation of the role and value of diaspora to Jewish history, *And Europe Will Be Stunned* offers a nuanced consideration of both the possibilities and the pitfalls of nationalism, diaspora, and utopia.

5

The Neue Diaspora

Diasporic Hebrew in Berlin

The complex relationship of Israel to the diaspora, in practical terms, has been no more evident than in the Jewish state's history with regard to Germany. The new state of Israel, established in the wake of the Holocaust and home to more than a hundred thousand survivors of Nazi genocide, perhaps understandably had a fraught relationship to German language and culture as well as to the country itself. But after more than half a century, the tide of globalization, and the advent of the internet, young Israelis see Germany as no different than any other European country and even as one of the more amenable destinations for immigration. This phenomenon, as well as movements for the creation of Hebrew and Israeli culture that is specifically European, has led to the establishment of a particularly intentional expatriate Israeli community in Germany, one that has made a conscious effort to create a multilingual, transcultural, diaspora Israeli culture for explicitly political purposes.

The hostility and suspicion with which Israel viewed all things German in the early years of the state was evident in both Israeli attitudes and political policies regarding Germany. Although many immigrants to the prestate Yishuv spoke it, there were strong taboos against the use of German, and German language instruction was banned at the Hebrew University of Jerusalem, Israel's flagship institution of higher education, between 1934 and 1953.[1] For eight years after the establishment of the state, it was forbidden to enter Germany on an Israeli passport, which contained the admonition "Good for all countries but Germany."[2] The

Holocaust, conceived not just as a defining event of Jewish history but also as a crucial catalyst in the realization of Jewish sovereignty, drove a deep wedge between Israel and Germany both practically and imaginatively.

However, beginning in the late 2000s, Israeli Jews began immigrating—some temporarily and some permanently—in significant numbers to Germany, most settling in or around Berlin. This trend is prominent enough that it has visibly impacted Berlin's local culture. Larissa Remennick notes, "The general feeling is that the presence of Israelis in Berlin's ethno-cultural mosaic is constantly growing: the sounds of Hebrew are commonly heard on public transport and in cafés, clubs, and other city venues."[3] Remennick has identified the main reasons Israelis immigrate to Germany as economic, professional, educational, and personal, to be with German partners; but she also notes that emigration from Israel (to Germany and elsewhere) is often either a temporary escape or a protest against the political situation, particularly the Occupation.[4] In addition, recent changes to German laws have allowed many Israelis to obtain German passports due to ancestral ties, prompting Michael Brenner's observation that "many Israeli Jews have a right of return to Europe, just as diaspora Jews have a right of return to Israel."[5]

Brenner's formulation emphasizes the extent to which emigration from Israel, and particularly to Germany, violates a long-standing taboo and represents a rejection and even reversal of the Zionist project of ingathering of the exiles. This is evident in the history of Israeli policy: until 1959 Israelis had to apply for an exit permit to even travel outside of Israel. Although emigration, even during the early years, has always been a large part of the story of the Zionist project in Palestine, and later the state of Israel, its history has largely been elided and its practice has remained taboo. As Gur Alroey has shown, even during the Second Aliyah, or wave of immigration to Palestine, in the early twentieth century, somewhere between 40 and 80 percent of immigrants in a given year emigrated, whether back to their countries of origin or to a new location.[6]

Over time, emigration from Palestine, and later Israel, took on negative connotations. In Hebrew, special language is reserved for migration to and from the land of Israel: *aliyah*, or ascent, for immigration to the land; and *yeridah*, or descent, for emigration from the land. Israel itself is known in Hebrew simply as "ha'aretz," or "the land," implying a special position for Israel, much like celebrities who use only one name, as the one and only place of importance. This vocabulary conveys a certain moral judgment with its quasi-religious implications of rising up to a better, or holier, place. Thus, emigration has usually been defined as a negative or even illegitimate move, a betrayal of the Zionist project and the homeland of the Jewish people.[7] This is compounded, in the case of Israeli immigration to Germany, by the history of the Holocaust and Germany's early fraught relationship to the Jewish state. As Hadas Cohen and Dani Kranz describe it, "Emigrating from Israel stands for the return to a diasporic existence and a betrayal of the Israeli Jewish community as a whole. Migrating to Germany adds another dimension to a downward spiral, given this particular history."[8]

Many reasons for Israeli emigration in general, and to Germany specifically, have been identified by social scientists. Some of these, called "push" factors, might apply to most Israeli emigrants: economic, professional, or political reasons. Others, thought of as "pull" factors, are often more specifically related to place: education, ties to German partners, or historical factors that allow for legal immigration, such as having ancestors born in Germany.[9] A subset of Israeli emigrants, however, claim artistic and political reasons, often linked, for their choice to settle specifically in Germany. This loosely organized group of writers, artists, and scholars has established a number of cultural initiatives, mostly in Berlin, that seek to redefine Hebrew culture away from its present in Israel and toward its past in Europe, while at the same time forming alliances with expatriates from other Middle Eastern countries that rely on notions of a pan-Levantine culture, and attempt to subvert Zionist claims on both Hebrew and Jewishness.

In the last decade, Israeli migrants to Berlin have created a Hebrew library; an online Hebrew magazine, *Spitz*; a series of lectures and seminars at Humboldt University called the Gymnasia Project; community organizations; and Hebrew-language classes for children. In addition, an artistic and scholarly community has sprung up that has developed new modes for artistic expression in Hebrew and in collaboration with other ethnic and linguistic communities that specifically reference Hebrew's diasporic history, as well as integrating Mizrahi Israelis into a multi-ethnic European culture. These varied modes of artistic production and the movement to deterritorialize Hebrew and reconnect it with a diaspora Jewish history reflect the most explicitly political diaspora Israeli culture considered in this volume. Often, the diaspora Israeli literature and art produced in Berlin is intentionally linked to a critique of Zionism and contemporary Israeli politics and makes use of diaspora as a motivating force in its critique. At the same time, it reflects a desire for Hebrew, and Israeli culture, to be more fully integrated into European, and global, cultural movements that foster a multicultural and multi-ethnic ethos and serve as points of connection for otherwise disconnected, and sometimes hostile, communities of people.

THE POLITICS OF DIASPORIC HEBREW

One of the primary projects of the Israeli diaspora in Berlin has been to create a new culture of what has been called "diasporic Hebrew." This phrase was first used by Tal Hever-Chybowski, one of the driving forces behind the Hebrew renaissance in Berlin and the rest of Europe. Hever-Chybowski (b. 1986), who grew up in Jerusalem, left Israel in 2008, at age twenty-one, because, as he has said, "I didn't want to start my life in Palestine-Israel."[10] In 2014 he moved to Paris to become the director of the Paris Yiddish Center–Medem Library. In the inaugural issue of *Mikan ve'eylakh* (From This Point Onward), a Hebrew journal published in Paris that he founded in 2016, Hever-Chybowski defines "diasporic Hebrew" as "a minor, hybrid, heterogenous Hebrew" facilitated by "the *duality* between the local presence and the trans-local presence of Hebrew."[11] Elsewhere, Hever-Chybowski connects this contemporary movement for the creation of a diasporic Hebrew culture to the history of Hebrew in Berlin, which in the modern period had always been one of the main

centers for the creation of Hebrew culture.[12] The function of contemporary diasporic Hebrew in Berlin, according to Hever-Chybowski, "is not
only an instrument for remembering that which has been forgotten, but
also for fundamentally resisting the historical forces which sought to
remove Hebrew from this place. Reclaiming Jewish diasporic languages
and literatures (and this holds for Yiddish as much as it does for Hebrew)
in Berlin is an act of historical defiance."[13] The Holocaust destroyed Jewish culture in Germany, but the revival of Hebrew in Berlin can be seen
partly as a mode of remembering, or even recuperating, that history, as
well as a political tool for reinstating Jewish history and culture into the
troubled space of Germany.

However, diasporic Hebrew, for much of the Israeli artistic community in Berlin, also has another political function connected to Hebrew's
role in Zionist ideology and the creation of Israeli culture. Hila Amit,
a scholar and writer who is another of the Berlin circle of Israeli emigrants, claims that the revival of Hebrew in Berlin is an activist project,
one that sees radical potential in "Hebrew's deterritorialization and the
reclamation of its diasporic and 'open' character."[14] Amit claims diaspora Hebrew, along with the process of emigration itself, as a critique
or even contradiction of the Zionist project. Mati Shemoelof, another of
the Israeli writers in Berlin, has written of what he sees as an Israeli
impulse to close off cultural dialogue with the diaspora, citing as an example the decision to restrict the Sapir Prize to writers living in Israel only.[15]
He notes, "This reaction [to close off borders, deny Israeli diaspora] is
reminiscent of the neoconservatism that we see in fundamentalist movements, which oppose globalization and freedom of information—and
are explicitly against cosmopolitan identities. Is it even possible to create imaginary borders between Hebrew, Jewish, and Israeli works in the
Internet age?"[16] Even the title of his article, "Creating a Radical Hebrew
Culture in the Diaspora," refers to the political possibilities attached to
the project of a contemporary diaspora Hebrew culture that explicitly
engages its relationship to Israel.

Some of those political possibilities are manifest in the participation of Berlin's Hebrew writers in an ongoing project of Arab-Jewish

dialogue. In 2015, the poet Mati Shemoelof and the artist Barak Moyal, both Israelis living in Berlin, hosted the first Poetic Hafla, an evening of literary readings, music, and performances in Hebrew, Arabic, German, and English. The term *hafla* is an Arabic word for a party or celebration and points to their intention to create a space of collaboration rather than conflict, as well as a place to acknowledge shared histories and languages, particularly for Mizrahi Jews whose families originated in Arab lands. Shemoelof has noted that the *haflot* (itself a Hebrew plural of the Arabic word) are intended to celebrate a pan-Middle Eastern culture that encompasses both Hebrew and Arabic and connects Israeli Jews with Arab roots to Palestinians and other Arabs also living abroad.[17] This also has a specifically political motive: "to diminish the colonial tension between Israel and Palestine, between Israel and the Arabic diaspora."[18] Both Shemoelof and Amit, with whom he has collaborated on similar initiatives, claim that these kinds of gatherings could not happen in Israel, a claim that echoes Larissa Remennick's finding that Israelis living in Berlin "enjoyed the mutli-ethnic and cosmopolitan cityscape of Berlin—rife with human encounters they had seldom experienced in Israel, with other Europeans and Middle Easterners, including Palestinians."[19]

Mati Shemoelof (b. 1972) has been living in Berlin since 2013, and while his initial move was temporary, he has since started a family in Germany. Born in Haifa to an Iraqi family, Shemoelof has long been involved in political and artistic activism. In 2007, he was one of the founders of Guerilla Tarbut (Cultural Guerilla), a group dedicated to the promotion of social and political causes through poetry. Members would perform work in Hebrew and Arabic during demonstrations around matters ranging from labor issues to the eviction of Palestinian families from their homes by Israeli authorities, and the group also published several anthologies of members' work. He met Hila Amit (b. 1985) in Berlin, where she was conducting research as a postdoctoral fellow. Amit holds a PhD in gender studies and writes both nonfiction and Hebrew fiction. In addition to her activist artistic work with Shemoelof, in 2014 she founded the International Hebrew School, which offers online Hebrew classes and tutors using a "queer, feministic and plural-istic method."[20] In 2020 she published a companion Hebrew textbook, *Hebrew for All*, marketed as "the first queer feminist Hebrew learning book," reflecting the same values that mark her activist work around Hebrew literature in Berlin.[21]

To advance their commitment to creating a diasporic Hebrew space that would also foster connections between writers from other parts of the Middle East, in 2018 Shemoelof and Amit created the organization Anu: Jews and Arabs Writing in Berlin (also sometimes known as Anu: Mizrahi Writers in Berlin). The group describes itself as "the very first literary group to bring together Jewish and Muslim authors & poets with heritage stemming from the Middle East, Asia, and North Africa. . . . Living together in exile in Berlin, Jews and Muslims are redefining their mutual existence in the diaspora."[22] Their goals are, in many ways, explic-itly political: to promote cultural dialogue and exchange, to bring Jews and Muslims together to work collaboratively to bridge divides, to open dialogue in Germany about historical narratives of the Other, to educate about Mizrahi Jewish history in Europe, and to promote feminist and queer representation. To accomplish this, they host symposia and events both promoting Middle Eastern writers in Berlin and analyzing the ques-tions at the center of their mission regarding identity, the relationship between Ashkenazi and Mizrahi Jews, and the relationship between Jews and Arabs from the Middle East.

Although the group, and the activists and writers who have estab-lished a diaspora Hebrew culture in Berlin, specifically attributes its mission to a diasporic setting, its work expands and continues a phe-nomenon that, like the founders of Anu, originated in Israel. In 2011 the Israeli singer Dudu Tassa released an album of Arabic songs orig-inally written by his grandfather and great-uncle, who performed in Iraq between the 1930s and the 1950s as the Al-Kuwaiti Brothers. Tassa learned Iraqi Arabic for the project, and he includes both Jewish and Arab (and Arab-Jewish) singers and musicians on the two albums he has now released of these songs. In 2014, the director Nissim Dayan released *The Dove Flyer*, a film based on Eli Amir's 1992 novel *Mafriach hayonim*, filmed entirely in the Judeo-Arabic of the Baghdad Jewish community. The Mizrahi Hebrew writers of Berlin have extended this Jewish reclamation of Arab roots to create a link between themselves and non-Jewish Arab writers from many parts of the Middle East also "in exile," as they say (some literally), in Berlin. In doing so, they have suggested that this space is only possible outside of the state of Israel.

The creation of a space for the meeting of Middle Eastern cultures in both Hebrew and Arabic, as well as a space for the acknowledgment of a dual Arab-Jewish identity, nods to Levantinism, an idea first articulated by the Israeli writer Jacqueline Kahanoff in the 1950s. Kahanoff herself, born in Cairo, never wrote in Hebrew, only English and French, and before settling in Israel had lived in both the United States and France. Using her cosmopolitan upbringing in prerevolutionary Cairo as a model, Kahanoff posited a pluralistic Levantine culture that would reflect the historic multicultural, polylingual, and diverse religious composition of the broader Middle East. She saw Israel as part of this Levantine culture and particularly saw Israeli Jews with origins in the Middle East as playing an integral role in establishing Israel as part of the Levant. Whereas Levantine, or oriental, culture had been viewed as inferior to the Western-oriented Israeli culture that Zionists wanted to establish in the new state, Kahanoff advocated for Levantinism as a positive value, encouraging a more pluralistic understanding of Israeli culture as comprising multiple cultural influences and as belonging to a broader multinational regional culture.

In her later work, Levantinism also came to have a utopian political bent. As she wrote in an introduction to a collected English volume of her essays that was never published, "I seek to discover traces of my own past here. But they cannot be separated from the history of other peoples who lived in or passed through this region; their roots and ours are intertwined, and so are our lives today, through the very intensity of the conflict that locks us in combat."[23] Shemoelof echoes Kahanoff's words when he writes of the reasons for the establishment of multicultural Hebrew-Arabic events in Berlin: "More than 100 years ago in the Middle-East, Jews, Arabs and other ethnic-religious groups lived in a fruitful dialogue and were culturally, spiritually and physically connected. After the disappearance of the Ottoman Empire, the two World Wars, and the rise of Jewish and Arab nationalism, the two peoples became disconnected. We lost our dialogue."[24] While these accounts of history may be somewhat revisionist in hindsight, nonetheless they describe a rationale for the revival of Hebrew culture in Berlin that is linked to a longing, even if falsely nostalgic, for a political Levantinism that stands as a critique of an Israeli culture that excluded both Mizrahi and Palestinian artists in the name of Zionism.

However, in the case of Berlin, this pluralistic Hebrew culture necessarily also includes the Ashkenazi history of the place itself, which, as Hever-Chybowski has noted, was forcibly erased. As he writes, "Hebrew was not just 'lost' here, but violently erased and burned down to oblivion."[25] The creation of a new diaspora Hebrew culture in Berlin, this time by Israelis, recalls Bartana's image of young Israeli pioneers returning to Warsaw to construct a kibbutz, to reoccupy the Polish homeland from which their ancestors were expelled. At the same time, as Shemoelof describes it, Berlin is a space in which meetings and cultural exchange between Arabs and Israelis, some of whom identify as Arab Jews, can produce an "alternative Arab-Jewish history." In this formulation, and the collaborations produced by it, Berlin becomes the site not only of an Israeli diaspora culture but also a Levantine diaspora culture in the style of Jacqueline Kahanoff. In this it may represent what Yael Almog has called "the struggle individuals face when they try to make a home in 'The Homeland'—a place that remains, for many, paradoxically elusive. When 'The Homeland' is elusive, so is the ability to see your immigration as a return to the place where you belong."[26] The Israeli diaspora in Berlin and the self-consciously political Hebrew culture they are creating elucidate this complicated conception of homeland, one that continues to locate itself in Israel yet embraces exile as a positive value.

HEBREW LITERATURE IN BERLIN

Shemoelof's 2017 poetry chapbook, *Ivrit mechutz le'ivreha hametukim* (Hebrew Outside Her Sweet Insides), which he wrote after his immigration to Berlin, addresses some of the questions raised by diaspora Hebrew culture in Berlin and the political dimensions of Israel migration there. Or, as the scholar Yael Almog has put it, "Is our presence here a critique of Israel? Is our diasporic community a manifestation of something *worse*?"[27] That "something worse" might be the attempt to decouple Hebrew from its Israeli context, reinstating it into its multilingual European context. The title of Shemoelof's chapbook itself situates it within the project of the revival of diasporic Hebrew, while at the same time acknowledging its connection to Israel, the "sweet insides" of the title. The word here translated as "(her) insides," *ivreha*, refers to the internal organs of the body, a natural metaphor that envisions Hebrew as housed or bounded within a particular geography. The chapbook announces itself as an act of creation outside of that seemingly natural space.

The poems in this collection return again and again to the subject of language and the concept of diaspora, particularly the tension inherent in diaspora Hebrew, a language that sees itself in exile even in the place where it was born. The first untitled poem of the collection begins: "Lover of two continents / Wanderer in a body without a foundation."[28] This sets the tone for the collection, which indeed wanders between Israel and Germany, Hebrew and German, exploring the possibilities of language unmoored from any fixed location. The poem "Eifo zeh chul?" (Where Is Abroad?) uses the specific vocabulary of home and exile built into the Hebrew language to explore this process. The word in Hebrew for "abroad" is actually an acronym used as its own word, *chul*, which stands for "chutz la'aretz," or "outside of the land." As noted, in Hebrew, Israel is not typically referred to by name but simply as "ha'aretz" or "the land." This renders the title of the poem, while simple to translate linguistically, difficult to translate culturally, since so much about Israeli self-perception and the notion of Israel as homeland is packed into that phrase. Just this difficulty sets the stage for the complex understanding of home and abroad presented in the poem.

The speaker writes of waiting for friends to return from *chul*, from abroad, "because I didn't believe that there was anything outside this land."[29] But now, he says, "I am the one who lives outside" and "abroad there is no word 'outside the land' [*chul*]." The absence of this very word in the world outside "the land," Israel, suggests that the status it confers is meaningless outside the land and the language that has been coupled with it. Israel's self-valorization, its visualization of itself, even in language, as the center, is contradicted by the untranslatability of this valorizing idiom. Rather, in the world "outside the land," "people wander freely from outside, to outside, / from land to land, from language to language." The move to the outside detaches the language from the land, allowing it to circulate along with the global movement of people and languages.

This movement, and the engagement of Hebrew with other places and languages, is best represented by the poem "Ich bin yuden dichter" (I Am a Jewish Writer), a mix of Hebrew and German written in Hebrew characters.[30] Perhaps more than any other, this poem speaks to the revival not just of Hebrew in Germany but also of the return to multilingualism as a particularly Jewish mode of expression. The poem begins with a line in German transliterated into Hebrew characters, "Ich schreibe hebraisch," meaning "I write Hebrew," followed by a Hebrew line: "Ish kotev ivrit," or "A man writes Hebrew." The lines are connected by the play on "ich/ish" (I/man)—pronounced nearly identically and spelled the same way when the German is transliterated. The line also recalls the title and first lines of Salman Masalha's poem "Ani kotev ivrit" (I Write Hebrew):

אֲנִי כּוֹתֵב בַּלָּשׁוֹן הָעִבְרִית,
שֶׁבִּשְׁבִילִי אֵינֶנָּה שְׂפַת אֵם

I write in the Hebrew language
which is not my mother tongue[31]

Masalha, a Palestinian citizen of Israel and native Arabic speaker, is a Hebrew poet who here, like Shemoelof, expresses his affiliation with a language that is both foreign and his own. This reference to another bilingual and translingual Hebrew writer, with a different kind of Arab heritage than his own, reinforces the slippage between languages and cultures that in Shemoelof's poem connect German and Hebrew and model the intermixture of languages in the German context.

This poem also plays with the two languages to create a secret or hidden narrative that suggests the invisibility of minority languages, as well as those who speak them, within the dominant culture. In answer to the question of why the poet writes in Hebrew in Berlin, the narrator answers first in German: "Ich kann nich [*sic*] schreiben gut Engliz [*sic*] oder / naturlich kein gut Deutschen" (I cannot write English well or / native good German). But the next line, in Hebrew, seems addressed to a different audience, those like him, whose German is not native but whose Hebrew is: "Ve'ani ger becha" (and I am a stranger within you). Although the "you" addresses itself to the Berlin German-speaking community, it functions as a Hebrew aside, an inside commentary for those who can understand. At the same time, though the narrator insists that he writes in Hebrew, and the mistakes in the German indicate that his self-assessment of his language skills is accurate, he is still writing in German here. Yet the German itself is transposed into a Hebrew context, transliterated such that a German reader could not decode it. This has the effect of both claiming German—even bad German—for the Hebrew poet and at the same time alienating German from German readers, rendering the familiar foreign and the foreign familiar.

The transcription of German into Hebrew characters also recalls the history of diasporic Hebrew, and in particular the work of Moses Mendelssohn, one of the originators of the *haskalah*, or Jewish Enlightenment, in Europe. In 1783, Mendelssohn published his *Biur* (Explanation), a translation of the Hebrew Bible into German, but one printed in Hebrew characters. At the time, most European Jews would have been literate in Yiddish, and possibly Hebrew, but not necessarily in German or Latin letters. Part of the goal of the translation was to help modernizing, "enlightened" German Jews to learn the language, and in particular the elegant High German of the translation. But Mendelssohn's project is also an example of the way that Hebrew circulated in diaspora Jewish communities for centuries before the establishment of the state of Israel and the way that it was part of a culturally and linguistically mixed European Jewish milieu.

Unlike Mendelssohn's elegant translation, partly designed to demonstrate the ability of Ashkenazi Jews to command European vernacular languages at the highest levels, Shemoelof's poem, just as he claims, is not written in "native" or "good" German. It is full of seeming mistakes (although the transliteration makes it difficult to know what a "correct" spelling might be) and neologisms. One of these is the word *lachman*, "funny man," which Shemoelof uses to refer to himself as the odd man out, in a longer line that reads: "I am a funny man [*lachman*], I am a bad Jew, immigrant, from Iraq, / I am a Jew, and I am an Arab." This line, written in transliterated German, details all the ways in which the speaker does not fit into the German context but also includes the ways in which he does not fit into the Israeli context. In fact, each element of his "funniness" or oddity could apply equally to his being in Germany or in Israel: in Germany he is an immigrant, but the flexible application of the word "immigrant" here suggests that even in Israel his Iraqi heritage makes him a kind of immigrant or outsider. Likewise, the combination of two identities—Jew and Arab—considered antithetical in Israel excludes him from a unifying national discourse. The "funny" language of the German simply underscores his liminality, the way in which he exists outside of any "home" context or language.

This poem, and Shemoelof's work, is emblematic of the new diasporic Hebrew literature being created by the Israeli expatriate community in Berlin. Just as Ruby Namdar makes reference in his work to an earlier generation of American Hebrew writers, Shemoelof alludes to the origins of Hebrew literature in its European setting. In playing with notions of home and abroad, language and identity, Shemoelof insists on a restoration of Hebrew to its transnational and multilingual origins, questioning its singular association with the state of Israel and even with Israeli culture.

THE ANTHOLOGY AND THE PERFORMANCE

The last few years have also seen the introduction of new Hebrew periodicals in Berlin and Paris that recall the historical development of Hebrew literature in a variety of Hebrew periodicals published in European cities. The Hebrew press originated in Europe and was central to the promulgation of *haskalah* (Jewish Enlightenment) ideology. From the early nineteenth century, Menucha Gilboa writes, the Hebrew press intended to "inculcate into Jewish life the spirit of humanism and modernity."[32] The Hebrew periodicals of the *haskalah* period published a variety of material, from poetry and fiction to moral literature. In the late nineteenth century, weekly papers also began to incorporate news and feature articles. But these journals were crucial in the development of modern Hebrew literature, and as Hillel Halkin notes, "There is hardly a Hebrew writer who did not take his first literary steps in one of the newspapers."[33] Hebrew journals and periodicals in Europe were the crucible for the development of modern Hebrew literature and culture, long before the existence of the state of Israel.

Several journals and news outlets in Berlin have consciously styled themselves in the likeness of these early Hebrew periodicals, recalling the diasporic origins of Hebrew literature. One of these is *Mikan ve'eylakh* (From This Point Onward), subtitled *Me'asef le'ivrit 'olamit* (Gatherer of World Hebrew), an appellation that recalls the title of one of the earliest Hebrew journals, *Ha'me'asef*, which appeared first in 1784 in Königsberg. That periodical, like many of its time, was designed to disseminate *haskalah* ideology and included original and translated Hebrew literature alongside articles on Judaism. As Rachel Seelig has noted, it also conveys the mission of *Mikan ve'eylakh*, much like the Hebrew journals of the *haskalah* period, to bring together both texts and people, not physically but culturally.[34] Likewise, as Hever-Chybowski writes in the introductory article, the word *'olam*, or world, "has a double-meaning—referring to both space and time. . . . Just as the Jewish people is a people of the world (and of eternity), so too Hebrew is an eternal world tongue."[35] Thus *Mikan ve'eylakh* places itself squarely within the tradition of European

Hebrew periodicals that fostered a transnational Jewish community and culture.

Indeed, the introduction to the second volume of *Mikan ve'eylakh* explicitly states that it "seeks to become a link" in a "chain of Hebrew printing in Ashkenaz" that dates itself to the period of the Hebrew Renaissance in Europe.[36] Like the Hebrew journals of the nineteenth century, which were passed along through the Jewish communities of Europe without regard to borders, the journal imagines itself as having "a utopian dimension that points to no place, to a place that is neither here nor there."[37] This description of the textual object as a space that is "no place," "a representation of the village of the book of a dispersed Hebrew,"[38] recalls George Steiner's notion of the homeland as text, while at the same time moving past it, rejecting the notion of the homeland entirely. Instead, they rely on a model of many centers, a heterogenous, nonbinary understanding that, like the cooperative artistic organizations established between Hebrew and Arabic writers, revalues the notion of exile.

The journal itself works to establish these multiple centers of Hebrew by publishing Hebrew writing from outside of Israel and through literary and linguistic experiments that playfully challenge the naturalness of language. For example, the second volume contains a short story by Tomer Gardi called "Broken Hebrew," which was originally written in German, not Gardi's native language, and translated by Cecile Neeser Hever into Hebrew, which is not her native language. This experiment nods to and extends the idea of Gardi's novel *Broken German*, which he, a native Hebrew speaker who has written almost exclusively in Hebrew, wrote in nonstandard (broken) German. Like the translingual literature examined in chapter 3, Gardi's novel works to detach language from its national affiliations as well as, by nodding to the inherent imperfection of its language, question the naturalness of a system governed by arbitrary, constructed rules of grammar.

This translingual translation extends the project of translingual literature almost into absurdity, as does the absurd premise of the story, which in some ways parallels its linguistic play. The story centers on an

Israeli mother and son traveling to Germany, who lose their luggage and take two random suitcases left at the baggage claim, which belong to a Lebanese man and an Eritrean woman. They try on the clothes of these absent characters and then change back into their own, but they continue to call each other by the names of the suitcase owners as they speak to each other in English (presumably the only common language of these two "others") while heading "outside into the German streets (mistakenly feminine adjective)."[39] The parenthetical is a translator's note denoting the mistake in the German, imported into the Hebrew but here explicitly exposed in an interruption to the narrative. These interruptions force the reader to consider the process of translation as well as translingual writing, thus also interrupting any ease or complacency about the naturalness of language in literary representation. It forces a consideration of language, what we speak and what we read, and how it comes to us whether on the page or in our own mouths. As the narrator says in the story itself: "My mother tongue is not my mother's mother tongue. My mother's mother tongue is not the mother tongue of her mother. Her mother's mother tongue is not the mother tongue, and afterward more. Afterward more, much more."[40] The "more, much more" seems to be the province of the journal itself, looking toward the future possibilities of a Hebrew denaturalized and deterritorialized.

Another new European journal that extends this tradition of diasporic, transnational Hebrew is the German-Hebrew bilingual *Aviv: Literature, Art, Culture*, founded by German journalist Hanno Hauenstein, whose first and only issue was published in 2016. Hauenstein learned Hebrew while working as a researcher and journalist in Tel Aviv during the social justice protests of 2011 and began translating Hebrew works into German a few years later. On its first pages, *Aviv* announces itself as "a bilingual journal presenting a variety of literary and contemporary artistic works, and seeks to awaken the relationship between German and Hebrew."[41] It is part Hebrew-German periodical and part art magazine, incorporating fiction, poetry, nonfiction prose, photographs, and paintings. All of the texts are printed in both Hebrew and German: the journal opens from each end and creates an imperfect mirror of the two languages.

In his introduction, Hauenstein notes that the journal's bilingualism has a political and social purpose: "As a journal that aims to provide a platform for writers and artists from different backgrounds, and to constitute a critical mass against expressions of racism, we see bilingualism as a gift, and our work is the result of a process whose point of departure is the understanding of the breadth of latent possibilities in linguistic variety."[42] The composition of the journal and its contributors reflect its mission to employ multilingualism as a tool for transnational conceptions of culture. As Hauenstein has said of the project,

> A lot of people have told me that we are trying to make something beautiful out of something that is not actually beautiful. And of course, I agree, that we are moving within a space that is very sensitive to a lot of people. But that's also a side note about the project: it's not based on Israel. It reflects back to it, but it doesn't necessarily play within its national boundaries. And we feel we have the privilege to feature artists who have never been to Germany or to Israel, by playing with these languages.[43]

The "sensitive space" he describes appears to refer to discussions around the topic of German Holocaust history and the history of Jews in Germany as well as debates about Germany's current relationship to Israel amid Israel's occupation of the West Bank. The creation of a visually beautiful, bilingual publication is thus intended as a kind of bridge, outside of these national conflicts and debates, on which cooperation and dialogue can occur. *Aviv* not only is another example of the new Hebrew diaspora culture of Berlin but also consciously styles itself as an example of a multilingual and transnational cultural project, one with explicitly political purposes, that includes Hebrew. This not only recalls the history of Hebrew literature's development in European journals but also looks to a globalized and transnational future in which Hebrew once again circulates among the languages of Europe.

Similarly, the poetic *haflot* organized by Shemoelof and Moyal refer back to an earlier era of the development of Hebrew culture in Europe:

that of the coffeehouse. Shachar Pinsker has demonstrated the integral role of the coffeehouse in the creation of modern Jewish culture and Hebrew literature. Like the Hebrew press in Europe, the coffeehouse functioned as a transnational space, part of what Pinsker calls a "network of mobility" that was "central to modern Jewish creativity and exchange in a time of migration and urbanization."[44] He argues for understanding cafés as a "third space," one that mediates between the real and the imaginary, public and private, migrant and native, and a host of other constructed binaries.[45] Coffeehouses, like the *haflot*, were places that opened themselves to cultural others, to those who may have been excluded from or not felt comfortable in institutional spaces, to those who spoke and read many different languages, and offered a space in which all of these elements mingled.

As noted above, the *haflot* are explicitly political in their invocation of a transnational Levantinism. But at the same time, they create a physical space that, like the coffeehouse, fosters creativity across the "networks of mobility" that characterize contemporary globalization. As Mati Shemoelof puts it, in writing about creating Hebrew culture in diaspora, "The discourse is not defined by the physical location of the writers, but rather by their consciousness, which is the product of diaspora. In the global age it is difficult to feel obligated to national borders, the borders of language, or the borders dictated to the citizen by his nation."[46] This vision is similar to the way that Pinsker describes the coffeehouse: "These urban cafés constituted not only the nexus of cultural migrant networks but spaces of refuge for people who could not find home elsewhere, spaces or shelters of cosmopolitan multilingualism that the pressure of nationalism and monolingualism threatened and sometimes destroyed."[47] The space of the *hafla*, like the "world Hebrew" of *Mikan ve'eylakh* or the nineteenth-century coffeehouse, carves out a space defined not physically but temporally and culturally for the creation of diasporic Hebrew culture.

At the same time that the *haflot* refer to the role of the coffeehouse in the development of modern Hebrew culture, they also, in a typically multicultural way, refer to the rich Arab-Jewish culture of the Middle

East before 1948. The *hafla* is a cultural event featuring performance, music, and poetry, which was popularized in the early twentieth-century Arab world by the singer Umm Kulthum. Michal Raizen, writing about Umm Kulthum's performances, broadcast via radio from Cairo, characterizes what she calls "hafla poetics" as "the constant gesture toward an elsewhere in time, place, or interpersonal relationships."[48] Like the coffeehouse, the *hafla* not only was a physical space but carved out a transnational web of connections linked by culture and language.

In the last decade or so, the *hafla* has been embraced by Mizrahi Israeli artists and writers as a mode of recovering an Arab-Jewish past. Raizen traces the use of the *hafla* as a poetic device in Israeli literature as a way of noting how it works symbolically as a marker of what Zionism erased or elided for immigrants from Arab lands, a "bridge between the here and now of Israel and the Arab Jewish past."[49] The contemporary literary-political movement Ars Poetica has adopted the *hafla* as a model for its poetic performances, an important part of its mission to create increased visibility for Mizrahi writers in Israel. However, these *haflot* are open to all and promote non-Mizrahi writers from other marginalized groups as well. Adi Keissar, one of its founders, has noted that it is a radically inclusive movement, calling it "guerilla, . . . an eruption, . . . undefined."[50] While evoking an Arab Jewish past, these writer-activists have also expanded its scope to carve out a space in Israeli culture that resists the elisions of a monolithic Israeli-Hebrew cultural assimilation.

In Berlin, Israeli Hebraists have used the *hafla* to define their movement toward diasporic Hebrew culture specifically as a partnership with Arabs from across the Middle East and North Africa. The description of the purpose of these events on the Poetic Hafla Facebook page reads,

> Hafla is a celebration. We will be celebrating culture and the future of our international culture here in Berlin. Culture through poetry and performance and live music. Our culture will be celebrated in English, French, Hebrew, Arabic and German at our Hafla. We will laugh and think and drink together. We will be warm and merry. Come and celebrate the warmth of poetic expression, song, dance and performance.

The talent will be various, interesting, and thrilling. We be a community in complete support of creative expression. Afterward we will laugh, talk and dance to the music of the world.[51]

The deliberate transnationalism of the Berlin Poetic Hafla points to its purposeful construction of a cultural and temporal space outside of geography similar to the "third space" of the café described by Pinsker. In the case of the *hafla*, this space is defined both by social and emotional warmth and by multilingualism and multiculturalism. In a sense, the Berlin Poetic Hafla attempts to create a utopian space disconnected from nationality, a home—in the Yiddish sense of *heymish*, a place that is "like home," familiar, welcoming, a place to belong—but not a homeland. It recognizes itself as a performance rather than a reality, an imaginary locale that offers a template for a contemporary diasporic Hebrew transnationalism.

More than any other manifestation of Israeli diaspora culture, the movement to re-create diasporic Hebrew in Europe aligns itself with an expressly political goal: a reclamation of Hebrew from its association with the Israeli nation-state and its instantiation as an element of a transnational Levantine culture that expressly forms bonds with those typically labeled as excluded Others (Arab Jews) or enemies (Arabs or Palestinians) within the context of Israeli society. In a sense, this movement seeks to create through organization and performance what the alternative histories of Jewish national realization create in the imagination: a utopian space that recovers a lost or elided Jewish history—in this case, both the diaspora history of Hebrew culture and the familial and cultural histories of Jews of Arab descent—in an effort to decouple the nation from language and culture. The conscious work of *Mikan ve'ey-lakh*, Anu, and the Poetic Hafla to create both intra- and intercultural connections, as well as to span time as a mode of bypassing the interventions of the nation-state, represents the creation of Israeli diaspora culture as political project. Whereas the alternative histories of Israel, Hebrew literature in America, and translingual Israeli literature may all have political implications or envision new modes of understanding the relationship between Hebrew, Israel, homeland, and diaspora, diasporic Hebrew in Berlin actively seeks to create a nonnationalized, deterritorialized Hebrew that might serve as a utopian political model as well as a form of protest against the imbrication of Hebrew with a Zionism that has, especially since 1967, become associated with Israeli hegemony and oppression.

Conclusion

Pandemic as Metaphor

In July 2020, in the midst of the ongoing coronavirus pandemic, the *New York Times Magazine* published a series of short stories by writers from around the world under the title "The Decameron Project." The idea behind the issue was to create a twenty-first-century Decameron, a contemporary adaptation of the fourteenth-century collection of novellas written in the midst of an outbreak of bubonic plague by the Florentine writer Giovanni Bocaccio. In the original, ten Florentines flee an outbreak of the Black Death in the city and quarantine themselves in a country villa, where they tell each other stories to pass the time and distract themselves from the catastrophe unfolding around them. Although many of the stories take place elsewhere, the frame is in many ways intensely local, the group cut off from news of the plague in Florence, their world shrunk to the walls of the villa. The stories themselves were told in the local Florentine dialect, limiting their circulation to the immediate region around the village where the characters are staying.

By contrast, the stories of the *Times*'s contemporary Decameron reflect a world changed by commerce, travel, and technology. These are stories of a community that exists only in the ether, on the internet, of writers who may never have met. Even the plague is not local: the forces of modernity have caused it to circulate around the globe. The project included one Israeli writer, Etgar Keret, a minor celebrity in Israel who is well known for his postmodern short-short fiction. Keret himself has long been popular outside of Israel as well: his work has been widely translated, and in 2006 one of his novellas was made into the full-length American feature film *Wristcutters: A Love Story*. His work has also appeared regularly on the podcast *This American Life*, confirming the degree to which national affiliation in an age of globalization and world culture is fungible. His recent memoir, *The Seven Good Years*, about the period between the birth of his son and the death of his father, was published in English before it was published in Hebrew, by Keret's choice. Keret is not American, nor does his work depict a typically American space; rather, it inhabits a kind of every space, enabling him to be both a representative of modern Hebrew literature, of Israeli culture, and a writer absorbed, at the same time, into various forms of American and global popular culture.

Keret's story in "The Decameron Project," titled "Outside," describes a post-pandemic future in which traumatized citizens have to be driven out of their self-isolation by the military and police.[1] A few months after its publication, Keret and his collaborator Inbal Pinto, a choreographer and director, released a short film based on the story, embedded in an interactive website.[2] The story itself has no conspicuous cultural markers and could be set in any contemporary city. The film adaptation exploits that ambiguity, placing the action squarely inside an unnamed woman's apartment (the story uses the second person—"you"—to convey a kind of universal protagonist).[3] Most interestingly, this film, though it is based on a story written originally in Hebrew, makes no use of Hebrew at all. It even places the narration in the voice of a Japanese television announcer, interrupted by only one word of English from the protagonist.[4]

The absence of Hebrew, the generic urban setting, the lack of distinct Israeli cultural markers, and the emphasis on the obviously foreign all recall many of the elements of the globalized, translingual, transnational, and transcultural literature and art explored in this book and might not be possible without it. Like the work discussed in this volume, Keret and Pinto's film turns away from the specificity of Hebrew and its hypernationalist associations with Zionism in order to consciously explore globalization and the role of language in national culture. Perhaps it's no accident that this appeal to the global comes at a moment when a new plague has demonstrated clearly the inextricable interconnectedness of the world. What greater evidence of globalization and its consequences can there be than a pathogen that skips between bodies as they traverse the world, irrespective of nation? Just as the novel coronavirus has exposed fault lines within and between nations, it has laid bare some of the dangers of cultural parochialism.

Political Zionism and the exclusively Hebrew culture it adopted and encouraged in Palestine were, in the early twentieth-century Yishuv, fiercely focused on the territory of the land of Israel and the Jewish people's exclusive claim to that territory, as well as the connection of all Jews around the world to that land and that culture. The negation of the diaspora built into Israeli culture overwrote the transnational history of Hebrew and the multilingual Jewish cultures of the world. Israeli culture has long insisted on borders for Hebrew culture that are more or less contiguous with Israeli national borders, which, in reality, have themselves been contested and shifting since the establishment of the state. But the developments of the twenty-first century—the internet, widespread travel, the reopening of European citizenship to the descendants of the expelled, and the circulation of television and film, as well as climate change and pandemic disease—have made clear that geographic and political borders are limited in their ability to protect any culture and even any body from whatever has been deemed "outside." The events of the last years, if not the last decade, have exposed the way that all of our territories are connected as they are devastated by climate change and development, as well as the way that our bodies are linked by our ability to pass pathogens one to the other, over oceans and across nation-states.

This book sought to show the consequences of narrow, binary understandings of diaspora as a space positioned in opposition to homeland, separate and distinct, and these consequences have been revealed to be monumental and sometimes deadly. Likewise, this book sought to show the consequences for a world Jewry, half of whose population lives, generally happily and by choice, in the diaspora, of privileging or valorizing either Israel or the diaspora as the authentic or politically utopian site of Jewish life and culture. The consequences of identifying Israel as the only authentic homeland for the Jewish people have had, in recent years, dangerous political effects. American public discourse in the last decade, influenced by the growing political power of evangelical Christians and their encouragement during the Trump administration, has increasingly featured antisemitic tropes of dual loyalty, the suggestion that, because Israel is the true homeland of the Jews, they are not fully loyal citizens of the United States. It is an antisemitism enabled at least partially by the representation of the state of Israel as the only true Jewish home.

However, increasingly complex interventions into the discourse of diaspora and homeland continue to appear, in both high and pop cultural forms. Shortly after Keret's story appeared in the *New York Times Magazine*, the winter 2021 issue of *World Literature Today* published a special section devoted to Hebrew literature in translation, the second such section in the last five years. What distinguished this special issue was the inclusion of material written by authors who live outside of Israel, writing in Hebrew about diaspora life. The editors, Yiftach Ashkenazy and Dekel Shay Amory, wrote in their introduction that they hoped the work they chose "allows for a different and complex outlook on Israeli society and the literature written from within it today." In particular, they note, "the voices arising from Hebrew literature in this issue present, in fact, movement and even restlessness; one story takes place by the Gaza border, others in the suburbs of New York, Jerusalem, and Tel Aviv, but also Georgia (the country) and Canada. Immigration looms strongly, to and from Israel, like a wandering Jew stepping side by side with literature and language."[5] Their expansion of the definition of Hebrew literature to include writers living outside of Israel or moving between Israel and the diaspora is reflective, in their understanding, of both the nature of the contemporary world as a globalized space and the history of Jewish transnationalism, moving between nation-states and languages, at home in many places.

One of the included poets, Maya Tevet Dayan, writes specifically about this connection to both past and present in her poem "Land," about the experience of receiving Canadian citizenship. She writes, "A land without a story / would always remain in exile," explicitly tying literature to the process of establishing a home. At the same time this formulation muddles the association between land, home, and literature or language. Does storytelling ground the land as home? Or is it an impossibility for a land to have a story and thus "return" from exile? After receiving Canadian citizenship, she writes that now "we" could "tell stories about this land / for the rest of our lives, tell of ourselves, / forget our previous chapters— / the wars, the anxiety, this whole business / of the persecuted Jew."[6] Here the settlement suggested by the land of the title is placed in opposition to the historical persecution that attended landlessness. At the same time, moving beyond this persecution requires storytelling, stories that, the poem itself suggests, may be fiction or may overwrite other stories, stories that may also be true. The tie to the land is not a physical or immutable one but one that may change with the plots of history and migration. Rather than privileging one story or the other, one land or the other, the poem reminds us that many narratives and histories, even conflicting ones, can exist simultaneously.

The shifting nature of Jewish history as a rebuke to the dichotomy of homeland and exile is also evident in the work of Alma Igra in the same issue, in an essay that she auto-translated into English, reflecting her comfort in both languages. Igra, a food historian, tells the story of her family through food, particularly chicken and chicken soup. She traces the migration of her family from Bessarabia, which her grandparents left to immigrate to Palestine, through Israel, and now to New York, where she lives and where her son was born. She notes the way that the pandemic has brought her back to the food practices of her grandparents: "I, who have never eaten anything I grew by myself, never lost a child on the road; I—who left my homeland on a plane and did not pack my things into a carriage, who never owned a silver spoon with the symbols of the twelve tribes of Israel—planted garlic in long beds."[7] The sense of circularity both in her food journey and in her journey around the world to establish a new home, a home signified and made concrete through the cultivation of food, is what distinguishes her family's Jewish experience. While *aliyah* was historically presented as the final immigration, Igra's own experience—having emigrated *from* Israel, her at-home-ness in New York, her distinctly American child, "who was born in the US and understands local cuisine like I never will"—is merely another chapter in the kind of story of the land that Tevet Dayan describes.

But this is not the only direction in which this migration goes. Ayelet Tsabari describes the way that even a return to "home" can also be a kind of exile. In 2019, after twenty years of living in Canada, Tsabari and her family moved to Israel. Her move from Israel to Canada, rather than seeming like a move away from home, rather felt like an opportunity to redefine the poles of home and exile and their relationship to each other. She writes of her emigration, "That loss of roots, language and cultural identity that is so often regarded as the cost of immigration felt liberating, an opportunity to reinvent myself." At the same time, after having established herself in Canada and as an English-language writer, the return to Israel is not only a homecoming but also another kind of exile. She writes, "Coming home after 20 years is not so much a return but an act of reverse migration. The country I returned to is not the same."[8] Rather, Tsabari sees both places as home(s) and also feels displacement from each. Her ability to both circle the globe and move between languages renders older understandings of homeland and exile obsolete.

Israeli popular culture, especially during the pandemic, has also evidenced this increasingly complex understanding of the position of Israel, Israeli culture, and Hebrew with regard to the rest of the world and the Jewish diaspora. In October 2020, the Israeli pop music phenomenon Static and Ben El released a song and video in collaboration with will.i.am of the Black Eyed Peas called "Shake Ya Boom Boom."[9] The video opens with Static video-calling Ben El and will.i.am, with all the action taking place on what looks like a typical smartphone screen. When will.i.am answers, he greets the two Israelis by saying, "What's up, *mishpukhe*?" This very Ashkenazi pronunciation of a Hebrew-derived Yiddish word by a Black American musician speaking to two Mizrahi Israeli singers indicates from the start that the song and the video are intended to blur the boundaries of identity and nation through the use of a common language of technology.

The video and the words of the song both confirm its transnational and translingual message. The entire video is shot as a series of clips that appear as various social media apps are opened on a phone screen, clips that include individual performers in various private settings as well as the singers themselves dancing along to the music. It specifically focuses on apps like TikTok, Instagram, and YouTube, tools of global internet communication and cultural exchange. The song makes similar reference to language as a tool of global communication. The refrain of the song goes, "Don't need words when you move like that / Shake ya boom boom boom boom like that / We communicate no conversation / Cuz your body talk no translation / No translation." The idea of communication through the body, superseding language, reflects the transnational universalism of the song, which adopts the basic unit of the human—the body—as its medium. Indeed, the videos of people dancing from all over the world reinforce this idea. The lyrics go on, "First sight I knew you a *mishpukhe* / Family, let's start a *familia* / I dunno your language but your body feels familiar / We can break the language barrier / . . . Ooh girl where you from? I'm curious / Baby baby, I don't speak Portuguese / I don't speak Français or know Chinese." The song goes on to incorporate more foreign words, especially in Spanish, while at the same time focusing on the inadequacy of languages, which are determined by geography and nationality, to communicate in a world in which those borders are routinely rendered obsolete through technology.

Many of Static and Ben El's songs reflect this understanding of the world as a global village and the body as a medium of communication across languages. They often collaborate with other well-known artists from around the world in various musical genres, like Pitbull and J Balvin, incorporating their partners' languages and musical genres into their songs. They also collaborate with Arab-Israeli artists like Nasreen Qadri, who sings with them in their tribute to gay pride, "Habib albi" (Love of My Heart), which was released a few months before "Shake Ya Boom Boom." The song, in English, Hebrew, and Arabic, again mixes languages with the message that love is universal and transcends national and linguistic barriers. In this case, they engage less with the diaspora and more with the implications of their transnational and transcultural ideals for Israeli society itself. In 2018, the Knesset passed a new Basic Law, one of the set of standards that are the basis for Israeli governance in the absence of a constitution. This new Basic Law, titled "Israel as the Nation-State of the Jewish People," defined the Israeli state as the nation-state of the Jewish people in particular, specifically excluding its Arab citizens, and redefined Arabic as a language with "special status" rather than as an official language of the state alongside Hebrew. Static and Ben El's music seems to deliberately redefine the relationship between nation and language set out in the new Basic Law, challenging some of its premises by envisioning transnational and translinguistic artistic communities within the state itself.

While this transnational understanding of Israel's place in the Jewish and broader world is not necessarily mainstream, even the public Israeli broadcasting network has expressed renewed interest in Israel's relationship to the diaspora and what that relationship might mean for Israelis. In early 2021, Kan, the Israeli public broadcasting network, released a show called *Hayehudi Hachadash* (The New Jew), hosted by actor and comedian Gur Alfi. The title of the show is a play on the Zionist ideal of the creation of a new kind of Jew for a new Jewish nation, one who would redeem the denigration of the persecuted Jew of the diaspora. In this case, the "new Jew" of the title refers, on the one hand, to the broad variety of American Jews Alfi meets and talks to on the show; on the other hand, it could refer to Alfi himself, and by extension all of the show's Israeli viewers, made new through this encounter with and understanding of the richness of Jewish life in the diaspora. In the course of the show, Alfi himself has a kind of personal revelation of the value of his encounter with the diaspora when he joins a woman known as the "adventure rabbi" for a bar mitzvah ceremony on a mountaintop outside of Boulder, Colorado, and reads his bar mitzvah portion from a Torah held by other members of the group. He says to her, speaking in English, "It was an immediate bond . . . and this is something that is happening to me in the course of this, I don't know, journey [here he uses the Hebrew word *masa*] that I'm going through. I'm going back to what Judaism is for me. Because I'm always talking as an Israeli and talking to Jewish Americans that is weird to me. All of it. And the thing is that it's doing something to me. It's turning me, like, inside out."[10]

This personal undoing also leads Alfi and some of his interlocutors to a less binary vision of diaspora and Israel, particularly around the question of homeland, like so many of the writers and artists discussed in this volume. Alfi's guide through the course of the show is Moshe Samuels, an Israeli *shaliach*, or representative of the Jewish Agency, who has been living in New York for twenty years educating Americans about Israel. When he takes Alfi to a farm in Maryland that is run as a Jewish agricultural and educational project, Samuels says to Alfi, "We, many times, as Israelis, think that our native land is Israel, and that the place that every Jew is connected to through his Judaism is Israel, but Jews who have been here already three, four, five generations, this is their home, and their connection to the land is to this land."[11] However, even in Samuels's seemingly nuanced understanding of Jewish homeland, the kernel of Israeli superiority is preserved through his description of Israel as "adama yelidit," or native land, an expression of the Zionist notion of Jews as indigenous to the land of Israel. By contrast, American Jews' connection to the land might go back a few generations but no more. Nonetheless, the acknowledgment of America as a homeland for Jews works against the notion of Israel as a unitary center.

Alfi's voiceover conclusion to the show sums up this idea, as well as its privileging of Jewish sovereignty over Jewish autonomism, and its preservation of the binary between Israel and diaspora. Over images of the people and places he has visited throughout the show, Alfi says, "In Israel they created a new Jew of one type, with a national, secular identity, with a sovereign nation, a deeply rooted language, and their own army. In America they create a new Jew of a different type, with a liberal religious identity and universal values, that tries with all its power to assimilate into the local culture and to fulfill the American dream."[12] At the same time, he notes that many American Jews, and here through the images the show particularly seems to refer to the American Jews of color Alfi interviewed, have a hard time identifying with Israel and seeing it as their "other home." While Alfi and his Israeli collaborators are able to see the diaspora as a home for Jews, a place for the people and especially for religious manifestations of Judaism, they nonetheless construct that space as entirely separate from and somewhat inferior to the nation-state, which insists on this distinction. But the mere existence of the show and Alfi's grudging admission at the end that "despite the fact that it was always clear to me that Jews had only one home in Israel, I have to admit that that assumption has weakened somewhat," nonetheless reflect a new willingness or even desire to contend with the reality of transnational Jewish culture and what it means for Israeli nationalism and identity in the twenty-first century.

In engaging with contemporary Israeli culture that reenvisions the diaspora within the context of Israeli society and culture, this book has sought to contend with the shifting meaning of diaspora in a world in which a sovereign Israel, one that increasingly insists on itself as *the* Jewish homeland, has positioned itself as the center of the Jewish world. The work in this volume grapples, in various ways, with the consequences of that positioning and envisions what it might mean to conceive of a world Jewish culture that is transnational, that preserves the communal goals of the Jewish state but exists beyond its borders. While many accounts of transnational Jewish culture and diaspora itself position these notions as ideals separate from the existence of Israel, diaspora Israeli literature and art insists on a nuanced understanding of transnationalism that refuses to valorize diaspora while also accounting for the problems of sovereignty, not just for Israel but for the Jewish world.

Israeli writers and artists now look to the history of Hebrew and transnational Jewish culture for inspiration and clues to better understanding and representing the place of Israel and Hebrew in Jewish life. When Etgar Keret won the Sapir Prize in 2020, which comes with a monetary award as well as the funds to translate the book into another language, he made the unusual choice to have his prize-winning book translated into Yiddish. When asked about his reasoning, Keret replied, "The diaspora Jewishness we Israelis have lost—the old Jewish way of reconciling our religion and our peoplehood with our absurd condition in the world—this is what I hope to reintroduce through my writing."[13] Yiddish, he felt, was the best vehicle for recapturing the spirit of diasporic culture consciously elided in Israel by the "negation of the diaspora."

That rejection of diaspora Jewish life and history by Zionism was born out of the tragedies and exclusions suffered by European Jews in the premodern world. Convinced they would never be accepted into European life or culture, early Zionists wanted to turn their backs on everything associated with it. But that model of separation is no longer desirable, or even possible, in the twenty-first century. Developments of the last several decades, including increased migration, ease of travel, and the rise of the internet, have allowed for and encouraged this reevaluation of the relationships between Israel and diaspora and even call into question the existence of a center around which the periphery is formed. Recent events, including the pandemic, have exposed the ways that travel and technology connect us but also how the uneven distribution of power means that these connections are not always equalizing. It is now even more clear how important it is to turn to imaginative spaces, to literature and art and film, in order to, in essence, think our way out of the restrictive boundaries we have created, whether those are national borders or the walls of our homes.

The artistic endeavors considered in this volume are all, in various ways, engaged in imagining new understandings and definitions of homeland for the contemporary, globalized world. Through recourse to fantasy and speculation about the homelands that might have been, the deliberate representation of and grounding of Hebrew in the American context, translingual experimentation, and a reclamation of the historical sites of Jewish diaspora life through artistic and cultural movements in Europe, the writers and artists surveyed here make varied appeals for a more complicated and nuanced understanding of homeland and diaspora that accounts for both a diasporic Jewish history and the sovereign Israeli present.

Notes

INTRODUCTION

1 Dominique Schnapper and Denise L. Davis, "From the Nation-State to the Transnational World: On the Meaning and Usefulness of Diaspora as a Concept," *Diaspora: A Journal of Transnational Studies* 8, no. 3 (1999): 238.

2 Ps. 137:1. From Robert Alter, *The Book of Psalms: A Translation with Commentary* (New York: Norton, 2007), 473.

3 *Hayehudim Baim*, "Al Neharot Bavel," season 2, episode 9. The show is known also for the political opposition to its irreverent and critical takes on these topics. In August 2020, hundreds demonstrated outside the television studio that creates the series, the public broadcasting station Kan. Organized by religious leaders and politicians, the demonstrators decried the show's satirical portrayals of religious figures and stories, calling them blasphemous. Transportation Minister Betzalel Smotrich went so far as to call for the public broadcasting authority to be defunded.

4 Because it's a comedy show, these actors speak modern Israeli Hebrew with a typical Iraqi accent—a joke but also a reminder that modern Iraqi Jews trace their ancestry back to the Babylonian Exile.

5 One could even say this is a central fact of proto-Jewish existence, since rabbinic Judaism would not come into being until many centuries later.

6 *OED Online*, s.v. "diaspora," accessed July 11, 2017, http://www.oed.com .ezproxy.rice.edu/view/Entry/52085?redirectedFrom=diaspora&.

7 Shimon Dubnov, "Diaspora," *Encyclopedia of the Social Sciences*, vol. 5, ed. Edwin R. A. Seligman (New York: Macmillan, 1951), 127.

8 Erich S. Gruen, "Diaspora and Homeland," in *Diasporas and Exiles: Varieties of Jewish Identity*, ed. Howard Wettstein (Berkeley: University of California Press, 2002), 20.

9 Sidra DeKoven Ezrahi, "Our Homeland, the Text . . . Our Text the Homeland: Exile and Homecoming in the Modern Jewish Imagination," *Michigan Quarterly Review* 3, no. 4 (1992): 468.

10 Stéphane Dufoix, *Diasporas* (Berkeley: University of California Press, 2008), 24.

11 Khachig Tölölyan, "The Nation-State and Its Others: In Lieu of a Preface," *Diaspora: A Journal of Transnational Studies* 1, no. 1 (1991): 6.

12 Daniel Boyarin, *Border Lines* (Philadelphia: University of Pennsylvania Press, 2004), 15.

13 James Clifford, *Routes: Travel and Translation in the Late Twentieth Century* (Cambridge, MA: Harvard University Press, 1997), 245.

14 Clifford, *Routes*, 251.

15 This phrase can be found in Schnapper and Davis, "From the Nation-State," 235.

16 Marianne Hirsch and Nancy K. Miller, "Introduction," in *Rites of Return: Diaspora Poetics and the Politics of Memory*, ed. Marianne Hirsch and Nancy K. Miller (New York: Columbia University Press, 2011), 3.

17 Nico Israel, *Outlandish: Writing between Exile and Diaspora* (Stanford: Stanford University Press, 2000), 11.

18 Schnapper and Davis, "From the Nation-State," 249.

19 Hirsch and Miller, "Introduction," 2.

20 For a thorough discussion of the use of the Jew as trope in modern European thought, see Sarah Hammerschlag, *The Figural Jew: Politics and Identity in Postwar French Thought* (Chicago: University of Chicago Press, 2010). For more on the problematics of the Jew as trope in European philosophy, and its appearance in the work of Yael Bartana, see chapter 4.

21 Daniel Boyarin and Jonathan Boyarin, "Diaspora: Generation and the Ground of Jewish Identity," *Critical Inquiry* 19 (Summer 1993): 711.

22 Daniel Boyarin, *Unheroic Conduct* (Berkeley: University of California Press, 1997), 2.

23 Tania Modleski, *Feminism Without Women* (New York: Routledge, 1991), 7.

24 Jonathan Boyarin and Daniel Boyarin, *Powers of Diaspora: Two Essays on the Relevance of Jewish Culture* (Minneapolis: University of Minnesota Press, 2002), 86.

25 Boyarin, *Unheroic Conduct*, 11.

26 Boyarin and Boyarin, *Powers of Diaspora*, 69.

27 Sefaria, Sanhedrin 14a:10, https://www.sefaria.org/Sanhedrin.14a?lang= bi. Translation from the William Davidson English edition of the Koren Noé Talmud. Emphasis added.

28 Boyarin and Boyarin, *Powers of Diaspora*, 56–57.

29 Boyarin and Boyarin, *Powers of Diaspora*, 70.

30 Omri Asscher, *Reading Israel, Reading America: The Politics of Translation Between Jews* (Stanford: Stanford University Press, 2020), 27.

31 Asscher, *Reading Israel, Reading America*, 190.

32 Gil Hochberg, *In Spite of Partition: Jews, Arabs, and the Limits of Separatist Imagination* (Princeton: Princeton University Press, 2007), 3.

33 Shaul Setter, "The Time That Returns: Speculative Temporality in S. Yizhar's 1948," *Jewish Social Studies: History, Culture, Society* 18, no. 3 (2012): 51.

34 Oz Almog, *The Sabra: The Creation of the New Jew*, trans. Haim Watzman (Berkeley: University of California Press, 2000), 91.

35 Uri Ram, *The Globalization of Israel: McWorld in Tel Aviv, Jihad in Jerusalem* (New York: Routledge, 2008), 212.

36 Amnon Raz-Krakotzkin, "Critique of 'The Negation of Exile' in Israeli Culture," in *The Scaffolding of Sovereignty: Global and Aesthetic Perspectives on the History of a Concept*, ed. Zvi Ben-Dor Benite, Stefanos Geroulanos, and Nicole Jerr (New York: Columbia University Press, 2017), 393.

37 Raz-Krakotzkin, "Critique," 415.

38 Eran Kaplan, *Beyond Post-Zionism* (Albany: SUNY Press, 2015), 48.

39 Amnon Raz-Krakotzkin, "Exile, History, and the Nationalization of Jewish Memory: Some Reflections on the Zionist Notion of History and Return," *Journal of Levantine Studies* 3, no. 2 (2013): 57.

40 Assaf Likhovski, "Post-Post-Zionist Historiography," *Israel Studies* 15, no. 2 (2010): 9.

41 Kaplan, *Beyond Post-Zionism*, 52.

42 Raz-Krakotzkin, "Critique," 395–96. At the conclusion of this article, Raz-Krakotzkin gives a sense of how this new ethics and politics might come into being through a revision of the Zionist understanding of exile, by accomplishing a conceptual deterritorialization in which the land as concept is detached from the land as a place, thereby creating "a space for the memory of the defeated" (416–18).

CHAPTER 1

1 Sidra DeKoven Ezrahi, "Our Homeland, the Text . . . Our Text the Homeland: Exile and Homecoming in the Modern Jewish Imagination," *Michigan Quarterly Review* 31, no. 4 (1992): 478.

2 Israel Zangwill, "Zionism and Charitable Institutions" (1903), in *Speeches, Articles and Letters of Israel Zangwill* (London: Soncino Press,

1937), 180. Quoted in Adam Rovner, *In the Shadow of Zion: Promised Lands Before Israel* (New York: New York University Press, 2014), 56.

3 Rovner, *In the Shadow of Zion*, xv.

4 Rovner, *In the Shadow of Zion*, 7.

5 Gavriel Rosenfeld, *The World Hitler Never Made: Alternate History and the Memory of Nazism* (Cambridge: Cambridge University Press, 2005), 6–8.

6 Rosenfeld, *The World Hitler Never Made*, 10.

7 Rosenfeld, *The World Hitler Never Made*, 3.

8 Shaul Setter, "The Time That Returns: Speculative Temporality in S. Yizhar's 1948," *Jewish Social Studies: History, Culture, Society* 18, no. 3 (2012): 45.

9 A couple of American novels that treat the subject of alternative homelands have also appeared in this period: Michael Chabon's 2007 *The Yiddish Policemen's Union* and Simone Zelitch's 2016 *Judenstaat*. Chabon's well-known novel imagines a Yiddish-speaking Jewish autonomous region in Sitka, Alaska; Zelitch's novel proposes a German-speaking postwar Jewish state in Saxony. As in the novels discussed in this chapter, in each of these, the state of Israel was not established in historical Palestine and a Jewish homeland was, instead, established in the diaspora.

10 Adam Rovner, "Alternate History: The Case of Nava Semel's *IsraIsland* and Michael Chabon's *The Yiddish Policemen's Union*," *Partial Answers: Journal of Literature and the History of Ideas* 9, no. 1 (2011): 140.

11 Eric Zakim, *To Build and Be Built: Landscape, Literature, and the Construction of Zionist Identity* (Philadelphia: University of Pennsylvania Press, 2006), 3.

12 Ben-Yehuda, in his autobiography, lamented that, as a nonnative speaker of Hebrew, he had moments in which other languages surfaced in his consciousness despite his best efforts. He wrote, "Then suddenly I realize that for a moment I have not been thinking in Hebrew, that from beneath the thought in Hebrew a few alien words have floated to the surface, words of Yiddish, Russian, or French!" Ben-Yehuda clearly juxtaposed a "pure" Hebrew, which he sought to create and use, with other European languages, and yet Hebrew nonetheless has many etymological roots in those languages. Eliezer Ben-Yehuda, *A Dream Come True*, trans. T. Muraoka, ed. George Mandel (Boulder, CO: Westview Press, 1993), 17.

13 Nava Semel, *E-srael* (Tel Aviv: Yediot Aharonot, 2005), 61. English taken from *Isra Isle*, trans. Jessica Cohen (Simsbury, CT: Mandel Vilar Press,

2016), 54. For future citations in the text, page numbers from the Hebrew version will be marked with an H and those from the English version with an E.

14 There are also other connections unrelated to geography: names that have special significance, which occur in various combinations attached to different characters in each section; timeline, in that the events of the first and last sections are both set in September 2001 and involve the September 11 attacks in their plots; genetics and "blood," in that each section focuses on characters who have familial ties to Noah, to the land, or, it is implied, to characters from other sections.

15 This translation is taken from the *JPS Hebrew-English Tanakh*, 2nd ed. (Philadelphia: Jewish Publication Society, 2003).

16 This tradition is also implicit in these names: the biblical Noah found refuge from the flood on Mount Ararat; likewise, the historical Mordecai Manuel Noah called his "city of refuge" on Grand Island Ararat.

17 In the English version, the timeline is described as "September 2001—An Alternate Story," which accords with Shaul Setter's understanding of "sovereign time" as uniquely linked with the history of Hebrew literature. Setter, "The Time That Returns," 51–52.

18 This section can be found on page 202 of the English edition, up to the italicized portion. The italics are my translation of the extra text in the Hebrew edition, found on page 211. The full sentence in Hebrew reads, "ספרינג היל. אחוזת בית. ככל שאני חוזר בליבי על השמות שהיו עדד אמש ריקים ממשמעות, כך הם הופכים לצירריופים טוענים, מעין לחש-כישוף שנועד לכונן גלות, אך מצמית את המקום עד חנק."

19 For ease of reference in English, I refer to the Hebrew *Herzl Amar* as *Herzl Said*, an exact translation of the title (which differs from the publisher's English title, *What If*). For purposes of clarity, I will differentiate the "Israel" of *Herzl Said* with quotation marks to distinguish it from the present-day state of Israel; similarly, when referring to the inhabitants of *Unholy Land*'s Palestina as "Palestinians" I will do the same. That I even need to create such a system of differentiation points to the ways these novels play with the political and cultural realities that underlie their creation of alternative homelands.

20 "Proclamation of the State of Israel (May 14, 1948)," in *The Jew in the Modern World*, 2nd ed., ed. Paul Mendes-Flohr and Jehuda Reinharz (New York: Oxford University Press, 1995), 629.

21 Lavie Tidhar, *Unholy Land* (San Francisco: Tachyon, 2018), 9. Future citations in the text will be referred to as UL.

22 Yoav Avni, *Herzl Amar* (What If) (Or Yehuda: Kinneret, Zmora-Bitan, Dvir, 2011), 119. Future citations in the text will be referred to as HA.

23 Homi K. Bhabha, *The Location of Culture* (New York: Routledge, 1994), 1–2.

24 Marianne Hirsch and Nancy K. Miller, "Introduction," *Rites of Return: Diaspora Poetics and the Politics of Memory*, ed. Marianne Hirsch and Nancy K. Miller (New York: Columbia University Press, 2011), 5.

25 Michael Weingrad, *American Hebrew Literature: Writing Jewish National Identity in the United States* (Syracuse: Syracuse University Press, 2011), 74.

26 Weingrad, *American Hebrew Literature*, 75.

27 Rachel Rubinstein, *Members of the Tribe: Native America in the Jewish Imagination* (Detroit: Wayne State University Press, 2010), 7.

28 Weingrad, *American Hebrew Literature*, 79.

29 While Native Americans are absent from Isra Isle, it is notable that they were forced out not by the Jewish population per se but by state forces of the U.S. government. But there is an oblique reference to the fact that Native American tribes still make claims to Grand Island as their native land, claims that are dismissed by Isra Isle and the U.S. government.

30 Rovner, "Alternate History," 141.

31 In *Herzl Said*, "Mumbo-Jumbo" is a derogatory, racist epithet used to refer to the Masai.

32 Karen Hellekson, *The Alternate History: Refiguring Historical Time* (Kent, OH: The Kent State University Press, 2001), 4–5.

33 In a slightly different manner, Israeli prime minister Benjamin Netanyahu has also concocted an alternate history of the Holocaust, although in his version the Grand Mufti of Jerusalem suggested the idea of the Holocaust to Adolph Hitler. In a 2015 speech to the World Zionist Congress in Jerusalem, Netanyahu claimed, "Hitler didn't want to exterminate the Jews at the time, he wanted to expel the Jew. And Haj Amin al-Husseini went to Hitler and said, 'If you expel them, they'll all come here (to Palestine).'" Netanyahu went on to say that when Hitler asked the mufti what to do, he replied "Burn them." This alternative version of Hitler's meeting with the mufti, which is not supported by most mainstream scholars of the Holocaust, allows Netanyahu to place blame for the genocide of European Jews on the Arabs he casts as Israel's present-day enemies. "Netanyahu: Hitler Didn't Want to Eliminate the Jews," *Haaretz*, October 21, 2015, https://www.haaretz.com/israel-news/netanyahu-absolves-hitler-of-guilt-1.5411578.

34 Adam Rovner, *In the Shadow of Zion: Promised Lands Before Israel* (New York: New York University Press, 2014), 46. In *Unholy Land*, Palestina still regards itself as a *Nachtasyl*, albeit now a permanent one.

35 Neil Leach, "9/11," *Diacritics* 33, nos. 3/4 (2003): 84.

36 Richard Gray, *After the Fall: American Literature Since 9/11* (Oxford: Wiley-Blackwell, 2011), 66.

CHAPTER 2

1 Robert Alter, *The Invention of Hebrew: Modern Fiction and the Language of Realism* (Seattle: University of Washington Press, 1988), 48.

2 Alter, *The Invention of Hebrew*, 33.

3 Shachar Pinsker, *Literary Passports: The Making of Modernist Hebrew Fiction in Europe* (Stanford: Stanford University Press, 2011), 8.

4 Allison Schachter, *Diasporic Modernisms: Hebrew and Yiddish Literature in the Twentieth Century* (Oxford: Oxford University Press, 2012), 7, 11.

5 Yaron Peleg, "A New Hebrew Literary Diaspora? Israeli Literature Abroad," *Studia Judaica* 18, no. 2 (2015): 322–23.

6 Peleg, "A New Hebrew Literary Diaspora?," 324.

7 Asscher, *Reading Israel, Reading America: The Politics of Translation Between Jews* (Stanford: Stanford University Press, 2020), 26.

8 Beth Kissileff, "Israel Has an Amazing Literary Diaspora," *The Tower* 22 (Jan. 2015), http://www.thetower.org/article/israel-has-an-amazing -literary-diaspora/.

9 Reuven Namdar, *Habayit Asher Nekhrav* (Or Yehuda: Dvir, 2013), 15. Translation from Ruby Namdar, *The Ruined House*, trans. Hillel Halkin (New York: Harper, 2017), 7. For future citations in the text, page numbers from the Hebrew version will be marked with an H and those from the English version with an E.

10 Walt Whitman, "Mannahatta," Poets.org, accessed May 14, 2018, https:// www.poets.org/poetsorg/poem/mannahatta.

11 See Michael Weingrad, *American Hebrew Literature: Writing Jewish National Identity in the United States* (Syracuse: Syracuse University Press, 2011), especially 3–4, 7, 10.

12 Quoted in Weingrad, *American Hebrew Literature*, 25.

13 Other Jewish writers of the same period, like Charles Reznikoff, writing in English, also represented New York as a particularly Jewish space. Ranen Omer-Sherman claims that one effect of overlaying Jewishness onto New York City is to "form an identification with a

wide-ranging humanity composed of differences: immigrants, the poor, minorities—the powerless rather than the strong." However, these seemingly powerless, marginal New Yorkers are also "are psychologically and sometimes even culturally the victors in defeat." Reznikoff's navigation between the identification with the powerless and the impulse to claim that identification as a strength is another way of adopting diaspora as a space central to Jewish identity and life. Ranen Omer-Sherman, *Diaspora and Zionism in Jewish American Literature: Lazarus, Syrkin, Reznikoff, Roth* (Hanover, NH: Brandeis University Press, 2002), 165–66.

14 Maya Arad, *Hamorah Le'ivrit* (The Hebrew Teacher) (Tel Aviv: Xargol, 2018), 9. Future citations are given in the text.

15 Danielle Drori, "Reading Maya Arad in North America Today: *The Hebrew Teacher* in Context." *Hebrew Higher Education* 21 (2019): 12–13. Indeed, Arad's novella satirizes, in many ways, the intellectual trends and theories that make up the foundation of this very book.

16 The word I've translated here as both "house" and "home" is *bayit*, the same one in the title of Namdar's book, which can flexibly specify both an individual home and a spiritual one.

17 This translation is taken from *Genesis Rabbah: The Judaic Commentary to the Book of Genesis: A New American Translation*, vol. 3, trans. Jacob Neusner (Atlanta: Scholars Press, 1985).

18 Arianna Dagnino, *Transcultural Writers and Novels in the Age of Global Mobility* (West Lafayette, IN: Purdue University Press, 2015), 7.

19 This is my own translation. I chose not to use Halkin's slightly more formal language here in order to maintain the rhythm of the original, which seems crucial to the sense of flow and movement conveyed in the passage. In addition, Halkin deemphasizes the use of the impersonal form here (סתמי) in favor of the personal pronoun "he," which has the effect of emphasizing Andrew as the subject rather than, as in the Hebrew, the action of taking the subway, and thus takes the focus away from movement. Halkin's translation reads, "How does one get to the Lower East Side? It was at the other end of the world. He would have to take the 1 or 9 train to 14th Street, follow the underground passage that led to the orange lines of the F, B, or D train, and continue to Lower Manhattan, making sure to get off at the right stop. A year ago, immersed in a book, he had missed it and found himself in Brooklyn" (35).

20 Adriana X. Jacobs, *Strange Cocktail: Translation and the Making of Modern Hebrew Poetry* (Ann Arbor: University of Michigan Press, 2018), 36. For an overview of the influence of foreign translation on the

development of Hebrew poetry specifically, see *Strange Cocktail*, chapter 1: "Voices Near and Far: Historical Perspectives on Hebrew Poetry and (Its) Translation," 25–46.

21 This is one of the overall conclusions of Asscher's *Reading Israel, Reading America*.

22 Alan Mintz, "Introduction," *Hebrew in America: Perspectives and Prospects*, ed. Alan Mintz (Detroit: Wayne State University Press, 1993), 15.

23 Personal communication from the author, May 14, 2016.

24 Adam Rovner, "Language Lessons: Maya Arad's 'The Hebrew Teacher.'" *Curated: Thinking with Literature*, August 17, 2020, https://arcade.stanford .edu/content/language-lessons-maya-arad%E2%80%99s-hebrew-teacher -0#_edn.

25 Benjamin Harshav, *The Meaning of Yiddish* (Stanford: Stanford University Press, 1990), 21.

26 According to Namdar, this section was not translated into English simply because of the extreme difficulty of doing so. Personal communication from the author, June 15, 2018. The decision to leave certain elements of the original Hebrew text out of the English translation, even more than the difficulty of the original texts, speaks to some of the cultural translation issues connected with language and the historical layers of Hebrew, which will be discussed in more detail later in the chapter.

27 Personal communication from the author, June 15, 2018.

28 See Asscher, *Reading Israel, Reading America*, 66–79, 87–93, 103–12.

29 Avrum Sutzkever, "Der aleynflier" (The Loner), *Di goldene keyt* (The Golden Chain) 91 (1976): 5.

30 Meir Wieseltier, "Chatakh orekh beshirato shel natan zach" (A Cross-Section of Natan Zach's Poetry), *Siman kriah* 10 (1980): 405.

31 Chana Kronfeld, *On the Margins of Modernism: Decentering Literary Dynamics* (Berkeley: University of California Press, 1996), 64.

32 Yael Feldman, *Modernism and Cultural Transfer: Gabriel Preil and the Tradition of Jewish Literary Bilingualism* (Cincinnati: Hebrew Union College Press, 1986), 33.

33 Linda Hutcheon, "Postmodern Paratextuality and History," *Texte: Revue de critique et de théorie littéraire* 4 (1986): 303.

34 Drori, "Reading Maya Arad," 4.

35 This history is detailed by Adriana X. Jacobs in "The Place of Hebrew: Maya Arad's Another Place, a Foreign City," in *Disseminating Jewish Literatures: Knowledge, Research, Curricula*, ed. Susanne Zepp, Ruth Fine,

Natasha Gordinsky, Kader Konuk, Claudia Olk, and Galili Shahar (Berlin: De Gruyter, 2020), 257.

36　Jacobs, "The Place of Hebrew," 263.

37　Drori, "Reading Maya Arad," 15.

38　Although Hammerstein was raised as an Episcopalian, his father was Jewish, and his biography, even or especially his parents' intermarriage, reflects some of the typical patterns of twentieth-century American Jewish life.

39　Hana Wirth-Nesher, *Call It English: The Languages of Jewish-American Literature* (Princeton: Princeton University Press, 2006), 57.

40　Benjamin Harshav, *The Polyphony of Jewish Culture* (Stanford: Stanford University Press, 2007), 27.

41　This quote is taken from Brenner's famous essay about Hebrew literature, "Hadzhaner ha'eretz yisraeli va'avizrayhu" (The Land of Israel Genre and Its Accouterments). The full text can be found on Project Ben-Yehuda, https://benyehuda.org/read/854.

42　Wirth-Nesher, *Call It English*, 14.

43　Jacques Derrida, "*Des Tours de Babel*," trans. Joseph F. Graham, *Semeia* 54 (1991): 22.

44　Drori, "Reading Maya Arad," 16–17.

45　Dagnino, *Transcultural Writers and Novels*, 2.

46　Harshav, *The Polyphony of Jewish Culture*, 22.

47　Harshav, *The Polyphony of Jewish Culture*, 22.

48　Haim Weiss, "Israel Doesn't Have a Monopoly on Great Hebrew Literature," *Forward*, June 8, 2015, http://forward.com/opinion/309641/great-hebrew-literature-doesnt-come-only-from-israel/#ixzz3r7Jl1GdZ.

49　Irin Katz, "Interview with the Writer Maya Arad," *Koreh Basfarim: Magazin le-sifrut*, November 24, 2015, (Hebrew), https://www.korebasfarim .com/2015/11/24/ראיון-עם-הסופרת-מאיה-ערד/.

CHAPTER 3

1　Shachar Pinsker, *Literary Passports: The Making of Modernist Hebrew Fiction in Europe* (Stanford: Stanford University Press, 2011), 8.

2　Yael Chaver, *What Must Be Forgotten: The Survival of Yiddish in Zionist Palestine* (Syracuse: Syracuse University Press, 2004), 16. Chaver traces some of the ways in which Israeli literary historiography accomplished this task by appropriating Yiddish writers into the Hebrew canon or eliding the literary works of certain iconic Hebrew writers that were written in other languages. Chaver, *What Must Be Forgotten*, 45–53.

3 Chaver, *What Must Be Forgotten*, 6. Emphasis added.

4 The organization is very active and maintains a website to document members' publications, publish their own newsletter, and publicize their calendar of events, https://www.iawe.org.il.

5 Steven G. Kellman, *The Translingual Imagination* (Lincoln: University of Nebraska Press, 2000), 24.

6 Irene Gilsenan Nordin, Julie Hansen, and Carmen Zamorano Llena, *Transcultural Identities in Contemporary Literature* (Amsterdam: Editions Rodopi, 2013), x.

7 Motti Regev, "To Have a Culture of Our Own: On Israeliness and Its Variants," *Ethnic and Racial Studies* 23 (2000): 227.

8 Liora Halperin, *Babel in Zion: Jews, Nationalism, and Language Diversity in Palestine, 1920–1948* (New Haven: Yale University Press, 2015), 24.

9 Rela Mazali, *Maps of Women's Goings and Stayings* (Stanford: Stanford University Press, 2001), 10. Future citations are given in the text.

10 M. M. Bakhtin, *The Dialogic Imagination: Four Essays*, ed. Michael Holquist, trans. Caryl Emerson and Michael Holquist (Austin: University of Texas Press, 1981), 61.

11 Jacques Derrida, *Monolingualism of the Other or the Prosthesis of Origin*, trans. Patrick Mensah (Stanford, CA: Stanford University Press, 1998), 25.

12 Derrida, *Monolingualism of the Other*, 64.

13 Yasemin Yildiz, *Beyond the Mother Tongue: The Postmonolingual Condition* (New York: Fordham University Press, 2012), 5.

14 Yildiz, *Beyond the Mother Tongue*, 204.

15 Paul Jay, *Global Matters: The Transnational Turn in Literary Studies* (Ithaca, NY: Cornell University Press, 2010), 43.

16 Shani Boianjiu, *The People of Forever Are Not Afraid* (New York: Hogarth, 2012), 17, 16. Emphasis added. Future citations are given in the text.

17 Ayelet Tsabari, "Tikkun," in *The Best Place on Earth* (Toronto: Harper-Collins, 2013), 3, 5, 7. Future citations are given in the text.

18 Esther Fuchs, *Israeli Mythogynies: Women in Contemporary Hebrew Fiction* (Albany: State University of New York Press, 1987), 7.

19 Miri Kubovy, "Inniut and Kooliut: Trends in Israeli Narrative Literature, 1995–1999," *Israel Studies* 5, no. 1 (2000): 263.

20 Karen Grumberg, "Ricki Lake in Tel Aviv: The Alternative of Orly Castel-Bloom's Hebrew-English," in *Anglophone Jewish Literature*, ed. Axel Stähler (London: Routledge, 2007), 246.

21 Schachter, *Diasporic Modernisms*, 58.

22 See Eric Zakim, "Stalagim: At the Limits of Israeli Literature," in *Since 1948: Israeli Literature in the Making*, ed. Nancy Berg and Naomi Sokoloff (Albany: State University of New York Press, 2020), 183–203.

23 I am indebted to Ranen Omer-Sherman for pointing out that this quality has a precedent in the Hebrew fiction of Ronit Matalon and Orly Castel-Bloom.

24 Not coincidentally, Boianjiu's book also derives its title from a bumper sticker slogan, a religious message that is applied with some irony. This, too, comments on the constant relocations of a fluid contemporary global culture, carried around in pithy aphorisms on moving cars.

25 Robert Alter, *Defenses of the Imagination: Jewish Writers and Modern Historical Crisis* (Philadelphia: Jewish Publication Society, 1977), 257.

26 Eric Zakim, *To Build and Be Built: Landscape, Literature, and the Construction of Zionist Identity* (Philadelphia: University of Pennsylvania Press, 2006), 183.

27 Daniel Boyarin, *Unheroic Conduct: The Rise of Heterosexuality and the Invention of the Jewish Man* (Berkeley: University of California Press, 1997). See, in particular, 271–312.

28 Max Nordau, "Jewry of Muscle," in *The Jew in the Modern World: A Documentary History*, ed. Paul Mendes-Flohr and Jehuda Reinharz, 2nd ed. (Oxford: Oxford University Press, 1995), 547.

29 It is yet another mark of the globalization of culture that the Marlboro Man, the iconic cowboy of American cigarette advertisements, is here the model of the ideal Israeli soldier and New Hebrew Man.

30 Quoted in Susan Sered, *What Makes Women Sick? Maternity, Modesty, and Militarism in Israeli Society* (Hanover, NH: University Press of New England), 75.

31 Sered, *What Makes Women Sick?*, 80–81. A 2015 internet furor over photos of female IDF soldiers in sexually suggestive poses also goes to the heart of questions of the Israeli military's misogyny. The photographs, in which female soldiers pose partially clothed with their weapons and other symbols of military belonging, seem to parody and deconstruct the way in which the military itself constructs them as both sexual objects and victims.

32 See Rela Mazali, "'And What About the Girls?' What a Culture of War Genders Out of View," in *Nashim: A Journal of Jewish Women's Studies and Gender*, no. 6 (Fall 5764/2003): 39–50.

33 Sered, *What Makes Women Sick?*, 79.

34 Sered, *What Makes Women Sick?*, 7.

35 Fuchs, *Israeli Mythogynies*, 26.

36 Sered, *What Makes Women Sick?*, 69.

37 Fuchs, *Israeli Mythogynies*, 32–33.

CHAPTER 4

1 Thanks to Yael Bartana and Petzel Gallery for allowing me access to the video trilogy, as well as Richard Gersch for assisting with permissions and images.

2 Yael Bartana, Sebastian Cichocki, and Galit Eilat, "Jewish Renaissance Movement in Poland (JRMiP)," in *A Cookbook for Political Imagination*, ed. Galit Eilat and Sebastian Cichocki (Berlin: Sternberg Press, 2011), n.p.

3 "About," Jewish Renaissance Movement in Poland, accessed August 21, 2017, http://www.jrmip.org/?page_id=2.

4 "Biography," Yael Bartana, https://yaelbartana.com/biography.

5 The Bilu, "Manifesto (1882)," in *The Jew in the Modern World: A Documentary History*, ed. Jehuda Reinharz and Paul Mendes-Flohr (Oxford: Oxford University Press, 1995), 532.

6 Theodor Herzl, *The Jewish State*, trans. Sylvie d'Avigdor, ed. Jacob M. Alkow (New York: Dover, 1988), 76.

7 Herzl, *The Jewish State*, 146.

8 Max Nordau, "Zionism" (1902), in *The Zionist Ideas: Visions for the Jewish Homeland—Then, Now, Tomorrow*, ed. Gil Troy (Philadelphia: Jewish Publication Society, 2018), 20.

9 David Ben Gurion, *Rebirth and Destiny of Israel*, ed. and trans. Max Nurock (New York: Philosophical Library, 1954), 137.

10 Misrad Haklita, "Yom Hazikaron" (Memorial Day), YouTube video, https://youtu.be/FP3gJN_YScM.

11 Misrad Haklita, "Higia hazman lachzor leyisrael lifnei shechanukah yahafoch leChristmas" (The Time Has Come to Return to Israel before Hanukkah Becomes Christmas), YouTube video, https://youtu.be/JQmE -jUZU_Y.

12 *Mary Koszmary* (Nightmares), dir. Yael Bartana, 2007, one-channel video and sound installation, 11 mins.

13 "The Jewish Renaissance Movement in Poland: A Manifesto," in Eilat and Cichocki, *Cookbook*, 121.

14 "The Jewish Renaissance Movement in Poland: A Manifesto," 121.

15 Sara Ahmed, *The Cultural Politics of Emotion* (Edinburgh: Edinburgh University Press, 2004), 35.

16 Ahmed, *Cultural Politics*, 35.

17 Sarah Hammerschlag, *The Figural Jew: Politics and Identity in Postwar French Thought* (Chicago: University of Chicago Press, 2010), 30.

18 Hammerschlag, *Figural Jew*, 8.

19 Hammerschlag, *Figural Jew*, 5.

20 *Avodah* (Labor), dir. Helmar Lerski (1935; Waltham, MA: National Center for Jewish Film, 2008), DVD.

21 *Summer Camp/Awodah*, dir. Yael Bartana, 2007, two-channel video and sound installation, 12 mins., https://yaelbartana.com/work/summer-camp-awodah-2007.

22 Sharon Rotbard, "Wall and Tower," in *A Civilian Occupation: The Politics of Israeli Architecture*, ed. Rafi Siegel, David Tartakover, and Eyal Weizman (New York: Verso, 2003), 48.

23 Gish Amit, "When Suffering Becomes an Identity: On the Moments of Catastrophe and the Contours of Hope," in Eilat and Cichocki, *Cookbook*, 210.

24 Avi Pitchon, "Save Europe Now Ask Me How," in Eilat and Cichocki, *Cookbook*, 365.

25 George Steiner, "Our Homeland, the Text," *Salmagundi* 66 (Winter–Spring 1985): 21.

26 Michael Rothberg, *Multidirectional Memory: Remembering the Holocaust in the Age of Decolonization* (Stanford: Stanford University Press, 2009), 5.

27 James E. Young, *The Texture of Memory* (New Haven: Yale University Press, 1993), 174.

28 This historical narrative, along with the explicitly nationalist intentions of the sculptor, accounts at least partially for the decision, in 1975, to install a reproduction of the monument at Yad Vashem, the Israeli Holocaust museum.

29 In the historical and political context in which the film was made, it also evokes the separation barrier that had begun to be built by the state of Israel roughly (but not precisely) along the Green Line.

30 James E. Young, *At Memory's Edge: After-Images of the Holocaust in Contemporary Art and Architecture* (New Haven: Yale University Press, 2000), 95.

CHAPTER 5

1 Amir Eshel and Rachel Seelig, "Editors' Introduction," in *The German-Hebrew Dialogue: Studies of Encounter and Exchange*, ed. Amir Eshel and Rachel Seelig, vol. 6 of Perspectives on Jewish Texts and Contexts (Berlin: De Gruyter, 2018), 3.

2 Hadas Cohen and Dani Kranz, "Israeli Jews in the New Berlin: From Shoah Memories to Middle Eastern Encounters," in *Cultural Topographies of the New Berlin*, ed. Jennifer Ruth Hosek and Karin Bauer (Oxford: Berghahn, 2017), 325.

3 Larissa Remennick, "The Israeli Diaspora in Berlin: Back to Being Jewish?," *Israel Studies Review* 34, no. 1 (2019): 89.

4 The Occupation refers to the continuing Israeli military occupation of Palestinian lands conquered from Jordan in the 1967 Six-Day War. Remennick, "Israeli Diaspora in Berlin," 93–95.

5 Michael Brenner, *In Search of Israel: The History of an Idea* (Princeton: Princeton University Press, 2018), 237.

6 Gur Alroey, "The Jewish Emigration from Palestine in the Early Twentieth Century," *Journal of Modern Jewish Studies* 2, no. 2 (2003): 114.

7 Cohen and Kranz even suggest that emigrants have been historically considered "traitors to the Zionist project of the Jewish state." Cohen and Kranz, "Israeli Jews in the New Berlin," 322.

8 Cohen and Kranz, "Israeli Jews in the New Berlin," 327.

9 Remennick, "Israeli Diaspora in Berlin," 89.

10 Maya Rosen, "Reclaiming a Minor Literature," *Jewish Currents*, February 21, 2022, https://jewishcurrents.org/reclaiming-a-minor-literature.

11 Tal Hever-Chybowski, "Mikan ve'eylakh" (From This Point Onward), trans. Rachel Seelig, in *The German-Hebrew Dialogue: Studies of Encounter and Exchange*, ed. Amir Eshel and Rachel Seelig, vol. 6 of Perspectives on Jewish Texts and Contexts (Berlin: De Gruyter, 2018), 249.

12 See, most recently, Tal Hever-Chybowski, "Diasporic Hebrew in Berlin," *JMB Journal* 20 (June 5, 2019): 53–59. For more on the modern history of Berlin as a center of Hebrew culture, see Shachar M. Pinsker, "Between the Scheunenviertel and the Romanisches Café," in *Literary Passports: The Making of Modernist Hebrew Fiction in Europe* (Stanford: Stanford University Press, 2011), 105–46.

13 Hever-Chybowski, "Diasporic Hebrew in Berlin," 59.

14 Hila Amit, "The Revival of Diasporic Hebrew in Contemporary Berlin," in *Cultural Topographies of the New Berlin*, ed. Jennifer Ruth Hosek and Karin Bauer (Oxford: Berghahn, 2017), 254.

15 For more on this decision and its origins, see chapter 3.

16 Mati Shemoelof, "Creating a Radical Hebrew Culture—in the Diaspora," *+972 Magazine*, August 19, 2016.

17 The Ars Poetica movement in Israel, which showcases Mizrahi writers, also uses the *hafla* as its model for events, for similar reasons. And some of the Berlin expatriates, like Shemoelof, have been involved in this movement as well. This loose connection between the two groups indicates the extent to which the connection to Israel still exerts influence even on these deliberate expatriates and advocates of diasporic Hebrew.

18 Sami David Rauscher and Noa Amiel, "Performing Identity," *Politikorange*, December 3, 2018.

19 Remennick, "Israeli Diaspora in Berlin," 89.

20 "About," International Hebrew School, https://www.learnhebrewnow.com/about.

21 "Hebrew Teaching," Dr. Hila Amit, https://www.hilaamit.com.

22 "About Us," Anu: Jews and Arabs Writing in Berlin, https://arabjewsberlin.wordpress.com/about/.

23 Jacqueline Kahanoff, "Afterword: From East the Sun," in *Mongrels or Marvels: The Levantine Writings of Jacqueline Shohet Kahanoff*, ed. Deborah A. Starr and Sasson Somekh (Stanford: Stanford University Press, 2011), 244.

24 Mati Shemoelof, "Creating Our Own Alternative Arab-Jewish History in Berlin," *Plus 61J*, December 11, 2018.

25 Hever-Chybowski, "Diasporic Hebrew in Berlin," 59.

26 Yael Almog, "Illusory Diasporas," *Shofar: An Interdisciplinary Journal of Jewish Studies* 37, no. 2 (2019): 65.

27 Almog, "Illusory Diasporas," 64.

28 Mati Shemoelof, "[Me'ahev shel shtei yebashot]" (Lover of Two Continents), in *Ivrit mechutz le'ivreha hametukim* (Hebrew Outside Its Sweet Insides) (Haifa: Pardes, 2017), 7.

29 Shemoelof, "Eifo zeh chul?" (Where Is Abroad?), in *Ivrit mechutz le'ivreha hametukim*, 20.

30 Shemoelof, "Ich bin juden Dichter" (I Am a Jewish Writer), in *Ivrit mechutz le'ivreha hametukim*, 21.

31 Salman Masalha, "Ani kotev ivrit" (I Write Hebrew). Poetry International, https://www.poetryinternational.com/en/poets-poems/poems/poem/103-3455_I-WRITE-HEBREW#lang-en.

32 Menucha Gilboa, "Hebrew Press," *Encyclopedia of Modern Jewish Culture*, vol. 2, ed. Glenda Abramson (New York: Routledge, 2005), 704.

33 Hillel Halkin et al., "Newspapers, Hebrew," in *Encyclopaedia Judaica*, ed. Michael Berenbaum and Fred Skolnik, 2nd ed., vol. 15 (Detroit: Macmillan Reference USA, 2007), 155.

34 Rachel Seelig, "Introduction," *In geveb: A Journal of Yiddish Studies*, https://ingeveb.org/texts-and-translations/mikan-veeylakh-foreword.

35 Hever-Chybowski, "Mikan ve'eylakh," 243.

36 Tal Hever-Chybowski, "Introduction," *Mikan ve'eylakh* 2 (2016): 11.

37 Hever-Chybowski, "Introduction," 20.

38 Hever-Chybowski, "Introduction," 21.

39 Tomer Gardi, "Broken Hebrew," trans. Cecile Neeser Hever, *Mikan ve'eylakh* 2 (2016): 123.

40 Gardi, "Broken Hebrew," 124.

41 *Aviv: Literatur, Kunst, Kultur/Aviv: sifrut, omanut, tarbut* (Aviv: Literature, Art, Culture), no. 1.

42 Hanno Hauenstein, "Editorial/Petach Davar," *Aviv: Literatur, Kunst, Kultur/Aviv: sifrut, omanut, tarbut* (Aviv: Literature, Art, Culture), no. 1, n.p.

43 Lila Nazemian, "Aviv Magazine: Reviving German/Hebrew Linguistic Legacies," *Daily Pnut*, Oct. 11, 2016, https://medium.com/daily-pnut/aviv-magazine-reviving-german-hebrew-linguistic-legacies-4af01c7b4528#.g2uhhs2lm.

44 Shachar M. Pinsker, *A Rich Brew: How Cafes Created Modern Jewish Culture* (New York: New York University Press, 2018), 5.

45 Pinsker, *A Rich Brew*, 10.

46 Shemoelof, "Creating a Radical Hebrew Culture."

47 Pinsker, *A Rich Brew*, 306.

48 Michal Raizen, "Sounding the Mizrachi Voice: *Hafla* Thematics from the *Ma'abarah* to the Post-Arabic Novel," in *Since 1948: Israeli Literature in the Making*, ed. Nancy Berg and Naomi Sokoloff (Albany: State University of New York Press, 2020), 44.

49 Raizen, "Sounding the Mizrachi Voice," 45.

50 Ayelet Tsabari, "Mizrahi Artists Are Here to Incite a Culture War," *Forward*, March 16, 2016, https://forward.com/opinion/335653/mizrahi-artists-incite-culture-war-against-israeli-elite/.

51 Poetic Hafla, "Home," Facebook, https://www.facebook.com/poetichafla/ ?ref=page_internal.

CONCLUSION

1 Etgar Keret, "Outside," trans. Jessica Cohen, *New York Times Magazine*, July 7, 2020, https://www.nytimes.com/interactive/2020/07/07/magazine/ etgar-keret-short-story.html.

2 Etgar Keret and Inbal Pinto, dirs., *Outside*, 2020, one-channel video and sound installation, 7 mins., https://youtu.be/Su2g7WilBlc.

3 In the Hebrew version, "you" is rendered using the feminine form (there is no ungendered second person in Hebrew), so the protagonist being envisioned by the story is clearly a woman. In Hebrew, the "neutral" second person is typically rendered using the masculine form, so this deliberate use of the feminine also functions to push back against the gendered norms of the Hebrew language.

4 While the story itself was originally written in Hebrew, it appeared first in the magazine in English translation by Jessica Cohen.

5 Yiftach Ashkenazy and Dekel Shay Amory, "An Introduction to Hebrew Lit: Congruency, Clash, and Collision," *World Literature Today* 95, no. 1 (2021): 57.

6 Maya Tevet Dayan, "Land," trans. Sarit Blum, *World Literature Today* 95, no. 1 (2021): 70.

7 Alma Igra, "Chicken Soup: The Story of a Jewish Family," *World Literature Today* 95, no. 1 (2021): 60.

8 Ayelet Tsabari, "After 20 Years in Canada, I Returned to Israel. But the Country I Returned to Is Not the Same Country I Left," *Globe and Mail*, April 5, 2019, https://www.theglobeandmail.com/opinion/article-after-20 -years-in-canada-i-returned-to-israel-but-the-country-i/.

9 Static and Ben El x Black Eyed Peas, "Shake Ya Boom Boom," YouTube video, https://youtu.be/-2EZbz22iNg.

10 *Hayehudi Hachadash* (The New Jew), episode 3, "Ha'atid" (The Future), dir. Daniel Adar (Israel: Kan broadcasting network).

11 *Hayehudi Hachadash* (The New Jew), episode 4, "Habayit" (The Home).

12 *Hayehudi Hachadash* (The New Jew), episode 4, "Habayit" (The Home).

13 Barbara Finkelstein, "Why Etgar Keret Wanted His Prizewinning Book Translated into Yiddish," *Forward*, February 4, 2020, https:// forward.com/forverts-in-english/439388/why-etgar-keret-wanted-his -prizewinning-book-translated-into-yiddish/.

Bibliography

Abramson, Glenda. " 'The first of those who return': Incarnations of the New Jew in Modern Hebrew Literature." *Journal of Israeli History* 30, no. 1 (2011): 45–63.

Adar, Daniel, dir. *Hayehudi Hachadash* (The New Jew). Israel: Kan Broadcasting Network, 2021.

Ahmed, Sara. *The Cultural Politics of Emotion*. Edinburgh: Edinburgh University Press, 2004.

Almog, Oz. *The Sabra: The Creation of the New Jew*. Trans. Haim Watzman. Berkeley: University of California Press, 2000.

Almog, Yael. "Illusory Diasporas." *Shofar: An Interdisciplinary Journal of Jewish Studies* 37, no. 2 (2019): 63–70.

Alroey, Gur. "The Jewish Emigration from Palestine in the Early Twentieth Century." *Journal of Modern Jewish Studies* 2, no. 2 (2003): 111–31.

Alter, Robert. *The Book of Psalms: A Translation with Commentary*. New York: Norton, 2007.

———. *Defenses of the Imagination: Jewish Writers and Modern Historical Crisis*. Philadelphia: Jewish Publication Society, 1977.

———. *The Invention of Hebrew: Modern Fiction and the Language of Realism*. Seattle: University of Washington Press, 1988.

Amit, Gish. "When Suffering Becomes an Identity: On the Moments of Catastrophe and the Contours of Hope." In *A Cookbook for Political Imagination*, ed. Galit Eilat and Sebastian Cichocki, 209–12. Berlin: Sternberg Press, 2011.

Amit, Hila. "The Revival of Diasporic Hebrew in Contemporary Berlin." In *Cultural Topographies of the New Berlin*, ed. Jennifer Ruth Hosek and Karin Bauer, 253–71. Oxford: Berghahn, 2017.

Arad, Maya. *Hamorah Le'ivrit* (The Hebrew Teacher). Tel Aviv: Xargol, 2018.

———. *Sheva Midot Ra'ot* (Seven Moral Failings). Tel Aviv: Xargol, 2006.

Ashkenazy, Yiftach, and Dekel Shay Amory. "An Introduction to Hebrew Lit: Congruency, Clash, and Collision." *World Literature Today* 95, no. 1 (2021): 56–57.

Asscher, Omri. *Reading Israel, Reading America: The Politics of Translation Between Jews.* Stanford: Stanford University Press, 2020.

Avni, Yoav. *Herzl Amar* (What If). Or Yehuda: Kinneret, Zmora-Bitan, Dvir, 2011.

Bakhtin, M. M. *The Dialogic Imagination: Four Essays.* Ed. Michael Holquist. Trans. Caryl Emerson and Michael Holquist. Austin: University of Texas Press, 1981.

Bartana, Yael, dir. *Mary Koszmary* (Nightmares). 2007. One-channel video and sound installation, 11 mins.

———. *Mur I Wieża* (Wall and Tower). 2009. One-channel video and sound installation, 15 mins.

———. *Summer Camp/Awodah.* 2007. Two-channel video and sound installation, 12 mins. https://yaelbartana.com/work/summer-camp-awodah-2007.

———. *Zamach* (Assassination). 2011. One-channel video and sound installation, 35 mins.

Bartana, Yael, Sebastian Cichocki, and Galit Eilat. "Jewish Renaissance Movement in Poland (JRMiP)." In *A Cookbook for Political Imagination*, ed. Galit Eilat and Sebastian Cichocki, n.p. Berlin: Sternberg Press, 2011.

Ben-Gurion, David. *Rebirth and Destiny of Israel.* Ed. and trans. Max Nurock. New York: Philosophical Library, 1954.

Ben-Yehuda, Eliezer. *A Dream Come True.* Trans. T. Muraoka. Ed. George Mandel. Boulder, CO: Westview Press, 1993.

Berdyczewski, Micha Yosef. "Urvah Parakh." In *Kol sipure Micha Yosef Bin-Gorion (Berdichevsky).* Tel Aviv: Am Oved, 1951.

Bhabha, Homi K. *The Location of Culture.* New York: Routledge, 1994.

The Bilu. "Manifesto (1882)." In *The Jew in the Modern World: A Documentary History*, ed. Jehuda Reinharz and Paul Mendes-Flohr, 532–33. Oxford: Oxford University Press, 1995.

Boianjiu, Shani. *The People of Forever Are Not Afraid.* New York: Hogarth, 2012.

Boyarin, Daniel. *Border Lines.* Philadelphia: University of Pennsylvania Press, 2004.

———. *Unheroic Conduct: The Rise of Heterosexuality and the Invention of the Jewish Man.* Berkeley: University of California Press, 1997.

Boyarin, Daniel, and Jonathan Boyarin. "Diaspora: Generation and the Ground of Jewish Identity." *Critical Inquiry* 19 (Summer 1993): 693–725.

———. *Powers of Diaspora: Two Essays on the Relevance of Jewish Culture.* Minneapolis: University of Minnesota Press, 2002.

Brenner, Michael. *In Search of Israel: The History of an Idea.* Princeton: Princeton University Press, 2018.

Chabon, Michael. *The Yiddish Policemen's Union.* New York: Harper Perennial, 2007.

Chaver, Yael. *What Must Be Forgotten: The Survival of Yiddish in Zionist Palestine.* Syracuse: Syracuse University Press, 2004.

Clifford, James. *Routes: Travel and Translation in the Late Twentieth Century.* Cambridge, MA: Harvard University Press, 1997.

Cohen, Hadas, and Dani Kranz. "Israeli Jews in the New Berlin: From Shoah Memories to Middle Eastern Encounters." *Cultural Topographies of the New Berlin*, ed. Jennifer Ruth Hosek and Karin Bauer, 322–46. Oxford: Berghahn, 2017.

Cooper, Simon, and Paul Atkinson. "Graphic Implosion: Politics, Time, and Value in Post-9/11 Comics." In *Literature after 9/11*, ed. Ann Keniston and Jeanne Follansbee Quinn, 60–81. New York: Routledge, 2008.

Dagnino, Arianna. *Transcultural Writers and Novels in the Age of Global Mobility.* West Lafayette, IN: Purdue University Press, 2015.

Dayan, Maya Tevet. "Land." Trans. Sarit Blum. *World Literature Today* 95, no. 1 (2021): 70.

Derrida, Jacques. "*Des Tours de Babel.*" Trans. Joseph F. Graham. *Semeia* 54 (1991): 3–34.

———. *Monolingualism of the Other or the Prosthesis of Origin.* Trans. Patrick Mensah. Stanford: Stanford University Press, 1998.

Drori, Danielle. "Reading Maya Arad in North America Today: *The Hebrew Teacher* in Context." *Hebrew Higher Education* 21 (2019): 1–19.

Dubnov, Shimon. "Diaspora." *Encyclopedia of the Social Sciences*, vol. 5, ed. Edwin R. A. Seligman, 127–30. New York: Macmillan, 1951.

Dufoix, Stéphane. *Diasporas.* Berkeley: University of California Press, 2008.

Eshel, Amir, and Rachel Seelig, eds. *The German-Hebrew Dialogue: Studies of Encounter and Exchange.* Vol. 6 of Perspectives on Jewish Texts and Contexts. Berlin: De Gruyter, 2018.

Ezrahi, Sidra DeKoven. "Our Homeland, the Text . . . Our Text the Homeland: Exile and Homecoming in the Modern Jewish Imagination." *Michigan Quarterly Review* 31, no. 4 (1992): 463–97.

Feldman, Yael. *Modernism and Cultural Transfer: Gabriel Preil and the Tradition of Jewish Literary Bilingualism.* Cincinnati: Hebrew Union College Press, 1986.

Finkelstein, Barbara. "Why Etgar Keret Wanted His Prizewinning Book Translated into Yiddish." *Forward*, February 4, 2020. https://forward.com/forverts-in-english/439388/why-etgar-keret-wanted-his-prizewinning -book-translated-into-yiddish/.

Fuchs, Esther. *Israeli Mythogynies: Women in Contemporary Hebrew Fiction.* Albany: State University of New York Press, 1987.

Gardi, Tomer. "*Ivrit shevurah*" (Broken Hebrew). Trans. Cecile Neeser Hever. *Mikan ve'eylakh* 2 (2016): 121–26.

Gilboa, Menucha. "Hebrew Press." *Encyclopedia of Modern Jewish Culture*, vol. 2, ed. Glenda Abramson. New York: Routledge, 2005.

Gilsenan Nordin, Irene, Julie Hansen, and Carmen Zamorano Llena. *Transcultural Identities in Contemporary Literature.* Amsterdam: Editions Rodopi, 2013.

Gray, Richard. *After the Fall: American Literature Since 9/11.* Oxford: Wiley-Blackwell, 2011.

Gruen, Erich S. "Diaspora and Homeland." In *Diasporas and Exiles: Varieties of Jewish Identity*, ed. Howard Wettstein, 18–46. Berkeley: University of California Press, 2002.

Grumberg, Karen. "Ricki Lake in Tel Aviv: The Alternative of Orly Castel-Bloom's Hebrew-English." In *Anglophone Jewish Literature*, ed. Axel Stähler, 234–48. London: Routledge, 2007.

Halkin, Hillel, et al. "Newspapers, Hebrew." *Encyclopaedia Judaica*, ed. Michael Berenbaum and Fred Skolnik, 2nd ed., vol. 15. Detroit: Macmillan Reference USA, 2007.

Halperin, Liora. *Babel in Zion: Jews, Nationalism, and Language Diversity in Palestine, 1920–1948.* New Haven: Yale University Press, 2015.

Hammerschlag, Sarah. *The Figural Jew: Politics and Identity in Postwar French Thought.* Chicago: University of Chicago Press, 2010.

Harshav, Benjamin. *The Polyphony of Jewish Culture.* Stanford: Stanford University Press, 2007.

Hauenstein, Hanno. "Editorial/Petach Davar." *Aviv: Literatur, Kunst, Kultur/ Aviv: sifrut, omanut, tarbut* (Aviv: Literature, Art, Culture), no. 1.

Hellekson, Karen. *The Alternate History: Refiguring Historical Time.* Kent, OH: The Kent State University Press, 2001.

Herzl, Theodor. *The Jewish State.* Trans. Sylvie d'Avigdor. Ed. Jacob M. Alkow. New York: Dover, 1988.

Hever-Chybowski, Tal. "Diasporic Hebrew in Berlin." *JMB Journal* 20 (June 5, 2019): 53–59.

———. "Mikan ve'eylakh" (From This Point Onward). Trans. Rachel Seelig. In *The German-Hebrew Dialogue: Studies of Encounter and Exchange*, ed. Amir Eshel and Rachel Seelig, 241–52. Vol. 6 of Perspectives on Jewish Texts and Contexts. Berlin: De Gruyter, 2018.

Hirsch, Marianne, and Nancy K. Miller, eds. *Rites of Return: Diaspora Poetics and the Politics of Memory*. New York: Columbia University Press, 2011.

Hochberg, Gil. *In Spite of Partition: Jews, Arabs, and the Limits of Separatist Imagination*. Princeton: Princeton University Press, 2007.

Hutcheon, Linda. "Postmodern Paratextuality and History." *Texte: Revue de critique et de théorie littéraire* 4 (1986): 301–12.

Igra, Alma. "Chicken Soup: The Story of a Jewish Family." *World Literature Today* 95, no. 1 (2021): 58–60.

Israel, Nico. *Outlandish: Writing between Exile and Diaspora*. Stanford: Stanford University Press, 2000.

Jacobs, Adriana X. "The Place of Hebrew: Maya Arad's *Another Place, a Foreign City*." In *Disseminating Jewish Literatures: Knowledge, Research, Curricula*, ed. Susanne Zepp, Ruth Fine, Natasha Gordinsky, Kader Konuk, Claudia Olk, and Galili Shahar, 257–66. Berlin: De Gruyter, 2020.

———. *Strange Cocktail: Translation and the Making of Modern Hebrew Poetry*. Ann Arbor: University of Michigan Press, 2018.

Jay, Paul. *Global Matters: The Transnational Turn in Literary Studies*. Ithaca, NY: Cornell University Press, 2010.

JPS Hebrew-English Tanakh. 2nd ed. Philadelphia: Jewish Publication Society, 2003.

Kahanoff, Jacqueline. "Afterword: From East the Sun." In *Mongrels or Marvels: The Levantine Writings of Jacqueline Shohet Kahanoff*, ed. Deborah A. Starr and Sasson Somekh, 243–59. Stanford: Stanford University Press, 2011.

Kaplan, Eran. *Beyond Post-Zionism*. Albany: SUNY Press, 2015.

Katz, Irin. "Interview with the Writer Maya Arad." *Koreh Basfarim: Magazin le-sifrut*, November 24, 2015 (Hebrew). https://www.korebasfarim.com/2015/11/24/ראיון-עם-הסופרת-מאיה-ערד/.

Kellman, Steven G. *The Translingual Imagination*. Lincoln: University of Nebraska Press, 2000.

Keret, Etgar. "Outside." Trans. Jessica Cohen. *New York Times Magazine*, July 7, 2020. https://www.nytimes.com/interactive/2020/07/07/magazine/etgar-keret-short-story.html.

Keret, Etgar, and Inbal Pinto, dirs. *Outside*. 2020. One-channel video and sound installation, 7 mins. https://youtu.be/Su2g7WilBlc.

Kissileff, Beth. "Israel Has an Amazing Literary Diaspora." *The Tower* 22 (Jan. 2015).

Kronfeld, Chana. *On the Margins of Modernism: Decentering Literary Dynamics.* Berkeley: University of California Press, 1996.

Kubovy, Miri. "Inniut and Kooliut: Trends in Israeli Narrative Literature, 1995–1999." *Israel Studies* 5, no. 1 (2000): 244–65.

Leach, Neil. "9/11." *Diacritics* 33, nos. 3/4 (2003): 75–92.

Lerski, Helmar, dir. *Avodah* (Labor). 1935; Waltham, MA: National Center for Jewish Film, 2008. DVD.

Likhovski, Assaf. "Post-Post-Zionist Historiography." *Israel Studies* 15, no. 2 (2010): 1–23.

Masalha, Salman. "Ani kotev ivrit" (I Write Hebrew). Poetry International. https://www.poetryinternational.com/en/poets-poems/poems/poem/103 -3455_I-WRITE-HEBREW#lang-en.

Mazali, Rela. "'And What About the Girls?' What a Culture of War Genders Out of View." *Nashim: A Journal of Jewish Women's Studies and Gender*, no. 6 (Fall 5764/2003): 39–50.

———. *Maps of Women's Goings and Stayings.* Stanford: Stanford University Press, 2001.

Mintz, Alan. "Introduction." In *Hebrew in America: Perspectives and Prospects*, ed. Alan Mintz, 13–26. Detroit: Wayne State University Press, 1993.

Misrad Haklita. "Higia hazman lachzor leyisrael lifnei shechanukah yahafoch leChristmas" (The Time Has Come to Return to Israel before Hanukkah Becomes Christmas). YouTube video. https://youtu.be/JQmE-jUZU_Y.

———. "Yom Hazikaron" (Memorial Day). YouTube video. https://youtu.be/ FP3gJN_YScM.

Modleski, Tania. *Feminism Without Women.* New York: Routledge, 1991.

Namdar, Reuven. *Habayit Asher Nekhrav.* Or Yehuda: Dvir, 2013.

Namdar, Ruby. *The Ruined House.* Trans. Hillel Halkin. New York: Harper, 2017.

Nazemian, Lila. "Aviv Magazine: Reviving German/Hebrew Linguistic Legacies." *Daily Pnut*, Oct. 11, 2016. https://medium.com/daily-pnut/aviv -magazine-reviving-german-hebrew-linguistic-legacies-4af01c7b4528# .g2uhhs2lm.

"Netanyahu: Hitler Didn't Want to Eliminate the Jews." *Haaretz*, October 21, 2015. https://www.haaretz.com/israel-news/netanyahu-absolves-hitler-of -guilt-1.5411578.

Neusner, Jacob, trans. *Genesis Rabbah: The Judaic Commentary to the Book of Genesis: A New American Translation.* Vol. 3. Atlanta: Scholars Press, 1985.

Nordau, Max. "Jewry of Muscle." In *The Jew in the Modern World: A Documentary History*, ed. Paul Mendes-Flohr and Jehuda Reinharz, 2nd ed., 547–48. Oxford: Oxford University Press, 1995.

———. "Zionism." (1902). In *The Zionist Ideas: Visions for the Jewish Homeland—Then, Now, Tomorrow*, ed. Gil Troy, 20–21. Philadelphia: Jewish Publication Society, 2018.

Omer-Sherman, Ranen. *Diaspora and Zionism in Jewish American Literature: Lazarus, Syrkin, Reznikoff, Roth*. Hanover, NH: Brandeis University Press, 2002.

Peleg, Yaron. "A New Hebrew Literary Diaspora? Israeli Literature Abroad." *Studia Judaica* 18, no. 2 (2015): 321–38.

Pinsker, Shachar M. *Literary Passports: The Making of Modernist Hebrew Fiction in Europe*. Stanford: Stanford University Press, 2011.

———. *A Rich Brew: How Cafes Created Modern Jewish Culture*. New York: New York University Press, 2018.

Pitchon, Avi. "Save Europe Now Ask Me How." In *A Cookbook for Political Imagination*, ed. Galit Eilat and Sebastian Cichocki, 353–69. Berlin: Sternberg Press, 2011.

Poetic Hafla. "Home." Facebook. https://www.facebook.com/poetichafla/?ref=page_internal.

"Proclamation of the State of Israel (May 14, 1948)." In *The Jew in the Modern World*, 2nd ed., ed. Paul Mendes-Flohr and Jehuda Reinharz, 629–30. New York: Oxford University Press, 1995.

Raizen, Michal. "Sounding the Mizrachi Voice: *Hafla* Thematics from the *Ma'abarah* to the Post-Arabic Novel." In *Since 1948: Israeli Literature in the Making*, ed. Nancy Berg and Naomi Sokoloff, 43–58. Albany: State University of New York Press, 2020.

Ram, Uri. *The Globalization of Israel: McWorld in Tel Aviv, Jihad in Jerusalem*. New York: Routledge, 2008.

Rauscher, Sami David, and Noa Amiel. "Performing Identity." *Politikorange*, December 3, 2018.

Raz-Krakotzkin, Amnon. "Critique of 'The Negation of Exile' in Israeli Culture." In *The Scaffolding of Sovereignty: Global and Aesthetic Perspectives on the History of a Concept*, ed. Zvi Ben-Dor Benite, Stefanos Geroulanos, and Nicole Jerr, 393–420. New York: Columbia University Press, 2017.

———. "Exile, History, and the Nationalization of Jewish Memory: Some Reflections on the Zionist Notion of History and Return." *Journal of Levantine Studies* 3, no. 2 (2013): 37–70.

Regev, Motti. "To Have a Culture of Our Own: On Israeliness and its Variants." *Ethnic and Racial Studies* 23 (2000): 223–44.

Remennick, Larissa. "The Israeli Diaspora in Berlin: Back to Being Jewish?" *Israel Studies Review* 34, no. 1 (2019): 88–109.

Rosen, Maya. "Reclaiming a Minor Literature." *Jewish Currents*, February 21, 2022. https://jewishcurrents.org/reclaiming-a-minor-literature.

Rosenfeld, Gavriel. *The World Hitler Never Made: Alternate History and the Memory of Nazism*. Cambridge: Cambridge University Press, 2005.

Rotbard, Sharon. "Wall and Tower." In *A Civilian Occupation: The Politics of Israeli Architecture*, ed. Rafi Siegel, David Tartakover, and Eyal Weizman, 39–58. New York: Verso, 2003.

Rothberg, Michael. *Multidirectional Memory: Remembering the Holocaust in the Age of Decolonization*. Stanford: Stanford University Press, 2009.

Rovner, Adam. "Alternate History: The Case of Nava Semel's *IsraIsland* and Michael Chabon's *The Yiddish Policemen's Union*." *Partial Answers: Journal of Literature and the History of Ideas* 9, no. 1 (2011): 131–52.

———. *In the Shadow of Zion: Promised Lands Before Israel*. New York: New York University Press, 2014.

———. "Language Lessons: Maya Arad's 'The Hebrew Teacher.'" *Curated: Thinking with Literature*, August 17, 2020. https://arcade.stanford.edu/content/language-lessons-maya-arad%E2%80%99s-hebrew-teacher-0#_edn.

Schachter, Allison. *Diasporic Modernisms: Hebrew and Yiddish Literature in the Twentieth Century*. Oxford: Oxford University Press, 2012.

Schnapper, Dominique, and Denise L. Davis. "From the Nation-State to the Transnational World: On the Meaning and Usefulness of Diaspora as a Concept." *Diaspora: A Journal of Transnational Studies* 8, no. 3 (1999): 225–54.

Schweid, Eliezer. *The Jewish Experience of Time: Philosophical Dimensions of the Jewish Holy Days*. Northvale, NJ: Jason Aronson, 2000.

Seelig, Rachel. "Introduction." *In geveb: A Journal of Yiddish Studies*. https://ingeveb.org/texts-and-translations/mikan-veeylakh-foreword.

Semel, Nava. *E-srael*. Tel Aviv: Yediot Aharonot, 2005.

———. *Isra Isle*. Trans. Jessica Cohen. Simsbury, CT: Mandel Vilar Press, 2016.

Sered, Susan. *What Makes Women Sick? Maternity, Modesty, and Militarism in Israeli Society*. Hanover, NH: University Press of New England.

Setter, Shaul. "The Time That Returns: Speculative Temporality in S. Yizhar's 1948." *Jewish Social Studies: History, Culture, Society* 18, no. 3 (2012): 38–54.

Shemoelof, Mati. "Creating a Radical Hebrew Culture—in the Diaspora." *+972 Magazine*, August 19, 2016. https://972mag.com/creating-a-radical-hebrew -culture-in-the-diaspora/121470/.

———. "Creating Our Own Alternative Arab-Jewish History In Berlin." *Plus 61J*, December 11, 2018. https://plus61j.net.au/plus61j-voices/creating -alternative-arab-jewish-history-berlin/?fbclid=IwAR1LxqslZ4pndj eeRz33eeL_W8iS-NPxLxk35fDZW0hOuv_HPQXeS1KTxlk.

———. *Ivrit mechutz le'ivreha hametukim* (Hebrew Outside Its Sweet Insides). Haifa: Pardes, 2017.

Silberstein, Laurence, ed. *Postzionism: A Reader*. New Brunswick: Rutgers University Press, 2008.

Static and Ben El x Black Eyed Peas. "Shake Ya Boom Boom." YouTube video. https://youtu.be/-2EZbz22iNg.

Steiner, George. "Our Homeland, the Text." *Salmagundi* 66 (Winter–Spring 1985): 4–25.

Sutzkever, Avrum. "Der aleynflier" (The Loner). *Di goldene keyt* (The Golden Chain) 91 (1976).

Tidhar, Lavie. *Unholy Land*. San Francisco: Tachyon, 2018.

Tölölyan, Khachig. "The Nation-State and Its Others: In Lieu of a Preface." *Diaspora: A Journal of Transnational Studies* 1, no. 1 (1991): 3–7.

Tsabari, Ayelet. "After 20 Years in Canada, I Returned to Israel. But the Country I Returned to Is Not the Same Country I Left." *Globe and Mail*, April 5, 2019. https://www.theglobeandmail.com/opinion/article-after-20-years-in -canada-i-returned-to-israel-but-the-country-i/.

———. *The Best Place on Earth*. Toronto: HarperCollins, 2013.

———. "Mizrahi Artists Are Here to Incite a Culture War." *Forward*, March 16, 2016. https://forward.com/opinion/335653/mizrahi-artists-incite-culture -war-against-israeli-elite/.

Weingrad, Michael. *American Hebrew Literature: Writing Jewish National Identity in the United States*. Syracuse: Syracuse University Press, 2011.

Weiss, Haim. "Israel Doesn't Have a Monopoly on Great Hebrew Literature." *Forward*, June 8, 2015. http://forward.com/opinion/309641/great-hebrew -literature-doesnt-come-only-from-israel/#ixzz3r7Jl1GdZ.

Whitman, Walt. "Manahatta." Poets.org. Accessed May 14, 2018. https://www .poets.org/poetsorg/poem/mannahatta.

Wieseltier, Meir. "Chatakh orekh beshirato shel natan zach" (A Cross-Section of Natan Zach's Poetry). *Siman kriah* 10 (1980).

Wirth-Nesher, Hana. *Call It English: The Languages of Jewish-American Literature*. Princeton: Princeton University Press, 2006.

Yildiz, Yasemin. *Beyond the Mother Tongue: The Postmonolingual Condition.* New York: Fordham University Press, 2012.

Young, James E. *At Memory's Edge: After-Images of the Holocaust in Contemporary Art and Architecture.* New Haven: Yale University Press, 2000.

———. *The Texture of Memory.* New Haven: Yale University Press, 1993.

Zakim, Eric. *To Build and Be Built: Landscape, Literature, and the Construction of Zionist Identity.* Philadelphia: University of Pennsylvania Press, 2006.

———. "Stalagim: At the Limits of Israeli Literature." In *Since 1948: Israeli Literature in the Making,* ed. Nancy Berg and Naomi Sokoloff, 183–203. Albany: State University of New York Press, 2020.

Zangwill, Israel. "Zionism and Charitable Institutions" (1903). In *Speeches, Articles and Letters of Israel Zangwill.* London: Soncino Press, 1937.

Zelitch, Simone. *Judenstaat.* New York: Tom Doherty Associates, 2016.

Index

diasporic Hebrew, 147–50, 166–67; *haflot* and performance of, 163–66; literature in Berlin, 156–59; periodicals in Berlin, 160–63; politics of, 150–55

Dove Flyer, The (2014), 153–54

Drori, Danielle, 63, 78, 79, 85

Dubnov, Shimon, 4

Dufoix, Stéphane, 5

"Eifo zeh chul?" (Where Is Abroad?) (Shemoelof), 156–57

Eilat, Galit, 121

emigrants, in English-language Israeli literature, 104–8

emigration (*yeridah*), 105, 107, 124, 148–49

English, in Hebrew Literature, 96

English-language Israeli literature, 87–89; as challenge to Zionist dream, 99–104; as challenging link between Hebrew and Israeliness, 92–95; and globalization, 95–99; immigrants and emigrants in, 104–8; and New Hebrew Man, 108–18; and transcultural and alternative Israeli identities, 118–20; and translingualism, 89–91. See also *Best Place on Earth, The* (Tsabari); *People of Forever Are Not Afraid, The* (Boianjiu)

epigraphs, in *The Ruined House*, 75–78

E-srael (Isra Isle) (Semel). See *Isra Isle* (Semel)

Even-Zohar, Itamar, 72

exile: Babylonian, 1–2; diaspora and Jewish, 2–4; in *Hayehudim Baim* (The Jews Are Coming), 1–2; "imaginary of," 6–7; in Israeli consciousness and historiography, 17; in Jewish self-conception, 2; negation of, 17, 83, 122–25, 129; return to home as, 174

Ezrahi, Sidra DeKoven, 4, 25

Feldman, Yael, 77

femininity, in Boyarins' critical construction of Jewish identity, 9–11, 13

figural Jew, 128–29

Fink, Ida, 88

foreign workers in Israel, 100–101

Frankel, Alona, 138–39, 140–41

Fuchs, Esther, 95, 115, 118

Gardi, Tomer, 161–62

gender: in Boyarins' critical construction of Jewish identity, 9–11, 13; and English-language Israeli literature, 94, 108; and masculinity, 109–10, 112–14; and New Hebrew Man, 108–18; Zionist expectations of, 116, 117–18. *See also* women

Germany, 147–50. *See also* Berlin, Arab-Jewish collaboration in

Gilboa, Menucha, 160

Ginzburg, Shimon, 62

globalization, 93, 95–99, 100–101, 164, 169–70, 192n29

Gnessin, Uri Nissan, 55

Golden Gate, The (Seth), 78–79

Grand Island, New York, 28, *29*, 30, 31, 32, 49

Gray, Richard, 52

Greek, Hebrew as influenced by, 75

Greenberg, Uri Tzvi, 76–77

Grumberg, Karen, 96

Guerilla Tarbut (Cultural Guerilla), 152

"Habib albi" (Love of My Heart), 175

hafla / haflot, 152, 163–66, 196n17. *See also* Poetic Hafla

hafla poetics, 165

Halkin, Hillel, 65, 160, 188n19

Hall, Stuart, 5

Halperin, Liora, 89

Hammerschlag, Sarah, 128, 129